INTEGRATING EUROPE

International Studies in Economics and Econometrics

VOLUME 37

The titles published in this series are listed at the end of this volume.

INTEGRATING EUROPE

The Transition Economies
at Stake

Jozef M. van Brabant

KLUWER ACADEMIC PUBLISHERS
Dordrecht / Boston / London

Distributors for North America:
Kluwer Academic Publishers
101 Philip Drive
Assinippi Park
Norwell, Massachusetts 02061 USA

Distributors for all other countries:
Kluwer Academic Publishers Group
Distribution Centre
Post Office Box 322
3300 AH Dordrecht, THE NETHERLANDS

Library of Congress Cataloging-in-Publication Data
Brabant, Jozef M. van
    Integrating Europe : the transition economies at stake / Jozef M.
van Brabant.
        p.   cm. -- (International studies in economics and
econometrics ; v. 37)
    Includes bibliographical references and index.
    ISBN 0-7923-9806-8
    1. European Union--Europe, Eastern.   2. Europe--Economic
integration.   3. Post-communism--Europe, Eastern.   I. Title.
II. Series.
HC241.25.E83B73   1993   96-40977
337.1'4--dc20   CIP

Printed on acid-free paper.

Printed in the United States of America

To Miyuki: May you yet
see Europe's (dim?) light!

Preface

Bringing the eastern European economies in transition (defined more precisely in the Introduction) under the economic, political, and security umbrella of the European Union (EU) has been an ambition of many of these countries from the very start of the so-called *annus mirabilis* in 1989. The road to gratification of this aspiration since then has been rather bumpy, however one wants to look at recent events. Indeed, since 1989 the relationship between the EU and the economies in transition has been ebbing and flowing with the evolution of two main strands of policy stances in the EU. One has been deep skepticism about bringing these countries into the Union at all in any foreseeable future. This in spite of the fact that, after long hesitation, in mid 1993 the EU Member States committed themselves eventually to explore accession with selected transition economies, as well as Cyprus and Malta. The other has been their evolving attitude toward their own integration endeavors. Hence the dilemmas, in the EU's parlance, of the "deepening versus widening" conundrum. That indeed constitutes the paramount issue addressed in the present investigation.

This deliberately modest and compact volume has had a rather strange backdrop, and a word of explanation is therefore in order. First of all, I tried to discuss the need to forge a constructive relationship between eastern and western Europe, hence the veritable remaking of Europe, in a book completed in June 1994 (Brabant 1995a), that is, at a time when the EU leadership was still rather lukewarm in their response to the expressed desire of some economies in transition to join the organization as soon as possible (Hungary and Poland applied in early April 1994). For technical reasons, the book was not published until a year and a half later. Although not completely up-to-date by the time it appeared in late October 1995, and it certainly is not at this juncture, I nonetheless regard it still as the only broad overview not only of the postwar integration attempts in Europe but also of the inherent obstacles to merging the two parts of Europe, precisely in the light of recent experiences. It was in December 1994 that the Essen

European Council decided to consider accession negotiations with as many as ten economies in transition once the planned 1996 Intergovernmental Conference (IGC) successfully completed. Subsequent developments concerning engineering such entry into the Union deserve to be analyzed in their own right, of course. As argued in Brabant 1995a (and slightly updated in 1995b, c; 1996a), by its very nature economic integration is and remains political economy in the broad sense. So economic rationale, which is what has primarily been motivating my writing of this book as well as earlier contributions to the subject, may well not be the overriding concern in arriving at an unambiguous decision on whether or not – and how best – to fuse the transition economies with 'Europe.' But economic tangents certainly can be ignored only at the cost of arriving at nearly irrelevant propositions or recommendations.

Second, I consider the remaking of Europe as a momentous, a truly historical event with ramifications in a wide array of activities intrinsically of interest to the broader international community, not just to the countries of eastern or western Europe. It was with this as backdrop that, within my capacity as Principal Economic Affairs Officer in the Department for Economic and Social Information and Policy Analysis of the United Nations Secretariat in New York and then, in early 1996, on assignment at the Economic Commission for Europe (ECE) in Geneva, Switzerland, I tried to draw more than casual attention to the myriad of problems arising from any eastern accession. That ambition has been repeatedly thwarted. While at the ECE, I drafted two chapters, as commissioned, for *Economic Survey of Europe in 1995-1996* (UNECE 1996a) on the subject. After these materials had been thoroughly vetted through the organization, including the leadership, the latter resolved *ex cathedra*, abruptly and inexplicably, no reason given, not to publish them.

There may well have been *raisons d'état* for this decision. After all, some such excuse can always be contrived when a more substantive justification cannot reasonably be upheld. Just the same, I very much regret this mode of adjudication. Throughout my career as an international civil servant, I have felt very strongly that any international secretariat, such as ECE or that of the United Nations Organization (UNO), should be impelled immanently to preserve its independence and autonomy in principle; at least to stand behind a cogent position arrived at in a professionally warranted manner once the basic parameters of the investigation have been thoroughly agreed upon and the ordinary vetting process has run its course. That this maxim was not observed in this case is regrettable. Alas, it was not the first time I have been deeply disappointed; and it probably will not be the last either if my understanding of behavior of the cited organizations is anywhere near the mark.

I have given the above explanation after considerate deliberations with myself for two reasons. One is that I cannot in all honesty claim to have written the present volume completely on my own time utilizing my own resources; though I do so for two derivatives (Brabant 1996b, c) on the basis of which I gave seminars at the *Institut Universitaire de Hautes Études Internationales* and *Institut Européen de l'Université de Genève*, both in Geneva (Switzerland) that incited numerous questions and comments, for which I am most grateful. Also, it would be dishonest on my part to pretend that the product as it was crystallizing at ECE during that extraordinary 1996 winter-into-spring season in Geneva, did not benefit greatly from numerous discussions with and comments on various drafts by my colleagues at ECE. I am particularly grateful for advice during the various rounds of drafting, but not the ones that led to this volume, to Messrs. Dieter Hesse, Paul Rayment, and Claus Wittich. The latter two introduced many improvements in language and style in the Geneva drafts, and indeed all three suggested useful alternative ways of presenting the case for and against quick accession of the transition economies to the EU. We never had disagreements about the substantive parts, however.

Since I completely reworked the drafts that were suppressed and expanded them considerably for the present publication by myself on my own time, without further consultation with my ECE colleagues, if only to avoid the onus being drawn onto them, I alone must and do bear full and final responsibility for the present end product, whatever its consequences. That holds for the merits of the piece as well as for whatever failings there may be in the various analyses presented. Again, this should not be read as a disrespect of the entirely friendly and professional assistance I was privileged to receive from my colleagues at ECE.

Two further acknowledgments, also without implying the principals in the responsibility for this product, are in order. It was largely thanks to Claus Wittich that I agreed to take advantage of the opportunity to spend in early 1996 two months in Geneva and indeed benefit from his generous hospitality, freed from just about all domestic chores other than the free hand in cooking and eating he allowed me with alacrity. Among other convivial externalities, such as the budding spring in Geneva and the entirely peculiar management of oyster supplies in the city, especially the good food and wine contributed mightily to off-setting our funk following the suppression of the draft chapters. Without a doubt, the congenial atmosphere there, in spite of what transpired at work, impelled me to revise and expand the product, and thereafter to finalize it at 'home.' My thanks to him, if only on that score, are therefore entirely warranted.

Finally, it would be churlish on my part not to recognize the generosity and patience with which my family has tolerated my determination, once again, to wander off into yet another book-writing adventure under adverse circumstances, in spite of earlier resolutions to abandon that professional ambition. Daughter Anja J. tried valiantly to explain to me from afar the prions and related matters, not always genetic in origin, that soured EU relations in the first half of 1996; but I fear ultimately in vain as, to my mind the structure of cells and their incredible vanities outpace economic policy making, or the behavior of international civil servants for that matter, by quite some multiple. Aside from my aspiration – or hankering? – to persuade not only friends and acquaintances, but indeed some policy makers too, of the ultimate prize within reach if Europe can be constructively remade, I also hope in particular to dispel my spouse's less warranted skepticism about Europe. Even if I succeed only in the latter, and I trust the book's dedication to her might improve the chances of achieving that goal, the adventure will have been well worth it.

Table of Contents

Part Two: The Conference and New Accessions

Acronyms

CAP	common agricultural policy
CEFTA	Central European Free Trade Agreement
CFSP	common foreign and security policy
CIS	Commonwealth of Independent States
CJHA	cooperation in juridical and home affairs
CMEA	Council for Mutual Economic Assistance
EBRD	European Bank for Reconstruction and Development
EC	European Communities
ECB	European Central Bank
ECE	Economic Commission for Europe
ECSC	European Coal and Steel Community
EEA	European Economic Area
EEC	European Economic Communities
EFTA	European Free Trade Association
EIB	European Investment Bank
EMCF	European Monetary Cooperation Fund
EMI	European Monetary Institute
EMS	European Monetary System
EMU	Economic and Monetary Union
EPU	European Political Union
ERM	exchange-rate mechanism
EU	European Union
FDI	foreign direct investment
Fund	International Monetary Fund (IMF)
GATT	General Agreement on Tariffs and Trade
GDP	gross domestic product
G-7	Group of Seven
G-24	Group of Twenty-four
GSP	General System of Preferences
IBRD	International Bank for Reconstruction and Development
IGC	Intergovernmental Conference
IMF	International Monetary Fund

MFA	Multi-fibre Arrangement
NTB	nontariff barrier
OECD	Organisation for Economic Co-operation and Development
PHARE	*Pologne/Hongrie – assistance à la restructuration économique*
SDR	special drawing right
TACIS	Technical Assistance to the CIS
TEU	Treaty on European Union
UNO	United Nations Organization
WEU	Western European Union
World Bank	International Bank for Reconstruction and Development (IBRD)
WTO	World Trade Organization

Introduction

On 29 March 1996, the Heads of State and Government of the Fifteen Member States of the European Union (EU), assembled in an Extraordinary European Council, opened in Turin (Italy) yet another Intergovernmental Conference (IGC). They did so with all the customary ceremonial pomp, this time 'enlivened' by the vicissitudes of the so-called mad-cow disease (more formally, bovine spongiform encephalopathy) and its potential causal links with the lethal Creutzfeldt-Jakob disease for humans, as ineptly hinted at by key U.K. policy makers. The ensuing political furor over this in Europe seemed incomprehensible to all too many nonscience observers like myself. The all-around bungling of the affair, at least from the political and public-relations points of view, may yet set loose a particular set of prions to infect in due course the EU's integration process. The decision of the British Prime Minister, Mr. John Major, on 21 May 1996 to enact a policy of noncooperation, including invoking the veto on all EU matters that require consensus and obstructing deliberations otherwise, until the EU's ban on exports of British beef and its byproducts is lifted may signal arrival of the first wave of this onslaught. Though the policy was abandoned a month later, the outcome of the posturing induced by electoral calculations, is as yet unknown (Peel, Peston, and Southey 1996).

Many issues are at stake during this Conference, which is expected to last at least one year, and possibly through most of 1997. Given the deep divisions in western Europe, notably British opposition to and, in many respects, unwarranted skepticism about the very purposes of western European integration, the Conference may well become quickly infected by those elusive prions, which will eventually leave a 'European' brain shot through with gaping holes and otherwise subject to deadly convulsions. Even if tactical motives might persuade the Conference negotiators to await the outcome of the next British election, due at the latest in May 1997, in the hope that a new British Government might be more receptive to EU-style integration, a clear-cut move forward is by no means assured. As the opening rounds of the deliberations have already amply demonstrated, the IGC will by no means be clear sailing among the Member States. For, even excluding Britain, there exists palpable disagreement on how best to resolve the twin issues of the Union's fundamental integration dilemma of long standing: "widening versus deepening," using again the EU's lexicon.

In this introduction, I clarify the backdrop of the core issues around which the Conference will revolve one way or the other as well as the particular tangent I pursue in this volume: the Conference's importance for the transition economies, particularly those that wish to accede to the EU in the near term. Then I propose several conventions. Next I refine the monograph's purpose in particular with reference to the economies in transition. Thereafter I end with a road map to the volume.

1 – The Heart of the Matter at the Conference

In its very essence, "deepening" in EU speak means consolidating the achievements made since the integration process first got under way; I shall argue up front in Chapter 1 that one may just as well date this back to May 1950. But it also means forging ahead with new integration endeavors as enshrined in the quasi-constitutional documents of the Union – the Treaty of Rome as elaborated upon, admittedly rather clumsily (as explained in Chapter 2), in the so-called Treaty on European Union (TEU), better known as the Maastricht Treaty, as well as the various acts endorsed by the European Council since it first came into existence over two decades ago. By contrast, "widening" in the Union's lexicon simply means extending the geographical remit of the single market and other forms of common activities.

It is crucial to be aware of the fact that yet another enlargement of the Union *per se* is not specifically on the agenda of this Conference (for details, see Chaltiel 1995; Ludlow 1996b, c). Many other acute policy issues confronting the EU leadership are also officially not included in the Conference's purview. Most notable among them is monetary integration by 1999 for at least a core group of EU Member States. Indeed, the Conference is ostensibly concerned primarily with the review of the Maastricht Treaty as the latter originally called for it. Its main purpose is to strengthen the institutions and governance mechanisms of the EU to permit the Fifteen to forge ahead toward their so-called *finalité politique*. In the EU's terminology, that means essentially the ultimate federal or confederal form of a (western?) Europe remade, however the membership may come to determine that. And to do so with efficiency, openness, transparency, democracy, solidarity, cohesion, and accountability, among other ambitions that have been the subject of penetrating questioning since the early 1990s.

It should be clear from the outset, however, that innovating solutions to the core issues of "deepening" constitutes a precondition for enabling the accession of new countries. From this it follows directly that this Conference is about finding a suitable balance between forging ahead with integration and accommodating new members. It is also a make-it-or-break-it sequence of, what are undoubtedly, difficult deliberations precisely because widening cannot be envisaged, not even in principle, without deepening integration. The only exception could be entertained on the assumption that the paramount ambitions of the quasi-constitutional acts of the Union will be dramatically altered – hollowed out, in fact. None of the leaders of the Member States have thus far been willing to commit him/herself openly even to envisioning such a dilution.

However, some members have assiduously sought to go for the narrowest interpretation of these ambitions. This has been notably the case for Mr. John Major's conservative Government. Neither is it a carefully guarded secret that several Member States may well be bent on achieving precisely such a watering down of the EU's core ambitions, thus transforming the EU eventually into little more than a free-trading arrangement. That is a minority view, however. It has some appeal for the potential members, particularly those from the eastern part of Europe, for reasons that must be carefully spelled out and weighed. The majority of the present EU members, however, do not seem to favor such a dilution. Most would like to forge ahead rapidly with the consolidation of the achievements made over the past several decades and indeed move into new areas of collaboration, such as in coordinating foreign policy, home affairs, and social issues.

Precisely because widening is predicated on successfully moving forward with deepening, a positive, successful outcome of the Conference is especially important. This is notably so since the European

Council has committed itself to consider favorably applications for accession of ten transition economies, namely those with a Europe Agreement, as well as Cyprus and Malta, after the Conference's successful conclusion (on which more in Chapter 1). Particularly the extension of the EU's geographical remit toward the eastern part of Europe now poses severe economic, technical, political, and other problems. Without exaggeration, this is at the very heart of the Conference's debates, although no EU leader will officially acknowledge that much. It is also at the center of attention around contemporary European integration efforts.

Against this backdrop, the present compact volume seeks to highlight the core issues of the policies as well as of the mechanics of engineering the accession of the ten transition economies into the EU. Other issues around the Conference, notably on institutional and decision-making reforms, are not explored in detail (see Ludlow 1996c for a solid overview). I furthermore address many of the problems of forging ahead with the elaboration and implementation of a more constructive relationship with other transition economies. I do so by looking at actual and potential cooperation programs for economies in transition that will not be credible applicants for accession for decades to come. Moreover, I examine the paramount interests of the EU with respect to the economies in transition that are unlikely ever to become EU members, because either they are not European, however the continent's eastern borders in particular will in the end be delimited, or they may not wish to seek entry into the EU for their own reasons.

In all this, I wish to make it explicit that I have no intention of taking here any particular partisan position on matters debated at or surrounding the Conference. Thus I shall touch upon the core matters of monetary union without questioning in detail the inherent logic, economic justification, or the wisdom of the policy measures envisioned in order to introduce a common monetary policy with fixed exchange rates for a while, to be followed within three years by the introduction of a common currency. Similarly, the mechanics of the latter three items are not the subject matter here. Rather, I shall be concerned primarily with the way in which the debate on Economic and Monetary Union (EMU), monetary union in particular, as called for by earlier policy decisions, is currently encumbering the deliberations at the Conference. And even then I shall do so primarily in the light of what the debate may mean for the accession of the economies in transition to the EU.

2 – Terminological Conventions

Because so many policy makers are so very touchy about nomenclature I wish to put up front several propositions on the definition of the EU, the economies in transition, and my core purpose in crafting this volume.

Explaining the definition is perhaps the easiest. Rather than proceed with the identification of whatever the organizational format of western European integration may have been called over time, throughout this volume I shall use EU to refer to the institutional framework for postwar integration endeavors, starting from the serious discussions of the so-called Schuman Plan in 1950 and ranging all the way to the present. I shall deviate from this course only when the particular point under discussion would lose some of its accuracy or potency if I were not to identify the specific name of the organization at a particular point in time. Thus one could conceivably talk about the six founder members of the EU. But it would be silly to identify those six as having established the EU in January 1958.

I shall follow the same custom in describing the executive organ of the EU. This is presently known either as the European Commission or, more officially, as the Commission of the European Communities (EC), and before the merger of the three Communities (the EC, European Atomic Energy Community or Euratom, and the European Coal and Steel Community or ECSC) in 1967 as the Commission of the European Economic Community (EEC). I am aware of the finely hewn message that is intended to be thereby conveyed: The Commission is not authorized to meddle in the 'communautarian' manner with the two other pillars of the EU. Its remit is essentially the three cited Communities as unified in a fashion in 1967. Nevertheless, this is a cumbersome name. Unless there is room for misunderstanding or misrepresentation, I shall therefore utilize only the designation European Commission or Commission throughout the volume.

In this context also a brief word about 'communautarian' and 'accedent,' which are not quite commonly coined expressions in English, is in order. These notions do convey, however, the special flavor or character of the EU's integration process. One could conceivably prefer 'community' over 'communautarian,' for example. The former is certainly more common. Unfortunately, it is quite imprecise. The way actions are taken in the EU in general, and in the Commission in particular, is not really always in the community spirit. Rather it reflects more often than not the *sui generis*, quasi-supranational authority with which some aspects of the EU's behavior have been invested. It is this singularity that I hope to impart by preferring, when appropriate, the expression 'communautarian' and its derivatives over 'community.'

The designation communautarianism plays arguably no greater role than in delineating the so-called *acquis communautaire et politique*, something that in the earlier years of EU cooperation was referred to as the *acquis communautaire* (here both frequently abbreviated simply to the *acquis*). Clearly, it encompasses more than the legal and administrative rules and regulations that circumscribe the single market or designate the Union's own governance. Without exaggeration, it definitely refers to the totality of what the Member States have agreed upon as being their 'communautarian' approach to tackling problems, whatever their nature, at the quasi-supranational regional, rather than the lower, governance level. This includes the gamut of decision-making *modi operandi* set by the Member States in order to arrive at the preceding concertation of views and *sui generis* common approaches.

A similar special sense I would have liked to impart to 'accedent' by reserving the term for characterizing the very peculiar manner in which candidates for accession are eventually ushered into the EU and become full Member States. In the end, I decided to use that particular expression sparingly, if only to avoid offending the linguistic sensibilities of all too many readers.

Using the designation 'economies in transition' or 'transition economies' interchangeably for all the countries in Europe that used to be managed through some form of mandatory central planning under a single communist-party constraint is an altogether different matter. Many of these countries claim they do not want to be lumped together either under the above label or the post-Yalta concept of 'eastern Europe,' even if the latter is used purely for geographical rather than political or ideological purposes. I am fully aware of these sensibilities. Nonetheless, there are two features that are incontrovertible: These countries are by and large geographically located in the eastern part of Europe and they are without exception still continuing with their transformation from planned societies with a single-party dominance to pluralistic democracies with market-based resource allocation. Likewise these countries do not wish to be encompassed by the label postcommunist or postsocialist economies or agglomerated under any of the many other headings that have been used, rather confusingly, since 1989 (for details, see Brabant 1992, pp. 6-9).

However, referring to these countries individually or as the "economies of central and eastern Europe, the Baltic States, and the Commonwealth of Independent States (CIS)" is simply too clumsy. For one thing, one would then have to explain what precisely is behind the labels 'central Europe,' or more precisely 'east-central Europe,' invoking the region's western Christian background as opposed to the Orthodox Christian background of eastern Europe. That certainly poses problems, for example, for the two Caucasian States with a western Christian heritage. Moreover, these terms carry quite some historical baggage that I would wish to avoid here. Claims that some of these countries are "no longer in transition" are spurious at best. Indeed it is precisely because they are – and will be – in transition between an administratively planned society dominated by a singular political creed to a properly functioning – governable, if you wish – pluralistic democracy with a market-based allocation of resources for a long time to come – but for some countries far longer than for others, of course – that the problems of ushering some of these countries under the EU's umbrella are so involved and daunting.

There is no easy solution aside from asserting that I shall insist upon using the designation economies in transition or transition economies interchangeably, depending on euphony, to refer to the countries in the eastern part of Europe with which the EU is compelled – if only for its own security, economic, defense, ecological, health, political, and other interests – to build up and maintain a special relationship. The notion 'eastern part of Europe' I use occasionally as an alternative shorthand designation for the above twenty-seven countries. I have no other motivation whatsoever, and any accusation that may be made about my political, ideological, professional, or other biases, whether intended or not, I do categorically reject up front.

In this context, eastern Europe is utilized as distinct from the former Soviet Union. Unless I specify it differently, eastern Europe encompasses Albania, Bosnia and Herzegovina, Bulgaria, Croatia, the Czech Republic, Hungary, Macedonia, Poland, Romania, Slovakia, Slovenia, and Yugoslavia; when reference is to the period when Czechoslovakia and the former incarnation of Yugoslavia were still intact, I do, of course, mean those countries rather than the successor States. The designation CIS is here utilized solely as the complement of the post-Soviet Union other than the three Baltic States (Estonia, Latvia, and Lithuania); in this, I shall disregard the shifts in the composition of the CIS, whether formal or not, since it was first constituted in late 1991. When there is no room for misunderstanding, eastern Europe since late 1991 includes the three Baltic States. Otherwise I mention these countries separately.

3 – The Focus of the Volume

Finally, what I hope to achieve with this volume has determined part of the layout and indeed the way in which I present the arguments. This book is manifestly not meant to be a standard academic treatment of the economics or politics of (western) European integration. Such a treatise might well be warranted, given the confusion that exists even among otherwise well-equipped observers about the theory of comparative advantage and integration. Two examples from my recent experience and reading may suffice. In dealing with the Baltic States, a keen observer, Anatol Lieven (1993, p. 77), has stated to my chagrin that the Baltic Common Market does not really work, ostensibly because the opportunities for worthwhile trade between the three countries are limited as "[t]he Balts basically produce the same kind of goods, and none have [*sic*!] the raw materials they so desperately need." So much for intra-industry trade and specialization!

More to the point is the second example. From the moment the Council for Mutual Economic Assistance (CMEA) collapsed in the early 1990s, many of the newfangled participants in the debates about transition and its policies in the eastern part of Europe have underlined their view that the future of these countries lies in solidifying bonds with the western part of Europe, not in strengthening their reciprocal economic ties. Economic cooperation among these countries foundered after 1989-1990, though chiefly for other than good economic reasons. Recent trade behavior of the more vibrant of the central European economies in transition in particular has now proved the point earlier made on the available opportunities for bolstering intraregional economic cooperation (Brabant 1990, 1991; UNECE 1990, 1991a, b). That potential for fruitful regional cooperation should have been clear on the simple logical principle that any economically warranted trade deserves to be realized, unless there is a gross threat to, possibly a violation of, national security at stake.

But I shall not delve further into the more academic aspects of economic integration beyond assuming that the countries that have embarked on economic and political integration, as well as those seeking to join that movement, are indeed pursuing their own individual and, hopefully also, collective interests, including in economic respects. My main ambition is indeed to clarify fundamentally the crucial umbilical link between deepening EU integration and widening its remit, and that proceeding with the latter is inextricably contingent on forging ahead with the former. The arguments are deceptively simple; but only at first blush. The facile reductionist approach to dealing with matters of great complexity has produced a number of irritating misunderstandings. Many have been voiced so very often over the past five years, such as regarding the moral or historical claims of the transition economies to immediate and full membership in the EU, that some observers have come to accept them as self-evident verities. They are anything but!

4 – A Road Map

To cut through the thicket without obliging every interested reader into digesting every detail of the argument I marshal, I decided to present my case in two rounds. The first part provides an overview of the principal policy issues at stake in fusing some of the transition economies with the EU and forging a more productive relationship with the rest of the eastern part of Europe, always seen in the first place against the backdrop of the ongoing Conference. The second part, then, paints those same arguments in much greater detail with all the proper references, justifications, and reservations. I hope that the full arguments will be sufficiently persuasive to those who wish to test their skepticism against the actual evidence adduced as well as the logical arguments wielded in the process.

Chapter 1 sets forth the backdrop to the Conference in some detail. It traces in particular the broad contours of the political economy of new accessions and, because of the preconditions for successful accession negotiations in a fifth round and beyond, discusses the main parameters of the Conference. The latter's salience is underlined. The chapter also clarifies the main purposes pursued in this volume. It details the nature of an IGC and where precisely it belongs in the governance of (western) European integration. It then sets forth the three principal areas of concern that constitute the broad backdrop to the Conference's deliberations.

The aim of Chapter 2, in the absence of a clear-cut agenda, is to detail the likely areas of policy debate that are bound to inform the Conference, relying basically on the various documents that have already been prepared and on the wide-ranging debate that has been under way since the conclusions of the 1990-1991 twin IGCs at Maastricht. I argue the case for supporting a much broader agenda than is formally intimated by the Conference's purported mandate. Indeed, it is reasonable to conjecture that the most important agenda items will revolve around five broad problem areas. I examine briefly the so-called Westendorp Report and the issues tabled in Turin that have found their way into the mandate issued to the Council of Ministers of Foreign Affairs and their assistants, who have actually been doing the legwork negotiations. That process is explained in some detail. Then I argue the case for viewing matters more broadly, and I develop a functional catalogue of the issues that are bound to undergird the deliberations of the Conference. Finally, I point to the widening issues that emerge from considerations of the deepening that the Conference's outcome is supposed to ensure for decades to come.

Although forging ahead with monetary integration has evolved into one of the critical policy dilemmas of European integration at this juncture, and as such will willy-nilly impact on the course of the IGC's deliberations, I decided to take up the more detailed questions arising in that context in Chapter 3. The purpose is not to examine the *pro* and *contra* of monetary integration, such as in the context of the optimum currency area. Rather, I take it for granted that the EU members have decided to move toward monetary union. Accordingly, I focus on the problems encountered in progressing toward that fateful state and the difficulties that may arise once the union will come into force. I also clarify the prevailing policy dilemmas arising from the obligation to start up monetary union in 1999 at the latest and set forth some options available to policy makers interested in exercising sensible statecraft rather than adhering to a rigid schedule that in and of itself lacks economic logic in any case.

The rest of the book is devoted nearly exclusively to the economies in transition. Chapter 4 traces the evolving relationship, and the recent experiences of the interactions, between the EU and the economies in transition, but especially the ten that have in the meantime negotiated a Europe Agreement with the EU prior to any concrete discussion about accession. It starts from the state of affairs on the eve of the momentous economic, political, and social shifts in the economies in transition since 1989. Then I look at western Europe's reaction to this unprecedented opportunity. I trace the assistance efforts western Europe in particular engaged in. The nature and portent of the Europe Agreement as well as other EU agreements with economies in transition are detailed. I finally pose the question whether the interactions between the EU and the economies in transition have emerged from some well-defined strategy on the basis of which a constructive relationship leading up to full membership in the EU could be built prospectively. I sketch there also, in case of a negative answer, what could reasonably be entertained to fashion such a constructive strategy.

Chapter 5 discusses the core issues to be tackled on the road to full membership, while gathering as much pertinent information as possible pertaining to the eventual deliberations between the Union and one or more transition economies. I recall the essence of integration into Europe's single market. Then I clarify the much heated debate about the criteria determining suitability for accession. Next I treat the parameters of generic accession negotiations, while drawing as much relevant material as possible for the accession negotiations in which the economies in transition will soon be engaged. This is followed by some speculation about the date of entry and the key elements of the transition phase. The problems of eventually assimilating the so-called *acquis communautaire et politique* constitute, of course, the heart of the matter, both for potential entrants and the present EU membership.

Precisely because of the problems that arise in any effort to usher the transition economies swiftly into the EU, Chapter 6 discusses the usefulness and contours of a comprehensive pre-accession strategy. Reference is in particular to the economies in transition that are credible applicants for accession to the EU. I also examine there whether such an approach could usefully be considered by way of reshaping the cooperation programs that the EU has extended to other economies in transition since the early 1990s, both to those that in time may become credible candidates for membership and to others that are not European or do not wish to join the EU for their own political reasons.

The conclusion sums up the central arguments made: Because widening is by its very nature contingent on deepening integration in the EU, and it will be so very difficult, not just costly in budgetary terms, to fuse the selected transition economies with the EU, it would be highly desirable to formulate soonest a constructive and comprehensive interim approach, which I prefer to refer to as a pre-accession strategy, to facilitate eventual enlargement for all parties involved, but especially for the potential entrants from the eastern part of Europe. Since these countries fall into distinct categories of readiness for assuming the obligations of EU membership, as well as for availing themselves of the benefits potentially accruing from such membership, in particular untrammeled competition in the large single market for intraindustry trade, notably manufactures, such a strategy should be modulated according to "time-and-place" features, that is, in the first instance according to the capabilities of the individual transition economy seeking membership.

PART ONE

Overview of the Policy Issues

Overview of the Policy Issues

The Intergovernmental Conference that opened in Turin (Italy) on 29 March 1996 is expected to last for at least a year, possibly until late 1997. This is an important event, one with the potential of taking on truly historical dimensions, in the integration movement in Europe. Such a negotiating forum is rarely convened – the present one is only the sixth in the history of the postwar integration movement in western Europe. It is as a rule held only when policy decisions on fundamental constitutional and governance aspects of the integration process in the EU are at stake. Such is the case with the present Conference as well. Indeed, it is expected to proceed with refining the core ambitions of the Union as enshrined in the Treaty of Rome, and further elaborated in particular in the Maastricht Treaty, and to improve the institutional and decision-making mechanisms that will facilitate realization of these paramount targets.

Expectations about the salience of the Conference run very high, given its intrinsic significance, but arguably also because the Union has been confronted in recent years with a panoply of daunting problems around its integration process. Especially since the conclusion of the Maastricht Treaty, the range and scope of these difficulties have expanded in directions that have surprised policy makers as well as many observers of the EU's integration scene. Furthermore, a wide range of diverging views on the Union's desired future have recently come to the fore once again, almost with a vengeance.

The significance of the present Conference must therefore be assessed within that purview, including clarifications of the EU's core ambitions. Forging ahead with integration in the years to come, both in finalizing what has been under way for decades, by consolidating its achievements to date, and in extending the compass of integration in the Union to related endeavors belonging to its so-called *finalité politique*, is thus a high priority. It is the purpose of this book to contribute to clarifying what the Conference is all about and what it might conceivably mean for Europe and indeed the global community. But I hasten to add that the real focus here is on its implications for the economies in transition of the eastern part of Europe, in the first place those that are more credible candidates for accession.

Seen in the light of the above considerations, the significance of the Conference will reside in the extent to which it can contribute to imparting a new impetus to the integration process that has been under way for over four decades and extend it to a wider range of activities related to the Union's so-called *finalité politique* in the years to come. It is expected to build upon the Maastricht Treaty by 'deepening' integration and enacting changes in institutional and governance matters so as to permit further 'widening' in the years ahead. These are critical policy issues addressed to the present Member States. Consolidating the degree of integration achieved to date and forging ahead with new tasks – deepening, in other words – are preconditions to be met for an effective widening of the membership to succeed.

1 – The Importance of the Conference

It is against this backdrop, notably the centrality of deepening versus widening and the contingency of the latter on the former, that the Conference assumes such salience in reflecting upon Europe's future. Whether successful or not, the outcomes of this Conference are bound to have major implications for the chances of the economies in transition with a Europe Agreement (four of which are yet to be ratified) to accede to the Union in the foreseeable future. Failure to deal effectively with the major problems facing the Union, in the first instance regarding decision making and institutional efficiency, could very well block accession altogether and eventually fracture the integration policies and ambitions that have been at the core of the Union since the Treaty of Rome was first drafted. A successful outcome would fulfill the critical preconditions for the Union to move ahead with deepening its own integration format and, at the same time, facilitate enlargement to the eastern part of the continent as well as encourage a strengthening of cooperation programs with other economies in transition. Such an approach could also pave the way toward a thorough review of the Union's other types of preferential arrangements, given the changed international-policy environment prevailing at this juncture and its likely transformations ahead.

In other words, the Conference is not simply of importance to the present membership. The Union's political and economic weight in world affairs will alone guarantee much wider significance for the Conference. However, it will be of special importance to the transition economies and particularly those in eastern Europe that have applied – or intend to apply – for membership in the Union and desire that their requests be acted upon soonest. The results of the Conference will unavoidably exert a major influence on whether the process of negotiation and accession proceeds smoothly, and in a way that reinforces both the transformation of the economies in transition and the general security of Europe as a whole, or whether accession has become more difficult and uncertain. If the latter, negative effects on the construction of vibrant market economies and stable democratic institutions in eastern Europe will be unavoidable. For one thing, a firm anchor in Europe's single market will enable those countries eventually to catch up with levels of development and technology in western Europe and in and of itself sustain growth for some time, thus affording these countries some of the means by which they can prolong and strengthen their present economic recovery and embark upon a veritable growth dynamic.

The outcome will also have ramifications for the Union's relations with other economies in transition, which may not qualify because they are not conceivably European or may not wish to apply for membership in the Union for their own reasons. This is particularly so for Russia and many other members of the CIS with which the Union nonetheless shares important interests in a wide array of economic, environmental, foreign policy, health, security, and other matters.

The main focus of the discussion here, as it is in the fuller development of the arguments in Part Two, is on the implications of the Conference for the transition economies seeking entry to the Union and on how the process of accession might be assured. But the issues that crop up here are so complex and the views of participants, insofar as they have been expressed in the run-up to the Conference, so varied that it is desirable first to try to clarify what the Conference and the prevailing policy dilemmas are all about before discussing their implications for transition economies. Moreover, although some contributions to the policy discussion separate the issue of 'deepening' integration among the present members of the Union from that of 'widening' it to include new members from eastern (and southern) Europe, I marshal support for the view that 'widening' will not be possible without at least some 'deepening' if the basic ambitions of the Union, as expressed in the Treaty of Rome, are not to be abandoned. There are many factors that buttress this view. Better governance, efficiency, transparency, subsidiarity, cooperation in foreign policy and in home affairs; moving toward a common understanding on features of social policy; and improving many other aspects of working together in the Union, as policy makers and even the citizens of a number of Member States have been increasingly demanding in recent years, are the topics that the Conference will necessarily have to grapple with. Some discussion of the issues pertaining to the primordial need to forge ahead with consolidating achievements and further integration among the Fifteen is therefore necessary in order to identify the principal parameters that will inevitably shape the debate on widening.

The assertion that widening can hardly proceed without deepening, if the central purposes of the Treaties of Rome and Maastricht are to be preserved, is so fundamental in working toward a closer relationship between the Union and the economies in transition, especially, but not only, those that have applied for accession or are expected to do so soon, that I feel justified in calling attention to the dichotomy at crucial junctures of the exposition of the place of the economies in transition in all matters that affect the current Conference. The options at stake cannot simply be reduced to accession or not. Rather, the central focus is on how to make accession feasible and easier to achieve in the years ahead both for the Union and the actual and potential applicants, on the one hand, and how to improve the cooperative relationship between the Union and other economies in transition to enhance stability and governability of Europe.

2 – Backdrop to the Conference: The Challenges Ahead

The importance of the Intergovernmental Conference can be understood in the light of four major policy challenges currently facing the Union. First, the Union has grown to fifteen members through four enlargements. However, by and large, it is still trying to function effectively with institutions and governance mechanisms laid down in the Treaty of Rome in 1957 for the six founder Member States. To expedite decision making through appropriate majority voting and representation, and to improve the Union's efficiency and transparency, it is widely accepted that new rules need to be agreed upon. The Conference will therefore have to make progress in streamlining the management of the integration process in a number of directions, including in decision making, in enhanced institutional efficiency and transparency, in budgetary matters, and in formulating and implementing common policy stances.

As a result of such streamlining of the EU's governance, some Member States will lose in stature or decision-making power while others will correspondingly gain. This naturally creates tensions, frictions, and apprehensions that need to be removed in a constructive manner before it is possible to forge ahead with integration and expansion. Although such a review of institutional and decision-making arrangements was one of the original purposes in calling for the 1996 Review Conference when the TEU was concluded in December 1991, there is at present by far no unanimity of views on how best to proceed with these matters.

Second, the Union's ambitions have moved from economic integration in a single market, to monetary integration, now scheduled for 1999, and a common currency, now scheduled for 2002; and increasingly to elements of common policies in foreign relations, security, defense, juridical matters, and home affairs. In addition to consolidating those achievements, some of which remain highly fragile, some Member States favor transferring already at this stage new tasks to the European Commission, such as on issues pertaining to the environment, energy, civil protection, and social affairs. There are sharp differences of views among the Member States not only on this expansion of responsibilities but also on how effectively to proceed with the common policy stances on other than economic affairs narrowly interpreted. All of these bear on the issue of further 'deepening' integration.

These divergent outlooks on how best to forge ahead have been preventing integration from moving beyond EMU for some time now. Even on the latter's second component – monetary union by 1999 and a common currency by 2002 – considerable differences among the

Member States have come to the fore in recent years, and the task of keeping to the calendar agreed to in 1991 for monetary union is creating strains in a wide range of Union activities and of policy stances held by the Member States. These stem in part from the pressures to meet the criteria of economic convergence at a time when economic activity is cyclically weak. There are, however, also more fundamental objections to monetary union at play for some EU members, Denmark and the United Kingdom in particular.

Third, since 1993, a further enlargement of the Union toward the eastern part of Europe, as well as Cyprus and Malta, has been accepted in principle. This will probably occur in several waves spread out over a number of years. In the case of the economies in transition, a rapid accession is not possible for three reasons. Without fundamental changes in the Union's constitutional arrangements, a further 'widening' of the Union would probably paralyze its decision-making capabilities. Also, the economies in transition are not yet sufficiently far advanced in their economic and political transformations to be able to live up to, and thus fully benefit from, the essential rules and regulations of the *acquis communautaire*, and increasingly the *acquis communautaire et politique*, that govern competition in the single European market. But even if these countries were able to abide fully by these rules and regulations, with the Union's present transfer programs still in place their accession would probably be too costly for the current Member States. Moreover, the burden of increased budgetary costs and of the reallocation of benefits would be distributed asymmetrically within the Union. Arranging for suitable compensation of the losers will thus be one of the critical policy tasks ahead.

Finally, the Union would seem to be in need of formulating its own priorities more explicitly, including the specification of weights, and of ensuring that all Member States share them, not just with respect to the more credible applicants for membership among the economies in transition but also to others. Some of the latter will not be able to lodge a viable application for some decades to come. Others will not join at all, either because they are not European or for their own reasons.

It is against this broad canvas that a number of policy issues revolving around the Conference are discussed here and analyzed at length in the chapters that follow. I evaluate in particular how the further expansion of the Union's remit toward the eastern part of the continent could be facilitated and how a more constructive relationship with other economies in transition could be established, seen against the backdrop of the Conference. When projected against the agenda referring to the economies in transition – in the first place the ten with a Europe Agreement, all of which have already submitted their accession request – the Conference assumes an even more august, a truly historical dimension: The remaking of Europe.

In fact, I am fully aware that the principal preoccupation of the Conference will not formally be the further enlargement of the Union, nor has this topic figured prominently among the policy issues raised by individual participants before and around the Conference. Nevertheless, what happens at the Conference will play a major role in shaping the modalities by which the economies in transition, among other credible candidates for entry, will be enabled to accede in the not too remote future. But without hammering together satisfactory solutions to the many institutional and decision-making problems, the chances of the transition economies joining the Union with its main policy ambitions intact within the next decade or so would seem to be fairly remote.

3 – Policy Dilemma of Widening the Union

Another enlargement of the Union, to be engineered without changing the fundamental tenor and direction of the movement toward deeper integration, as first laid down in the Treaty of Rome, was in principle agreed to by the Union in mid 1993. This decision was arrived at only after long hesitation among the Member States and strong political pleas from the leadership of a number of transition economies. Also a large number of commentators, academics and others, had been urging the Union to reconsider its views on widening its remit yet again.

For the fifth and subsequent enlargements of the Union to become feasible, however, many conditions will have to be met. This holds as much for the criteria that the economies in transition will have to comply with as for the ability of the Union to accommodate new entrants, with the prospect of an eventual doubling of the present membership.

Expectations that the more advanced transition economies, particularly the central European ones, could be admitted into the European Union by the year 2000 seem to be extraordinarily optimistic, however. Even if the Conference were to be a full success by mid 1997 and further deepening of the Union's integration to proceed smoothly, accession of the candidate members would not be a *pro forma* matter; it simply could not be just that. The basic reason is that the gaps in institutional capabilities and in levels of development, technology, and trade participation of the economies in transition relative to those of the range of economies presently in the Union remain considerable. They will continue to pose a palpable obstacle for smoothly merging these countries into the single market and Europe-wide competition along established rules for some time to come.

Even if further deepening of integration in the Union were to be achieved smoothly in the near term, something that cannot simply be taken for granted, and the transition economies forged ahead with their transformation agenda at full speed, none of them are likely to achieve membership before, at best, the middle, but possibly not before the end, of the next decade. This follows even when one only contemplates the sheer mechanics of the accession negotiations and the ratification process. The politics and economics of new accessions may call for even more time to make enlargement feasible.

Deepening integration in the Union requires, in the first place fundamental changes in the institutional and governance structures within which the Fifteen pursue common policies of various degrees of intensity. These changes are required to ensure progress in European integration, even without contemplating another enlargement, and to avoid increasing tension in relations among the present Fifteen as well as between the Union and its other external partners. But it should be clear also that failure to deepen integration within the Union, in line with the ambitions specified in its quasi-constitutional treaties and the subsequent decisions of the Council, would effectively block the entry of the transition economies of eastern Europe into the Union. Decision making in the Union would be severely hampered, and in a number of important respects paralyzed. There are few, if any, Member States that favor such an outcome for the sake of accommodating the applicants for accession.

But, even if the Union does progress soon with its own deepening, the accession of some of the economies in transition is unlikely to be

easy unless these countries move ahead quickly with their own transformations and establish market economies that are able to function
effectively within the Union's single market. Despite the considerable
achievements with economic transformation and restructuring of many
of the transition economies since 1989, much indeed remains to be
accomplished before they can reach this stage. This applies especially
to institution building, rounding off the process of privatization, and
enacting further structural change so as to be able to participate effectively in full intra-industry competition.

Most economies in transition are still in need of strengthening
policy credibility and, at the same time, of obtaining a greater degree of
security to sustain their policies of socioeconomic transformation with
at least a minimal degree of popular support. They are also looking
forward to reaping the benefits of joining the single market, in part to
facilitate and ease the burden of painful adjustments at home. It is
possible, however, to attain many of these objectives to a considerable
degree, but admittedly not to the full extent, without rushing hastily
into a premature, fully-fledged membership of the Union.

A good part of the expected economic benefits can be mobilized by
supporting – indeed by actively facilitating – the general transformation
processes in the applicant countries, as has already to some extent been
achieved through the Union's various assistance programs, as well as
by helping them to prepare specifically for constructive competition in
the single market. A first step in that direction was set in the White
Paper released in mid 1995, which clarifies priorities on assimilating the
acquis communautaire. This was meant to be only one episode in putting together a pre-accession strategy by the European Commission.
Another was involving policy makers from the more advanced economies in transition in the Union's policy debates in selected areas. Other
elements are now being subsumed under this heading as well.

Whatever the intentions of the Essen Council, which recommended
the elaboration of such a strategy, what is presently in place does not
by a far shot constitute a comprehensive and coherent pre-accession
strategy. Indeed, a strategy worthy of that name must be more encompassing than, for example, simply informing the candidate countries
about the complexity of the *acquis* and the order in which these rules
and regulations could usefully be introduced and applied. Likewise,

allowing policy makers to be more closely in touch with Union affairs should not be confined to yet another photo opportunity. Much more is involved if effective assistance with a view to accelerating the preparedness of the economies in transition for accession is to be rendered in as constructive a manner as the Union's facilities truly allow and the clamor for safeguarding their just-recently won sovereignty permits, after considerable agony.

Participating effectively in the single market necessarily requires the capacities to take an active part in intra-industry trade and specialization, something that so far has not been high on the policy agenda pursued in most countries of the eastern part of Europe. It would be useful to combine these objectives, together with the myriad of assistance programs already in place, into a well-targeted, more comprehensive, and consistent assistance strategy, which for the candidates for Union membership would amount to a streamlined pre-accession strategy, as discussed later. At the same time, the Union, and indeed other members of the Group of Twenty-four (G-24), might find it useful to gather assistance efforts into a more coherent cooperation strategy, if only for a more effectual pursuit of their own economic, foreign policy, and other interests.

The rationale for such a strategy falls squarely within the analysis of the transition process and the implications for western assistance for the economies in transition that I have developed in earlier work (Brabant 1990, 1991, 1993, 1995a). It has also been a solid thread running through much of the recent work published in core ECE documents (notably the issues of *Economic Survey of Europe* and *Economic Bulletin for Europe* published since 1990), in some of which I have had the privilege to participate. These analyses, positioned within a political-economy framework, have placed considerable emphasis on the importance – and difficulties – of creating the new institutional infrastructure required so that a market economy can function effectively, a task which has been further complicated by the simultaneous need to build the political institutions of pluralistic democracy. They have also underlined that the reasonable time required to achieve these objectives is by no means a short period. For many countries and for some issues, it will take decades before sound delivery on the promises of "1989" can be assured.

4 – *The Most Likely Agenda for the Conference*

The concrete agenda of the Conference is not yet known. As per the agreement reached by the Heads of State and Government in Turin, the Ministers of Foreign Affairs and their immediate assistants were to work on the core issues in a series of meetings that started right after the conclusion of the Turin summit, from April to June 1996. These should have led up to a first assessment of what can and cannot be accomplished, in time for the European Council to be convened in Florence (21-22 June 1996). It had been anticipated that substantive issues could have been dealt with in time for that Council session to issue more concrete recommendations for the IGC under way. This has not proved possible, however. Instead, the assistants and the Council of Ministers since Turin succeeded only in 'reviewing' the issues. As a result, the chairman of the group of assistants, the Italian Silvio Fagiolo, presented his impressions to the Florence Council in his own name, not that of the negotiators. Current expectations are that under the Irish Council Presidency in the second half of 1996 the Council of Ministers of Foreign Affairs will set its own working agenda on substantive matters, relying in part on the preparatory consultations of the assistants and the European Commission. The latter will, however, continue until the Conference's conclusion.

Although it would be premature to speculate on what will eventually be tabled for intensive negotiations, beginning hopefully during the second half of 1996 with the impetus of the October 1996 Extraordinary Council, the agenda yet to be worked out is bound to be influenced by three groups of concerns: (1) the fine-tuning of the Maastricht Treaty with a view to deepening integration, which was the original purpose of the Conference; (2) seminal unforeseen events since 1990, notably the complicated transformations under way in the transition economies; the turbulence in financial markets that undermined the earlier arrangements for moving toward monetary union by early 1999 at the latest; and the recent slowdown in economic activity in major Member States at a time of already unprecedented levels of unemployment and social discontent; and (3) the need for credible arrangements to overcome obstacles encountered during ratification of the Maastricht Treaty.

Efforts are being made by some of the principals involved, including the European Commission, to confine the Conference's agenda chiefly to institutional reform and to the governance of the core European institutions – the original purposes of the Review Conference – augmented with some elements of the popular dissatisfaction expressed since then. This is understandable given the Commission's position and the original purposes of the Review Conference as it was called for in the Maastricht Treaty. Moreover, these matters alone are sufficiently daunting, given the continuing lack of agreement among the Fifteen on the direction of future integration with its consequences for institutional underpinnings and decision making. Britain's month-long noncooperation in mid 1996 only exacerbated finding a *modus vivendi*.

In practice, however, it is unlikely to be possible to adhere to this narrowly defined governance agenda. Given the range and complexity of the problems facing the Union, it will not be feasible to 'deepen' without addressing other important aspects of integration. Seminal decisions on the EU's compass, notably in the fields of foreign policy, defense, juridical matters, and home and social affairs, are expected by some Union members. Others attach a high priority to enlargement, however. The interdependence among the major issues in the debate is such that one cannot be pursued without affecting the others.

In that light, it might be more appropriate to consider the problems dealt with directly or indirectly by the Conference under five broad headings: (1) deepening the Union's policy remit, (2) completing EMU through pragmatic solutions to the prevailing policy dilemmas, (3) strengthening the Union institutionally and in governance matters, (4) evaluating the costs and benefits of widening for the present members, and (5) assessing the costs and benefits of accession for the economies in transition over time, as well as accommodating these countries within the Union's framework if early membership is not feasible.

5 – Striking a Balance Between Deepening and Widening

First, the Union will need to find ways and means to overcome the lethargy about moving ahead with integration – deepening, in other words – that set in soon after the endorsement of the Maastricht Treaty. This can only be accomplished by specifying more clearly Europe's *finalité politique* to which all Member States can commit or recommit themselves and which will serve as a solid point of reference, like a topological fixed point, for all countries desiring membership of the Union. Further drift in this respect risks not only undermining relations among the present members of the Union but also hampering the accession of the economies in transition possibly for years to come.

It should be crystal clear, however, that under the prevailing circumstances in the EU as well as in the transition economies, in the first place the ten with a Europe Agreement, a suitable balance between widening and deepening will have to be struck quite soon.

6 – *The Policy Dilemma of Monetary Integration*

Second, progress needs to be made with monetary integration in spite of the variations in policy commitment to achieving that stage of maturity of EMU observed already during the negotiations of the Maastricht Treaty and since the intermittent turmoil in the currency markets in late 1992 and mid 1993. Monetary union is essentially a logical extension of the single European market. Its merits cannot be decided by reference to whether the Union as a whole, or any meaningful subgroup of Member States (such as the 'core' that might start the monetary union), forms an optimum currency area, meaning a group of countries with maximum flexibility in resource allocation, particularly in markets for the factors of production, so that external shocks, particularly asymmetric ones, leading to temporary imbalances can be worked off reasonably smoothly; at least without provoking serious economic, political, or social tensions among various regional interest groups.

The Union is obviously not an optimum currency area, as defined, among other reasons because the flexibility of prices, notably of production factors, is limited particularly in the downward direction. This holds especially for the mobility of labor, which has remained quite confined in Europe. For various cultural, historical, political, religious, and other reasons that characterize Europe as Europe, labor mobility is likely to stay at this low level for decades to come, though some relaxation of prevailing institutional rigidities may yield an important degree of flexibility, notably in mobility within countries; that would strengthen the stability features of any monetary union. Until such price flexibility will be arranged, however, problems both in moving toward monetary union, given the diverse monetary situations in the Member States, and in sustaining the union in the event of asymmetric shocks disturbing the regional balance need to be tackled constructively.

The flexibility of adjustment, at least in the short run, provided by the possibility of currency devaluation, possibly at the direct expense of the competitive position of other Member States, will by definition no longer be available to participants in a monetary union. The adjustment should be steered by flexible wages and prices, but since these are on the whole rather sticky in a downward direction, as discussed, some room for greater fiscal federalism among the participants in the monetary union will need to be created in order to ensure the latter's stability. This requires coordination of stances on macroeconomic policy - among the participants, but not necessarily tight centralization.

The Maastricht Treaty and the decisions of the European Council since 1991 envisage moving toward monetary union in early 1999 on the basis of the so-called convergence criteria (on inflation, interest rates, budgetary imbalances, debt levels, and exchange-rate stability), and introducing the 'euro' as a common currency by 2002, as determined by the Madrid Council in December 1995. In this program, eligibility for admission to the monetary union will be determined on the basis of a relatively inflexible interpretation of the five convergence criteria as specified in the relevant protocol of the Maastricht Treaty. That poses the danger of creating monetary union as a formality or of provoking undesirable setbacks to policy credibility, particularly in real and financial markets. These may be very significant for Member States that do not join the monetary union, but whose policy flexibility could cause problems for participants. Competitive devaluations are simply not compatible with the functioning of a single market. In any case, the subsumed "small country" assumption in many of the arguments underlying the positions that favor retaining the exchange rate as a policy instrument is simply misplaced, given the preponderant share of intra-Union trade for all Member States.

It would have been more logical, and not just with the benefit of hindsight, to set the timetable for the initiation of monetary unification as the final step in a coherent strategy for harmonizing macroeconomic policy through which the chosen convergence criteria would have been met. This could conceivably have been programmed for a certain number of participants forming a critical minimum mass, provided rules of the game for other participants would have been put in place. Inception of the monetary union would then have been a natural, logical outcome of a process rather than a target to be met at all cost, regardless of what might be happening in the real economy. If expectations of medium- to long-term growth in the Union had been less optimistic than they were when the Maastricht Treaty was under negotiation, the target dates for monetary union or the specification of the convergence criteria would almost certainly have been quite different from those now invoked.

This episode suggests a number of lessons to be heeded when setting future integration deadlines, such as for the transition economies in the next round of accession negotiations. From an economic point of view, a deadline in and of itself is much less important than formulating a credible strategy on how to meet such a deadline, a theme to which I return on several occasions later in this volume when contemplating various aspects of bringing the economies in transition into the Union.

The Member States, however, are now committed to a pre-set date for inaugurating monetary union, lest a simple legalistic justification for another start-up date be agreed upon before the end of 1997. Unfortunately, the economic, let alone the political and social, circumstances for vigorously pursuing the policies required to secure compliance in time with the convergence targets are far from congenial at present. In particular, the fiscal criteria (levels of debt and budget imbalances in relation to gross domestic product or GDP) require tight fiscal policies, which is painful when economic performance in a number of key economies is weakening. Policy makers have at least four policy options.

• One is to proceed with monetary union as foreseen in the Maastricht Treaty, while observing the strict fulfillment of the convergence criteria, come what may, even as an empty shell or with very few participants. While entirely possible, this option would not be very credible to market participants and would probably exert negative repercussions on other components of the integration process.

• Second, the Member States could modify the convergence criteria sufficiently to enable a group of core countries to initiate monetary integration by the target date. This too is unlikely to be very credible, particularly among participants in financial markets, and might even infuse an element of instability into the union from the very beginning, which would be most undesirable. That outcome would almost certainly transpire if major deviations from the specified criteria were to be permitted, given the emphasis policy makers have placed in recent years on the importance of holding to the most rigid interpretation of the convergence criteria as conditions for admission.

• Third, in view of the timing problem – that is, the cyclical slowdown in economic activity in key Member States and the uncertainty as to whether a resumption of stronger growth will occur in late 1996 or in 1997, which creates difficulties in meeting the deficit criteria – the Fifteen could revise the Maastricht Treaty, or at least the interpretation of one article, and specify another date for starting the monetary union. While this would provide a breathing space for policy makers, there is no guarantee at all that conditions by the year 2000 or in 2001, or whatever new date is chosen, will make it any easier for most Member States, or even the critical core group, to abide by the convergence criteria. This objection could be removed if a genuine Treaty revision were to be agreed upon, entailing concurrence on the various policies to be observed by all or by a critical minimum of Member States before monetary union could be initiated. But the grave danger of this last option, which anyway would require restaging something similar to the 1990-1991 IGC on EMU, is that past efforts at launching monetary integration have shown that failure to implement an agreed program sets the movement back, on average, by at least a decade. In other words, postponing the start of monetary union at this point, which is the fourth attempt since 1962, may make it politically and diplomatically impossible to try again for quite some time.

• Finally, the Maastricht Treaty itself, although not the particular protocol that contains the quantitative magnitudes of the convergence criteria, provides for a measure of flexibility that would permit the monetary union to be inaugurated in 1999 with a larger membership without violating the spirit in which the specific convergence criteria – whatever their intrinsic economic merits – were set forth in the Treaty. After all, a number of countries *are* in a position to meet the commitments on inflation, exchange rates, and interest rates. Some even comply with the debt-to-GDP target. And marked progress toward reducing budget deficits has been recorded by several countries, although the situation in some has been aggravated by the current slowdown in economic growth. Note, however, that most have made significant progress with reducing the structural, as distinct from the conjunctural, component of the fiscal imbalance. Moreover, even the strict convergence criteria of the protocol will need to be interpreted anyway. Two examples thereof may suffice: Are the present wider exchange-rate bands regular or not? Must the comparison with the three best-performing Member States be in terms of the average, the best, or the worst?

The Union members might consider this fourth option, possibly during the Conference, if only as a fallback to ensure the start of monetary union in 1999. If a strong recovery were to occur later this year and to continue in 1997, it could permit a larger membership of the monetary union, which would be important because it would help to forestall problems of exchange-rate instability in countries that do not or cannot join the union. The rhetoric about adhering rigidly to the convergence criteria of the protocol could then be relaxed in favor of stressing the genuine progress in policies made in the spirit of the Treaty's specifications. This would permit the Member States to underline and cogently argue the room for constructive policy making through reasonable flexibility in the light of unanticipated economic circumstances.

7 – The Maastricht Treaty and Governance

The third range of concerns for the Conference is with finding a satisfactory solution to the Union's multiple governance issues. These have become particularly acute since the Maastricht Treaty was agreed to in late 1991. They include concerns about democracy, efficiency, subsidiarity, openness, transparency, and accountability. Engineering major improvements in these areas has become an urgent priority in order to regain and sustain popular as well as political support for the integration process. In particular, solutions to questions about representation in the European Parliament, the Commission, and the European Council and about the system of voting strengths on different categories of issues will have to be found through political compromise before another enlargement can realistically be entertained – underlining once again the need for suitably balancing widening and deepening.

Various formulae for resolving the multiple issues at stake have recently been suggested at the highest levels of policy making. Compromise solutions on electoral representation and on membership of the Commission would appear to be within reach. More difficult will be reaching agreement on the division of powers among the major Union institutions (the Commission, the Council, the Parliament, and the Court) and the cutoff for 'qualified majority' voting (possibly organized in several tiers) on all but a very few constitutional issues.

8 – Can the Union Afford to Admit the Transition Economies?

The fourth issue, bringing the economies in transition into the EU as full members, will take time and will involve substantial costs to be borne both by the present Union members and the transition economies. It is pertinent to be clear about the expected gains for Union members as well as for the potential applicants. And it is particularly germane to bear in mind as coherently as possible the time path of distributional asymmetries in the benefits and costs – not solely confined to budgetary effects – among and between Union members and applicants. Now that the reluctance to consider enlargement toward the eastern part of Europe has abated, it is time to examine how and when these applicants can realistically be accommodated. Political will is one factor; practical implementation, at least in this case, is quite another.

Budgetary matters have figured most prominently in current debates. This is a question of who pays what in order to apply the existing Union transfer programs to the economies in transition when they enter the Union. These are certainly important considerations, particularly at times of fiscal austerity in Member States. Even so, the obstacles arising from other aspects of the process of integrating with the Union, also in terms of benefits and costs, both those that can be quantified and others that can be assessed only more qualitatively, are arguably more daunting.

The overall impact of accessions on budgetary dues or receipts cannot be ignored, however imprecise the estimates. Entry into the Union of the ten economies in transition with a Europe Agreement, many observers fear, calls for a substantial expansion of the Union's budget. Estimates are difficult to prepare because the key parameters for assessing the impact of accession on the budget are simply not yet available; some will be determined only after the Union's deepening efforts take shape over the next several years and the next round of budgetary guidelines will be agreed upon by the end of 1999. Even so, the magnitudes emerging from some of the more credible estimates of the strict budget implications of applying present common policies, notably in agriculture and cohesion, to the ten economies in transition with a Europe Agreement usually lie between roughly 20 and 100 percent of the budget forecast for the Fifteen around 2000; in absolute value this would amount, very roughly, to between $36 and $130 billion at early 1996 exchange rates. For the four central European economies, if they were to enter soon, say, by the year 2000, with present transfer programs still in effect, some estimates put the budgetary transfers from the Union at between 12 and 20 percent of their GDP as compared to some 5 percent for the present four beneficiaries (Greece, Ireland, Portugal, and Spain). This inevitably raises the question of whether such large transfers, if accommodated by the Union, can be absorbed and productively invested in these countries.

One is well advised to take these and other estimates, however, with a very large grain of salt. Even so, they all suggest substantial increases in the magnitude of transfers, both for Union members and for the acceding transition economies. On present policy stances, any rise in the Union's budget by such orders of magnitude simply cannot be envisaged, if only because the bulk of the supplementary funds would have to come from the countries that are reluctant 'net contributors' (primarily France, Germany, Italy, the Netherlands, and the United Kingdom, and soon Austria and Sweden), all of which are presently under domestic budgetary pressures. But, in addition, any widening of the Union toward countries with an important agricultural sector and a comparatively low level of development will affect both the level and distribution of transfers accruing to the present beneficiaries (notably Greece, Ireland, Portugal, and Spain), and this in and of itself will necessitate painful political negotiations in the years ahead, at the latest by 1999, when a new budget strategy will have to be worked out, as determined in 1992 at the Edinburgh Council. It cannot be taken for granted that the losing beneficiary countries will automatically concur on the issue of another enlargement on favorable entry terms.

The various transfer programs and associated common policies (notably to serve agricultural and cohesion objectives) will therefore almost certainly have to be refashioned to permit the accession of new members. But such change is also imperative in the medium to long run for internal reasons. If the Union is to be sustained in spite of fiscal stringency in most Member States, and indeed be entrusted with new tasks, a reallocation of expenditure categories will be unavoidable. It is true that concrete measures in this direction are not due until 1999. However, whatever the choices made at the Conference, they cannot they are bound to affect future options on the transfer programs.

In addition to budgetary considerations, further enlargement, however managed, will require a range of adjustments in both the applicant countries and the present members of the Union. The magnitude of the costs of these changes cannot be estimated in value terms, not even approximately. For example, a failure to live up to the *acquis*, possibly for institutional reasons, may disadvantage other members in a variety of ways. Possessing the capacity to abide by and compete constructively within the single market is an unavoidable precondition of membership. For the economies in transition, it is not at all self-evident that they can, or even that they can afford to, narrow the gap sufficiently between what is demanded by the Union's rules and what they are able to deliver in the foreseeable future unless strenuous efforts are made to accelerate the transformation process.

9 – Can the Economies in Transition Afford to Join the Union?

The balance of costs and benefits of Union membership for the economies in transition is too often partially viewed in terms of transfer benefits for them and budgetary costs for the present Union members. Given the asymmetries between costs and benefits across countries and over time, it is not self-evident that, in the short to medium run, the transition economies, individually or as a group, would in fact benefit on balance (in a broader sense than just budgetary transfers, which do promise to be substantial). One can be reasonably certain, however, that in the longer run, with constructive accession and, later, cohesion policies to boost the potential for catching up with levels of development typical of the Union, the longer-term benefits of being fully integrated into the large market of the Union will be considerable.

It is useful to distinguish between the admission criteria that are primarily qualitative in their formulation and adjudication, and those that focus essentially on the narrower budgetary implications. Among the former, Union officials as a rule refer to democracy and human rights, being European, and having a functioning market economy, as set forth in the Treaty of Rome. These have been variously interpreted, and it may be useful to refine them into eight criteria – namely, domestic political pluralism; democratic maturity and political stability; good neighborly relations or peaceful coexistence; introduction and effective application of the rule of law; ability to comply with the Union's *acquis*; acceptance of the overall ambitions of European integration; having a European identity; and reasonably effective market-based resource allocation. Some of these may not be so easily met by some of the candidates for Union membership. This is especially the case for the rules and regulations circumscribing competition in the single market.

Before the benefits of Union membership materialize, however, a range of costs will have to be borne, largely by the candidate in its preparation for entry and adjusting to the *acquis*. There still exists a daunting array of institutional and policy problems, referred to above, that remain to be solved in all transition economies before any of them can hope to be a properly functioning market economy capable of facing competition in intra-industry trade, while conforming to, and applying in practice, the EU's rules and regulations. Standards on safety, health, the environment, financial intermediation, and so on are but one example. Having the institutions in place to effectively engage in constructive competition is another. But there are many other areas, depending on the individual candidate, that need further restructuring and strengthening. Attempting to do so rapidly will entail considerable costs in the first instance for the entrants; but it will at least indirectly affect also the existing membership.

In all of these respects, all economies in transition have some way to go before they can reasonably claim to have reached the position of, say, Portugal or Spain at the time of their accession in the mid 1980s. The Commission is rightly concerned about engineering a premature expansion of the membership. As recent experience has amply demonstrated, such as in the case of Greece, inability or reluctance on the part of a new entrant to abide by the *acquis* causes considerable tensions among members, because of the potential for free riding, and is divisive of Union policies.

The hopes of core policy makers in some countries, notably those in central Europe but also in some western countries, for these transition economies to enter the Union by the year 2000 are not very realistic. This can be assessed in terms of the sheer mechanics of the negotiation and ratification process. If, as expected, accession negotiations will commence in early 1998, accession by the year 2000 would leave, in effect, only two years for negotiation and ratification. No previous enlargement relevant to the case of the economies in transition has ever been completed in such a short period of time; five to ten years has been a more typical time span. Furthermore, several well-placed officials of the European Commission have intimated that accession by the year 2005 even of the most advanced economy in transition would be a very optimistic target. Leading members of the European Parliament have recently argued for the year 2010 as a more plausible target, even for the most advanced of the eastern applicants.

Based on what can reasonably be conjectured about the criteria for membership; the likely date for starting accession negotiations; the length, purposes, and major hurdles of the negotiations; the likely date of accession; and the transition regime at the end of which these countries will be full Member States, the economies in transition will have to mount considerable efforts for accession to be feasible even by the most likely earliest date – sometime toward the second half of the next decade. The effort required may well exceed the capacity or political will of some of the potential entrants. Rather than insisting upon the requirement that these economies wait with their accession until they will be able to comply with all the accession criteria on their own strengths, which would require much time and effort the economies in transition can ill afford now or in the foreseeable future, it might be more fruitful to think about the formulation and implementation of a strategy to facilitate the preparations for meeting this deadline for entry and for doing so at the least cost for both the present Fifteen and the potential entrants.

Another strategy deserves to be elaborated soon, especially for the economies in transition with credible claims to early membership. With such an interim strategy the Union could then hope to meet the transition economies' expectations not only of economic benefits, largely those emanating from market access and budgetary transfers, but also of gaining credibility for their transformation policies and of strengthening their general security. Such a strategy would also help to reconfigure the assistance formats that have been applied with varying degrees of success since 1990 in favor of various groups of transition economies.

Given the range of major dilemmas mentioned above, there would seem to be room for fashioning a coherent assistance and cooperation program also for other economies in transition, and indeed for non-member countries more generally, by reexamining the Union's multitier preference system. This topic is also not explicitly on the Conference's debating table, but along with many observers I believe that the matters at hand cannot be completely ignored there, if only because the present political and geostrategic environment differs substantially from what earlier motivated the Union to accord such preferences to selected groups of countries.

10 – Toward a Pre-accession Strategy

Several channels are available to ensure that the expectations of the economies in transition, notably as regards strengthening policy credibility and their overall security through a streamlined relationship with the Union, can be provided without pushing for membership in an overhasty manner. Many of the economic benefits can be secured and some of the costs forestalled by working in a more strategic manner to smooth the path leading toward membership. With such a strategy firmly in place the answer to the question of when a firm date for accession will be set would follow logically, and preferably automatically: Compliance with all the sequential stages in the strategy, which would be closely assessed, monitored, and occasionally fine-tuned to ensure its continuing relevance, would be tantamount to admittance into the Union. At the moment, no such strategy can be discerned, not even on the horizon.

The formulation and implementation of a program around a pre-accession strategy, consisting of a sequence of policy and institutional changes in both the economies in transition and in the Union, will, of course, have to be the outcome of political negotiations. They will almost certainly have to be tailored to concrete circumstances, notably of individual applicants for accession. Initially such a program could be constructed around six principles for which concrete measures would then be formulated for individual countries.

• First, the Union could play a much more active role as a strong partner in the economic and societal transformation of the ten potential entrants. It is not enough to stress further stabilization, privatization, and liberalization policies in these countries: The Union could help in actually designing effective strategies to accomplish them. It could also play a useful role in economic restructuring, particularly of the most 'sensitive' sectors, and in consolidating the 'institutions' that together actually constitute a 'market' and determine how well it functions. Thus it would be useful to remove the contingent protectionism presently enshrined in the Europe Agreement and to work through close negotiations to avoid exacerbation of the 'sensitivity.' Similarly, the Union could constructively take into account the peculiar decision making in some of the state firms in economies in transition and foster progress, among others, with corporate governance, particularly in sectors, such as iron and steel, that have recently been subject to conflicts because of 'sensitive' products. The Union could also help to mobilize financial resources, especially from official institutions, with a view to supporting so-called 'crowding-in' investments, including various European communication and transportation networks. Finally, the Union could helpfully widen access to its markets for candidate members beyond the provisions of the Europe Agreements.

• Second, it could extend considerable technical assistance to the transition economies, especially to help implement the detailed requirements of membership and of the transition period, and also to strengthen the role of public institutions in meeting those requirements. A pragmatic and close involvement on the part of the Union in the formulation and implementation of transformation policies could be very constructive. For example, the White Paper prepared for the ten candidates for accession contains very useful details of the *acquis* to be put in place prior to accession. This now deserves to be acted upon by both the Union and the applicants, rather than simply leaving it up to the individual transition economy to move ahead with assimilating and applying these rules and regulations. For a number of them, the economies in transition, given their postwar institutions and policies, and the comparatively short experience with building a market economy, will encounter problems that are of a different order of magnitude than those experienced by earlier entrants.

• Third, the Union might consider reshaping its own assistance programs with a view to strengthening the economic recovery under way in some of the economies in transition and helping others to quickly reach such a stage – this would contribute to underpinning robust and sustainable growth throughout the eastern part of Europe. An objective should be to encourage economic agents in the economies in transition to move toward active participation in intra-industry trade as a means of getting the economies as a whole onto a sustainable growth trajectory, one that would enable these countries eventually to catch up with western levels of income per head. Gains in the real economy will reinforce the capacity of the transition economies to compete effectively in the Union's single market and to sustain popular support for restructuring programs despite their often considerable short-run costs. It would also reduce the income gap between the candidate and the Union's average, thereby facilitating access if only because the budgetary implications would be easier to deal with.

• Fourth, there are other gaps between the economies in transition and the Union to be bridged, however. These are perhaps largest in terms of the institutions and the ability to compete effectively in the single market. It is important to ensure that these gaps between the Union and the economies in transition, and thus the hurdles to be overcome upon eventual accession, do not widen, especially in the event that the current Conference is successful in making progress with monetary union and further integration. A widening of these gaps would postpone still further the point at which the transition economies could conceivably enter the Union.

• Fifth, the Union could encourage and give practical support to economic cooperation among the transition economies themselves as a means of strengthening the foundations of sustainable growth. Robust economic links among these countries, rooted in market-based criteria of success, would strengthen their patterns of specialization and facilitate, as well as accelerate, accession to the Union. Several transition economies have recently, especially in 1995, recorded rapid growth in their intraregional trade. As I and others have underlined from the very inception of the transformations in the eastern part of Europe, opportunities for further expansion of such commerce, certainly now that the recovery under way is broadening and, in some countries, strengthening, are available. Some may need further institutional support, such as in effective payment, insurance, export-credit, and related arrangements. Sustaining this expansion would be particularly important at a time of the slowdown in aggregate demand in the Union, which is bound to have repercussions for the economies in transition that have considerably bolstered their EU trade ties.

• Finally, the Union can influence the psychological climate for 'Europe' in a number of ways, including the collection and dissemination of appropriate information, in the various national languages, with a view to informing both the citizens of the Union as well as those in the transition economies about each other. Such citizen-friendly openness would be entirely in line with the ongoing search for transparency, subsidiarity, democracy, accountability, and efficiency that marked the preparations for the Conference. Acting upon these commitments has, however, lagged far behind the expressed ambitions aired on those scores in particular since the early 1990.

Such a program should not, of course, be set in concrete. It should be closely monitored, periodically reviewed, and fine-tuned in response to experience. Close monitoring by the Union calls for a more practical and deeper involvement than the 'structured political dialogue' that the Union has been fashioning since the Essen Council in 1994. Such a dialogue undoubtedly provides useful contacts at the highest political level. As a strategy to facilitate entry of the economies in transition into the Union, however, it leaves too much uncertainty. Most of the admission criteria are still far too vague for the credible applicant to be able to map out a clear path toward compliance, which in the end will still involve a large measure of judgment, hence political good or ill will, on the part of policy makers whose concerns may not be completely focused on the EU's expansion.

The approach suggested here is a more structured one with a much larger involvement of the Union, the European Commission first of all, in the policy steps to be undertaken by the applicants than has been evident to date. Meeting the criteria and implementing the policies recommended in such a strategy would signal that the country is ready to join the Union with minimal further delay, and be enabled to do so forthwith. Such a program could usefully replace the present, dispersed assistance programs, some of which appear to be in disarray or not particularly effective, as recently adjudicated by the European Court of Auditors. Examples of the particular components of such a program can be easily identified, and the merits of some are set forth at length in Chapter 6 below. But many others need to be fashioned into a coherent whole. Such a program would benefit not only candidates for Union membership but, in several respects, also present Union members.

The proposal is not, of course, prescriptive. Nor is it aimed at bringing all western and international assistance efforts under the EU's umbrella. There is no need for that. Quite the contrary: What is required is an articulated strategy that is comprehensive, well coordinated, and credible. The argument advanced here is that the mere existence of such a program, leading up to the accession of the ten transition economies with a Europe Agreement, but not necessarily at the same date, will, in and of itself, act as a coordinating mechanism. Other partners in global cooperation are unlikely to ignore it; and since they support the basic objectives of the transition process anyway, they should see the advantage of orienting their own efforts to its basic structure. As a result, a coherent, strategic program, rather than aggravating bureaucratic turf battles, wasting assistance, or creating overlap in different approaches, would in all likelihood provide the basis for a more spontaneous coordination among the various actors assisting the transition process.

The more strategic approach suggested here should not of course be confined to the transition economies that are likely to be the first to join the Union. It should apply *a fortiori* to those countries (such as Albania, Croatia, Bosnia and Herzegovina, Macedonia, and rump Yugoslavia) all of which can be expected eventually to apply for membership. On present expectations, however, the transition process in these countries has much farther to go than in the countries in the first tier for joining the Union, given that they are by and large still early in their development or transformation phase.

But the Union also has many interests (such as economic, political, strategic, and environmental) that argue for developing a well thought-out, strategic cooperation and assistance program for countries that will never become members of the Union, either because they are not European or because they may not wish to join for their own political reasons. For these countries the involvement of the Commission would be much less intense than is the case of potential Union members. But the general approach could be justified as a way of responding to the dissatisfaction with the manner in which much international assistance, notably from within the EU itself, has been extended to the economies in transition since 1990.

11 – Outcomes Are Critical, Whether Positive or Negative

Whatever may transpire during the Conference's deliberations, the decisions taken, if only by default, by the time the Conference ends around mid 1997 should be of strategic interest not only to western Europe and its immediate neighbors, but also to the global community as a whole. This will certainly be the case if the Conference is success-ful in laying the basis for further integration. But even failure to reach some consensus on the most critical challenges facing the Union would have palpable consequences for the integration process and for the Union's relations with nonmember countries, especially those benefit-ing from preferential arrangements. It would also hamper the Union's negotiating strength in international negotiations scheduled for the next several years, such as the planned round of discussions around agricul-tural subsidies, which was agreed upon when the Uruguay Round was concluded, due towards the end of the decade.

Arguably, the outcome of the Conference will be nowhere of great-er significance than for the economies in transition, individually and as a group, and regardless of whether they will be able or want to join the Union in the foreseeable future. Any enlargement of the Union without coming to a *modus vivendi* on its deepening can only exacerbate the already marked deterioration over the past four years or so in the degree of commitment to integration. Many observers fear that if this were to happen the European integration process would eventually retrogress into some variant of a free-trading arrangement, which has never been among the Union's fundamental ambitions. Indeed, it has been inimical to them.

If western Europe is serious about its own architecture, it cannot disregard its eastern half, regardless of which individual countries will qualify for membership. Likewise, if the economies in transition are firmly bent on joining the 'Europe' that the Union embodies, they have to formulate new approaches toward building the necessary institutions and other foundations that are a requirement for full membership. If both sides accept these viewpoints, a realistic compromise on an approach to enlargement may then be in the offing.

12 – But There Is No Need for a Doomsday Scenario

While the Conference is critical in the sense that failure would signal a severe setback to the construction of an integrated Europe, there is, however, no need to elaborate doomsday scenarios for such an outcome. The disintegration of trade and integration among the Fifteen is unlikely to occur quickly, if at all. Thus, commercial and financial relations among the present Union membership are highly interdependent, particularly through intra-industry trade, and there are increasingly dense networks of cooperation in a wide and diverse range of noneconomic matters.

However, any failure at the Conference cannot but affect to a considerable extent the anticipated framework for economic relations on the continent in the medium to long run, including the trading opportunities for the Union's eastern and southern neighbors. Precisely because the Union's commercial relations with the economies in transition in the vast majority of traded goods is not yet far advanced when it comes to intra-industry trade, tensions and bickering within the Union because of lack of progress with deepening is, then, likely to affect negatively the chances of the economies in transition to prop up their recovery and catch-up efforts through vibrant competition.

This applies as well to monetary integration. Missing the inauguration of monetary union in 1999, for example, would not destroy the intricate degree of commercial or financial interdependence of the EU's economies. It would, however, adversely affect the more general economic, political, and social climate, not least by exacerbating uncertainty, which in turn could hardly avoid affecting the horizon of investment decisions. Compressed levels of fixed investment would be a consequence of any setbacks at the Conference. Clarity and transparency, especially in reemphasizing the commitment to forging ahead with integration, will be critical in laying out a more strategic, long-term perspective on the future of Europe. It is especially important to avoid imparting greater uncertainty to markets than need be the case.

13 – The Need for Statecraft

The international community at large can only hope that western Europe at this critical juncture in the evolution of its own affairs as well as with respect to its historical role in refashioning the continent as a major component of the global framework, will rise to the task at hand in depth and in breadth, and seize the opportunity this juncture in its history provides with magnanimity. It would be unwise, though, to bank on the formulation of once-and-for-all solutions applicable for decades to come at the Conference. But at least the decisions reached in the course of that meeting will exert a determining influence on the evolving long-term nature of union formation in Europe and presumably on matters reaching beyond that specific horizon.

Key policy makers of several of the economies in transition have pronounced themselves as being resolutely opposed to virtually any proposal that falls short of full membership in the Union at the earliest moment. As a result, any offer from the Union that would move them onto a fairly comprehensive pre-accession path with a firm strategy leading up to membership is likely to set off alarm bells. True, resistance to the idea has waned somewhat as the costly and painful realities of the economic, political, and social transformations under way as well as the hurdles to be overcome in joining the Union have taken ascendancy over ideology, politics, or any misguided moral or facile historical claim. Nevertheless, resistance to a paced accession strategy is still quite pronounced. It should not really be so as any well-conceived strategic program would provide greater credibility than any verbal calendar commitment. It would do so not only in relations between the

EU and the transition economies, but also among the transition economies and indeed between the latter and other agencies actively involved
in channeling bilateral and international assistance to the eastern part of
Europe.

The proposals that I have advocated here by way of illustration of
what could be done to benefit the meaningful accession of the selected
economies in transition and to strengthen the Union's cooperation with
other economies in transition are just that. I readily admit that much
more thought deserves to be given to how best to set about formulating
and implementing, let alone expeditiously negotiating, pre-accession
and cooperation strategies designed along some of the lines hinted at in
Chapter 6. Stitching together a tighter safety net for the economies in
transition requires coping with a number of diplomatic and political
knots whose tangles cannot be ignored with impunity. The Conference's outcome, whatever it will be, cannot but clarify matters in this
regard.

PART TWO

The Conference and New Accessions

1

The Core Challenge of the European Union: Widening versus Deepening

With the June 1993 decision of the European Council in Copenhagen, subsequently refined in particular at the Essen Council in December 1994, to entertain the future entry of up to ten economies in transition, as well as Cyprus and Malta, into the EU a new seminal step on the road to remaking Europe was set. The commitment made at Essen, which was given more concrete contents at Cannes (June 1995) and Madrid (December 1995), was to begin accession negotiations soon after the successful conclusion of the Intergovernmental Conference set to begin sometime in 1996 (hereafter Conference or IGC96). Interest in the Conference's preparation and policy deliberations, including notably on the part of the economies in transition, has since risen markedly. As already indicated, this Conference opened on 29 March 1996 in Turin (Italy) and is expected to last until well into 1997.

There is little doubt that the leadership of these potential entrants, as well as the policy makers of the EU Member States, are fully aware that yet another enlargement – "widening" in the EU's terminology – can be seriously entertained only with a successful consolidation of integration achievements, while forging ahead with new measures – "deepening" according to the above-cited lexicon. The ongoing Conference was initially intended to be concerned solely with the former. Its purview has since been extended *de facto*, by force of circumstances, although a major effort is being made by several Member States and indeed by the European Commission to confine the deliberations to the original purposes for which it was first envisaged already in 1991.

It is against the above backdrop that the present chapter analyzes the broad contours of the political economy of new accessions and, because of the preconditions for successful accession negotiations, it discusses the main parameters of the Conference. I first underline the salience of the Conference and clarify the main purposes pursued in this volume. Next I describe briefly the nature of an IGC and where precisely it belongs in the structure of governance of (western) European integration. The following three sections are devoted to the three principal areas of concern that form the broad backdrop to the Conference's deliberations. Conclusions follow and provide a road map to the more detailed discussion of eastern accession in the remainder of the book.

1 – Salience of the Conference

The ongoing Conference is expected to be a critical one to Europe's future, almost regardless of its outcome. One must be absolutely clear about this proposition. Failure to reach a minimal set of decisions about how to consolidate achievements made over the past forty-six years will fragment the Union's ambitions. The latter revolve around moving toward a single economic space with considerable concertation of economic, but also other, policies. Such an outcome would over time narrow the Union's integration format largely to free trading. Success at the Conference with institutional reform and a reshaping of the governance mechanisms, including decision-making rules and representation of the citizens and Member States in the Union's principal organs, will provide the platform from which policies regarding further deepening can be entertained and purposefully pursued. As such, a successful outcome in and of itself provides the precondition for moving ahead with further enlargement, which will probably take the form of several waves over a protracted period of time (see Chapter 5). This momentum needs to be sustained in spite of the many obstacles that can already be discerned and others that will undoubtedly crop up as substantive negotiations about accession get under way.

One brief word by way of explaining why I date the start of western European integration to 1950, even though the first incarnation of the EU – the establishment of the European Economic Community (EEC) – dates only from early 1958; March 1957 if the signing of the Treaty of Rome is taken as the marker for the inception of the EU's integration. One can legitimately argue that the founding of the EEC was politically made possible by the prior experience with postwar cooperation among the six countries that founded the EEC (Belgium, France, Germany, Italy, Luxembourg, and the Netherlands – the latter two and Belgium having earlier established the Benelux). The start-up of that cooperation can be variously dated. However, a good case can be made for anchoring it to the negotiations, started in 1950, about a treaty to jointly manage the coal and steel sectors, notably of France and Germany. That was the essence of the Schuman Plan (named for Robert Schuman, the French politician) about which agreement was reached in 1951 with the so-called Paris Treaty according to which the ECSC was inaugurated in January 1952. So I propose 1950 as the year during which the process of postwar western European integration, now led by the EU, was kicked off.

If we agree on the above convention, we must also be clear about Europe's current governance structures, which have varied somewhat over time. I shall provide details as required for the arguments made later. At this stage it is important to be aware of the paramount role of the Council's decisions, as referred to above, in the governance of the EU. The European Council is the highest deliberative-executive body of the EU. The amalgam should be borne in mind too for, unlike a national government, the EU's governance is ensured through overlapping responsibilities, as will be clarified in Section 2 below. Nonetheless, the European Council plays a unique role in EU decision making, although it is a relative newcomer in the Union's institutional development. It was first convened in 1974 by the then French President Valéry Giscard d'Estaing with a view to reactivating western European integration, following the setbacks incurred in the late 1960s and early 1970s, by bringing together key decision makers at the intergovernmental level.

By virtue of the fact that the Council is made up of the Heads of State or Government of the Member States, assisted at least by their respective Ministers of Foreign Affairs, and the President of the Commission, it has on occasion played an important role in setting strategy and determining common positions with regard to Union affairs and foreign policy (see European Commission 1995c, p. 2). It meets at least twice a year under the chairmanship of the Head of State or Government of the member that holds the Presidency of the Council, which rotates every six months (European Commission 1993, p. 25). As such, it is a special form of the Council of Ministers, an organ that was formally created as one of the EEC's governance pillars by the Treaty of Rome. In what follows, reference to a Council meeting at a particular city means a meeting of the European Council; otherwise Council refers to the Council of Ministers in charge of one particular area (such as finance or foreign affairs).

As already indicated, the primary focus in this book is on the extension of the EU toward the eastern part of Europe. To date, the Council has committed itself to starting up accession negotiations with up to twelve countries, provided they apply. By mid 1996, all had done so. Slovenia could join the group only on 10 June 1996, once its long-simmering dispute with Italy was resolved in a fashion and it could sign its Europe Agreement. Aside from Cyprus and Malta, as already indicated, ten economies in transition are included. These encompass the countries with whom the EU has concluded the so-called Europe Agreement (for details, see Chapter 4). Of those six agreements have been ratified (with Bulgaria, the Czech Republic, Hungary, Poland, Romania, and Slovakia) and four are in the process of being ratified (with Estonia, Latvia, Lithuania, and Slovenia).

Note that also Turkey has lodged an application for accession and did so formally already in 1987 (although it had wanted to table it already much earlier). It is not included in the Council's list. It is also pointedly omitted in recent visions on the EU's future advanced by key policy makers in Europe. For example, Jacques Chirac (1995) in his concept of Europe's future simply ignores Turkey. It is also glaringly, and quite noticeably, absent from the list in the so-called Westendorp Report (see point 20 of the annotated agenda in Reflection Group 1995, part II), which I discuss in some detail in Chapter 2. This is all the more curious in a sense, given that the EU and Turkey inaugurated their customs union in early 1996, after several delays. To the best of my knowledge, the European Council has not yet committed itself even in principle to look favorably upon Turkey's application.

I am singling out Turkey not because I want to draw attention to this anomaly in the EU's response. Rather, I consider it symptomatic of what may happen when other economies in transition in due course will knock at Brussels's doors. In addition to the countries that are currently being entertained for accession, the eventual relationship of the

EU with other economies in transition is at least implicitly on the agenda, including of the Conference. There can presently be little doubt that at some more distant future, the Union will have to face other applicants. In the first instance, the list of applicants for accession may in due course well include at least the remaining Balkan countries (Albania, Bosnia and Herzegovina, Croatia, Macedonia, and Yugoslavia). And at a further point in time, one might even envisage some of the western successor States of the Soviet Union (notably Belarus, Moldova, and Ukraine), other than the three Baltic States, following suit.

Thus, in the foreseeable future, the EU's membership may expand from the present fifteen to perhaps more than twice that number (twenty-seven if the present twelve candidates are included, thirty-two with Albania and the other successor States of Yugoslavia, and thirty-five with the three western successor States of the Soviet Union), though some case can be made for other potential applicants, as discussed in Chapter 6 in particular; hence the importance of the governance decisions to be reached at the present Conference.

Accession will take time, even for the economies in transition with a credible agenda for meeting the most vital membership criteria. I maintain this even if both these economies move ahead full speed with their transformation and the Union were to be prepared to be as generous as feasible in slipping these countries into its integration format. It is therefore useful to consider also what can be undertaken by the EU for these and other economies in transition in the interim. For them I propose the development of a pre-accession strategy. That will be the subject of our discussions in Chapter 6 for the more credible of those candidates. I also discuss there similar issues revolving around the format of a more comprehensive and coherent cooperation program for the other economies in transition, both those that may eventually join and others that will not join, because they either are not European or do not wish to merge with the EU, given their own interests. Whether as a whole or in part, such a strategy is very likely to be discussed at the Conference, at least implicitly. That is simply because many of the issues at stake in the EU's variously structured relationships with the transition economies, both credible candidates for accession and others, are highly pertinent to matters that will in all likelihood occupy a central spot on the agenda.

   As was the case for earlier IGCs, expectations about the impact of this meeting on the future evolution of European integration are running high, in some cases at fever pitch, even though in principle the formal matters to be discussed at the Conference concern essentially institutional and governance reforms of the present EU. A number of Member States as well as many observers of the European integration scene, including business interests and the wider public in a number of Member States, are reckoning with a more ambitious agenda, not only in terms of the issues to be covered but also as regards the nature of the decisions and recommendations to be reached. Their scope will not only shape the future development of integration but also affect a range of other policies for a long time to come. The current IGC will thus be critical for European countries and the continent's future.

   The rationale for this state of affairs is rather straightforward, given the recent policy differences among the Fifteen on the further course of their integration: The forthcoming IGC will be critical to Europe's future almost regardless of the decisions that will be reached there on the wide variety of paramount topics that figure prominently in the current economic, political, security, and social debates in Europe and beyond. If it is successful, the Conference's various outcomes will determine the "deepening" of the integration process in (western) Europe while laying the foundations for the "widening" of the Union in the years ahead. In effect, it will set basic markers that cannot but leave an indelible imprint on the remaking of Europe for decades to come.

   But, equally, if the IGC were to end in stalemate, that too would mold the future of the European integration process. If the latter were to happen, most observers agree that it would irrevocably alter the foundations and basic character of the EU as the focus of integration toward which so many countries are now attracted. Joining the EU is an important policy objective for many countries, especially those on the Union's eastern borders – and not solely for economic reasons. An inconclusive outcome of the Conference would be likely to transform the nature of the EU, away from being a quasi, *sui generis* supranational organization with ambitions extending far beyond free trading or the unification of national markets. It would also worsen the chances of the economies in transition quickly becoming integral parts of Europe's single market, a development that many observers regard as being of critical import to their realizing their envisioned strategies of modernization and catching up with the levels of economic development in western Europe. But to benefit fully from the single market, countries must accede to the EU. A part-way arrangement cannot possibly be equated with full membership.

2 – The Place of the IGC in Europe's Governance

An IGC is a fairly rare event in the EU. The present one is only the sixth in the Union's forty-six years, if its history is dated from the negotiations of the Paris Treaty, which established the ECSC, as argued in the preceding section. At the same time it is instructive to bear in mind that this is the fourth in eleven years, after an hiatus of nearly three decades. The latter 'blank space' suggests problems with moving ahead with integration. The former pace is indicative of the acceleration over the past decade or so of top-level deliberations about core integration matters (European Commission 1995c, p. 2).

An IGC does not as a rule develop the specific content of policies, but rather sets the legal and institutional framework and the procedures by which policy agreements are reached among the Member States. Such a Conference is as a rule devoted to negotiating a broad consensus among the Member States on paramount issues affecting their integration format, including their intragroup policies, institutions, cooperation mechanisms, governance issues, stances with respect to non-member countries, and the potential widening of the membership to the extent that these issues cannot be dealt with in the regular EU organs, such as the Council of Ministers or the European Council.

It is instructive to recall briefly that, without exception, all of the earlier Conferences marked crucial advances in building the foundations of European integration. The first, which began in May 1950, led to the Treaty of Paris signed in April 1951, followed by the establishment of the ECSC in early 1952. The second, which began in Messina in April 1955, led eventually to the Treaties of Rome, signed in March 1957, and the creation of the EEC and Euratom in January 1958. The third, which was started in September 1985, revolved around institutional reform, after a protracted period of stagnation in the building of Europe. As a welcome advance on the Euro-pessimism of the preceding decade or so, it culminated in the Single European Act in 1986 and the decision to create the Single European Market by the end of 1992. The fourth on EMU and the fifth on European Political Union (EPU), both initiated in 1990 and concluded in December 1991, were seminal in the preparation and conclusion of the Maastricht Treaty, formally the Treaty on European Union (TEU).

It should be pointed out, however, that recognizing the importance of the IGC in advancing the cause of integration in the EU does not imply endorsement of the position of some commentators (notably Moravcsik 1993) to the effect that the successive IGCs have reached intergovernmental bargains, each of which sets the agenda for an intervening period of consolidation. The intricacies of the bargains struck at these infrequent IGCs are quite distinct from the way in which the legislative agenda in the EU has been propelled over the years as a result of the interactions among the Council of Ministers, the European Commission, and the European Parliament (Garret and Tsebelis 1996).

It is, then, useful to maintain a perspective on the importance of the IGC, both the previous ones and the one under way. Regarding the latter, however, it is of critical importance to be aware of the contrast with earlier such meetings. Indeed, unlike in earlier IGCs, the present one is not expected to lead to a new treaty *ab ovo*. In its original conception, the present Conference was designed to clarify the fundamental, and in some cases constitutional, issues of how the Union will henceforth operate, as regards both the final goals of European integration as well as the *modi operandi* of moving toward the EU's so-called *finalité politique*. Originally, its principal purpose was indeed the refinement of the Maastricht Treaty. Thus, a renewed, streamlined, more comprehensive, and more coherent TEU should emerge from the Conference, at least in the view of some important observers of the European scene (Martin 1995, para. 24, p. 7).

Another way of assessing the potential importance of an IGC is to look into its very rationale. An IGC can be called by the membership whenever it is deemed necessary. This is usually done by consensus. As a rule, at least this has been the practice up to now, such a Conference is designed to be devoted to negotiating a consensus among the Member States on paramount issues affecting their mutual integration that cannot be dealt with in the regular EU organs, such as the Council of Ministers or the European Council. This is also the case for the present Conference. It too will be concerned, one way or the other (Martin 1995, para. 18, p. 6), with the more obdurate problems surrounding the issues of "widening" and "deepening" EU integration.

In many respects, the key institutional and governance topics to be addressed derive from the gradualist approach to integration enshrined in the Treaty of Rome and in later quasi-constitutional acts. Indeed, the Treaty of Rome is only firm on the formation of a customs union according to a precise schedule. The ambitions of moving toward economic union and a unified market, and indeed toward some form of political union, were stated as firm intentions. But how progress toward those goals would be achieved was left to later negotiations. The failure of the first attempts at monetary union in 1962 already underlined the problems in progressing beyond the customs union (Brabant 1995a, pp. 122-6, 176-86).

To appreciate this point more fully, recall that there are essentially four core levels of governance in the EU, although decision making is not neatly separated. The European Parliament and the European Council (including the regular Council of Ministers) are the so-called bicephalous legislative organs, in some cases overlapping through the so-called codecision rule; the European Commission, together with the European Council and the sectoral or topical Council of Ministers, forms the executive arm; the European Court of Justice constitutes the EU's juridical arm. Particularly since the disenchantment with the Maastricht Treaty set in almost before the signature ink was dry, the Heads of State and Government of the Member States have been insistent on strengthening the importance of the European Council, possibly at the expense of the Council of Ministers and of the European Commission, with only a streamlining of the relationship with, and a more focused mechanism of decision making in, the European Parliament, as well as a narrower place for law making by the European Court of Justice, held out for the near term.

Thus *qua* its importance in steering the integration process and giving it new impetus, going by earlier IGCs, the salience of the present Conference should be beyond question. It is arguably even more of a make-it-or-break-it venue than previous IGCs in view of the fact that, in more than one respect, the EU members have never been confronted with as many and as complicated a range of fundamental – truly existential – challenges as those that have arisen in the last few years (Gudin 1995, p. 3). But, at the same time, and unlike all of the preceding IGCs, the present Conference is not organized around a comprehensive, well-argued, and politically concerted policy document to be refined during the proceedings (Davidson 1996a).

The so-called Westendorp Report (Reflection Group 1995) could not have filled that role. It provides only a first attempt at formulating an agenda (see Chapter 2). The available text, as well as the conflicting commentary which it has generated, suggests that many core issues are likely to be avoided or resolved only in a minimal fashion (Hughes 1996). That commentary ranges indeed from the very optimistic (see, for example, Chirac 1995 for the view of a politician in power) to the most pessimistic (see, for example, Giscard 1995 for an equally important policy maker, but one out of executive, though not legislative, office).

As indicated earlier, the Conference is expected to last for at least twelve months, which would be end March 1997. But according to Nico Wegter, who as spokesperson for Commissioner Hans van den Broek (external political relations, particularly with eastern Europe) is well placed, it could conceivably last until mid 1997 (Interview 1996b, p. 23). However, if electoral political calculations enter into the debates, particularly in connection with the U.K. elections to be scheduled no later than May 1997, the Conference's conclusion could come possibly even later, but hopefully before the end of 1997 (European Commission 1996q, p. 2). Regardless, whatever happens during the course of the present Conference, the outcome is likely to exert a determining influence on the shape of European integration for decades to come (Guigou 1995). Another IGC in the near term is held by core insiders to be rather unlikely (Interview 1996a).

There are several reasons for believing that the present Conference will be critical, of truly seminal importance. Arguably the most important is that there are now too many EU matters that can no longer be adequately dealt with – 'governed' in the broad sense of that term – in the institutional framework originally created in 1958 for the six founding members of the EU. That is no longer adequate to an EU with fifteen Member States, and would certainly become an insuperable hindrance with any further enlargement. Moreover, the pressure for another enlargement of the EU's membership has been mounting for some time. Even though in principle both the accession negotiations and the transition period to full membership can be stretched out over a long period of time, this is not a tactical option likely to benefit the EU at this particular juncture, however. The political pressure from the eastern part of Europe is likely to be too intense to permit such non-committal dalliance. As a result, it would be preferable to identify more practical and pragmatic means for permitting the EU to move ahead with integration. Referring to the three pillars and the associated social compact signed by fourteen Member States (all but the United Kingdom), the European Commission (1995a, p. 70) has stated categorically that "there can be no question of trying to accommodate further enlargements with the present arrangements for their operations."

It should be borne in mind that although an IGC is as a rule opened and concluded in full diplomatic summitry mode, and Turin was no different, the operative deliberations take place elsewhere and in different fora. Indeed, it is foreseen that monthly meetings of the Council of Ministers of Foreign Affairs will actually negotiate about items on the agenda. This organ will examine the work undertaken and still to be accomplished on a nearly continuous basis by a group composed of delegates from the ministries of foreign affairs of the Member States (in previous IGCs as a rule permanent representatives of the Member States in Brussels) and the president of the European Commission, Mr. Jacques Santer. The latter group is expected to meet on nearly a weekly basis. Once the review of the Maastricht Treaty completed, the fifteen Governments must unanimously agree on the text of a revised Treaty, which will then be placed before all fifteen national parliaments for ratification in accordance with the national constitutions. I specify further organizational details in Chapter 2 (Section 2 in particular).

3 – Backdrop

Partly as a result of the buoyant optimism about western European integration aroused during the late 1980s, two IGCs were convened simultaneously in late 1990 and successfully concluded in Maastricht in late 1991. One focused on EMU as a logical sequel to – indeed twin component of – the Single European Market, which was formally completed at the end of 1992. It therefore dealt with a series of rather technical issues concerning the creation of a European Central Bank (ECB) and a European currency subject to a highly concerted monetary policy, in the view of both insiders (see Pöhl 1995) and the more academic assessment of the IGC on EMU (see Gros and Thygesen 1992). The other was devoted to EPU but did not take a clear stance on the fundamental constitutional issues surrounding the EU's so-called *finalité politique*. Nonetheless, in retrospect, both meetings marked without a doubt important milestones on the way to the drafting and subsequent endorsement of the Maastricht Treaty. It must be kept up front that the origin of the current Conference is precisely the haste with which that Treaty was completed for reasons of political expediency.

These extraordinary rounds of diplomatic activity in the EU conducted in 1990-1991 in particular stemmed in part from efforts to overcome the unease felt by a number of European economic and political leaders over the possible consequences, in the first place, of German unification, but also apprehensions about the then still pregnant socioeconomic and political changes transforming the face of the eastern part of Europe more generally. German unification had placed the 'German question,' which had been the hub of most of the conflicts during the postwar period, in a completely new light (Fritsch-Bournazel 1992). To allay the fears on the part of some western European leaders about the future strategic interests of a unified Germany, anchoring the new Germany irrevocably deeper into the European framework became an urgent priority of European policy. A firm commitment toward European political integration, as a step forward, thus moving beyond monetary integration and the single market, so it was thought, would irreversibly tie Germany to 'Europe' and prevent any weakening of its interests in (western) European integration. It was thought wise to proceed toward this goal rapidly, even without policy makers having reached a broad understanding, let alone a fundamental agreement, including about the proximate shape of EPU or the kind of strategy to be pursued to reach it. Hence the hurried endorsement of the Maastricht Treaty and the call for a Review Conference in 1996.

However, the interest of high-level policy makers in moving beyond the issues of economic union, which had dominated much of the agenda in the 1980s, also followed from the unexpected success achieved with the implementation of the single-market program inaugurated in the second half of the 1980s. That had been facilitated by, and in part gave rise to, the unanticipated and sharp economic upswing during the same phase with a noticeable decline in the high levels of unemployment that had emerged in part as a result of the particular policy response to the two oil shocks. But there was also a substantial increase in levels of productivity, although there was no return to the high growth of the so-called golden age (Marglin and Schor 1990). After a protracted period of Euro-pessimism, then, this upturn led, among other effects, to substantial GDP growth, a marked reduction in levels of unemployment, and an acceleration of productivity growth. All this was quite remarkable, certainly in comparison to what these countries had been able to achieve in the preceding decade.

Furthermore, the tumultuous developments in the eastern part of Europe with the near-demise of communism as a political and economic system, the replacement of central planning with market-based resource allocation, and the rapid unraveling of the economic and political ties between the former communist countries dramatically modified the traditional East-West conflict and opened up new prospects, economic and political, for the process of European unification (European Commission 1995c, p. 4). This has turned out to be not a one-off affair to be completed within a comparatively brief period of time, however. Rather, it should by now be crystal clear that from its very inception the process has been associated with a painful upheaval in economic, political, and social affairs whose end is not yet in sight, not even for the economy in transition that has advanced most toward its own *finalité politique*: pluralistic democracy anchored to private property with some constraints to ensure that income and wealth differentiation remains somehow acceptable to society.

The backdrop, therefore, of the Maastricht Treaty itself is quite convoluted. Only if that is firmly understood does it become clear why the then twelve Member States decided to schedule a Review Conference in 1996 as part and parcel of the negotiated Maastricht Treaty. At first sight this seems unusual: A Treaty that created a procedure for its own revision with a definite timetable to do so just over two years after it came into effect (on 1 November 1993). The basic reason, as mentioned above, was that Europe as a whole, and especially the Twelve, were at the center of wide-ranging and radical change, indeed in the grip of a vortex of seminal transformations. In the words of the European Commission (1995a, p. 59), "it was initially intended to introduce [EMU], as a complement to the single market. Consideration of further steps toward political union then became unavoidable, in response to the major upheavals that struck Europe at the turn of the decade. The Treaty undoubtedly shows signs of these mixed origins."

There is a widespread view that, as constituted by the debates of 1989-1991, the Union is no longer adequately equipped to deal with the changes occurring on the European continent (Ludlow and Ersbøll 1996, pp. 2ff.). This had been clear for some time. But it became noticeably pronounced soon after the Maastricht Treaty was agreed upon. In particular, institutional and core elements of decision-making mechanisms had been left aside in the negotiations of the two IGCs held in 1990-1991 in order to facilitate the process of reaching a firm commitment to political union, at least in principle, though many leaders have quite a diverging interpretation of what precisely that should entail. This expedient had been resorted to in view of the seminal changes taking place at the time in the make-up of Europe under impulse of the major transformations under way in the eastern part of Europe, particularly German unification in 1990 and the implosion of the Soviet Union.

With the successful conclusion of these two IGCs, in particular with the agreement at Maastricht in December 1991, the Review Conference was to have focused primarily on consolidating the integration achievements to date and forging ahead with new endeavors – deepening of integration, in other words – among the then twelve members of the Union; with the accession of Austria, Finland, and Sweden in 1995, this ambition was naturally extended to the Fifteen, albeit with some reservations, owing to these countries' earlier neutrality in the East-West conflict and reluctance to participate in full in particular in shaping the future security arrangements on the continent. But their earlier precept of "neutrality" is no longer well defined.

Under the final dispositions of the Treaty, as stated in article N(2), it was agreed that "a conference of representatives of the governments of the Member States shall be convened in 1996 to examine, in accordance with the objectives set out in articles A and B, those provisions of this Treaty for which revision is provided" (European Commission 1993, p. 56). This somewhat cryptic stipulation indicates that virtually any issue pertaining to the Union's objectives can in principle be addressed at the IGC96. Nonetheless, it was generally understood that the review exercise would focus conceivably on five areas.

The first concerned the completion of the monetary union, with a single currency and a highly concertized monetary policy, as one cornerstone, indeed one of the twin pillars, of the EMU; the other is the single European market. Since the details of monetary union had already been spelled out in the Maastricht Treaty, three broad issues were to be raised following phases 1 and 2 of EMU: the establishment of the timetable for and selection of membership in the monetary union with a common currency, a common monetary policy, and a unified ECB; an evaluation of the application of the Single European Market in law and in practice in the Member States; and an assessment of whether that single market was succeeding in promoting balanced economic and social progress. These matters should in principle have been dealt with in the context of Council decisions. But in view of the unexpected developments in financial markets in 1992 and 1993, the persistence of high levels of unemployment, the growing social discontent in many Member States, and the premature interruption of the economic upswing in late 1995, following the protracted recession earlier in the decade, leading to a marked slowdown and perhaps recession for most of 1996, it was inevitable that they would occupy a central position in the debates around and at the IGC96.

Second, the review exercise also called for forging ahead with the two other pillars of the Union: the Common Foreign and Security Policy (CFSP), which included explicit provisions for formulating a common defense policy, in part because the so-called Brussels Treaty of the Western European Union (WEU) expires in 1998 (Adam 1995, p. 16; Anon 1996, p. 31) and it was thought politic to forestall any withdrawal from the common defense organization, if only because membership of the EU and WEU already diverges and the leadership hoped to forge greater congruence, given the end of the Cold War; and Cooperation in Justice and Home Affairs (CJHA). Whereas the field of foreign and security policies are fairly well delineated, that of justice and home affairs is more variegated. This matter need not detain us here very long, however. Suffice it to take it to mean in particular cooperation among national police forces, combating drug trafficking, policies with respect to immigrants from outside the Union, the granting of asylum to political refugees, migration, terrorism, and such other topics as may be in need of a communautarian initiative because a solution is not available at the national level.

More important, however, is that, unlike the first pillar with the communautarian and in some respects supranational features of EMU, the second and the third pillars remained clearly anchored within the context of intergovernmentalism, at least until the Review Conference in 1996, it was hoped, could carry the political-integration process as a minimum one step forwards. It bears furthermore to point out immediately that there is wide agreement among policy makers and observers alike that little progress has been achieved in either of these two areas since 1991 (see Bourlanges and Martin 1995; European Commission 1995a, p. 20; Reflection Group 1995), thus complicating the negotiations at IGC96.

Governance of all these issues, as well as those arising within the existing framework of economic integration, formed the third major item originally envisaged for the review conference. More specifically, it was intended to amend the Maastricht Treaty in order to raise the efficiency and appropriateness of common integration mechanisms and institutions (article B). In that context, moreover, the issues of democracy, subsidiarity, transparency, efficiency, and accountability were all introduced as topics to be tackled in a determined manner in order to improve the 'quality' of community decision making, while ensuring that decisions be taken as closely as possible to the citizen, whose rights and interests were deemed to be in need of protection.

Fourth, it was also agreed, albeit much more vaguely because of the opposition of some Member States, the United Kingdom in particular, to strengthen greater coordination and, in some instances, harmonization of social policies so as to attain a greater degree of uniformity in social-policy stances and provisions than had been the case up to then; and, in particular, to elaborate on the social charter endorsed in 1989. Also the competencies of the Union in new domains – notably energy, civil protection, and tourism – were to be delineated to permit steady progress with these aspects of "deepening" for some period of time.

Before proceeding a word on the social agenda is required for there appears to be wide disagreement in the literature on what precisely is entailed. Some consider the social agenda as part and parcel of the third pillar, that is, CJHA. In my view, it might be preferable to consider it as a potential fourth pillar. In fact, in order of priority, it might even be treated as the second pillar of the EU. The reason is simple, as I shall elaborate in Chapter 2: The essence of the EU's approach to economic integration is ensuring fair competition based on genuine productivity differentials within a large single market. That cannot tolerate discriminatory exchange-rate movements for it would grant specific advantages to one country possibly at the express expense of other Member States. Hence the need in a nutshell for a common currency and monetary policy (on which more in Chapter 3 in particular). Likewise for social conditions: Wide divergences in approaches to social security, unemployment, welfare provisions, medical insurance, working time, leaves, and so on may confer benefits on economic agents of some Member States that have nothing to do with genuine productivity. These matters are intrinsically different from those that form the subject of the second and third pillars.

Precisely because social matters encompass a different category of concerns than home and juridical affairs, the social agenda worked out in 1989 was kept out of the Maastricht Treaty *strictu sensu* because of opposition mainly on the part of the United Kingdom to any kind of communautarianism in these matters; the British Government remains adamantly opposed to erecting anything like such a fourth pillar. This has been made crystal clear in its position on the ongoing conference (United Kingdom 1996a, in para. 60). The other fourteen members have, however, endorsed the Agreement on Social Policy. It thus forms an integral element of the spirit of the Maastricht Treaty. But the Agreement is not – at any rate, not yet – another pillar of the Treaty. This has given rise to special elements of incoherence (see European Commission 1995a, p. 47). The European Commission has advocated that the cited Agreement become part of the Treaty. Social matters must therefore be dealt with at IGC96 (see European Commission 1996a, b, c).

Finally, issues concerning the institutions and the governance of political union – notably the division of powers among the European Parliament, the European Commission, and the European Council and the rules for representation and decision making in these organs – were to be reexamined as part and parcel of the broader review of the functioning of these leading bodies in fostering economic, political, and social integration within the Union.

It should be borne in mind, however, that the above specific issues arising from the Maastricht Treaty constitute just one set of concerns informing the present IGC. Although several Member States and organs of the EU have been advocating that the Conference's remit be confined to the revision of the Treaty (European Commission 1996a, b, c), there are two other broad areas, namely, political and popular disaffection with the Treaty and unforeseen (mostly truly unforeseeable) events since 1991 that cannot be ignored in any analysis of the purposes of or the deliberations at the IGC. Disaffection with Maastricht set in quickly and became pronounced during the difficult ratification process in several Member States, particularly after the Danish vote against ratification in June 1992, which necessitated some further modifications of the Treaty via special protocols (European Commission 1993, pp. 607-10) similar to the one earlier arranged to accommodate the U.K.'s wishes (European Commission 1993, pp. 601-6).

Furthermore, a number of circumstances have arisen that could not have been foreseen, or were explicitly ignored, when the Treaty was drafted, including the implosion of the Soviet Union and the drawn-out and often very painful transformations in eastern Europe. But other arguments have been marshaled in recent years. These are presently very much encumbering the processes of consolidating achievements and forging ahead with integration in new economic and possibly political areas and taking in new members into the EU.

4 – Ratification Difficulties and Their Aftermath

Ratification of the Maastricht Treaty ran into unexpected obstacles, beginning with the Danish rejection in June 1992 (later reversed but only after important concessions had been introduced that may yet complicate the negotiations at the ongoing Conference) and ending with its weak endorsement in several other Member States, notably in France, in Germany, and in the United Kingdom. By that time western Europe was moving into its deepest and most protracted economic recession of the postwar period. It turned out to be convenient to blame many elements of the syndrome of recession on European integration in general and the Maastricht Treaty in particular, even though there was not even a remote connection. Western Europe's earlier approach to remaking the European continent had clearly become inadequate in order to proceed with constructive deepening and widening of the integration movement.

The recession gave rise to another round of concerns about the wisdom of European integration, fueled in part by high levels of chronic unemployment and popular disenchantment about government in general and integration in particular. What has been particularly surprising, although it should not have been for reasons that will become clear soon, is the widespread belief that the Maastricht Treaty process in general and EMU in particular are responsible for a whole range of domestic political ills in Member States that have no bearing whatsoever on the integration process, including on the scheduled transition to monetary integration. To cite but one example: EMU is being blamed, notably in France (France 1996a), for all kinds of actual or expected ills, such as the constraint on pension funds or the stark levels of unemployment. But these phenomena have nothing to do with monetary integration at all. Another instance is the widespread apprehension about the Common Agricultural Policy (CAP) and the Maastricht Treaty, even though the CAP was not even a consideration in the negotiations at the 1990-1991 IGCs, unlike in the budget round concluded in 1992 and in the Uruguay-Round negotiations.

Furthermore, the earlier approach toward EPU proved ineffective for several reasons: the political and economic changes in eastern Europe, including German reunification; the unraveling of the European Monetary System (EMS) in 1992 and the 'retreat' of some Member States to the earlier 'core' of monetary cooperation; and the governance issues that complicated the negotiations over the fourth enlargement with Austria, Finland, Norway (where the electorate subsequently rejected the deal), and Sweden.

The negotiations with the four countries that were then members of the European Free Trade Association (EFTA) and had requested accession to the EU ran fairly smoothly once the Single European Market's deadline had passed in early 1993. But the process leading up to the fourth widening of the Union in 1995 added three important topics to the Conference's agenda. One refers to the composition of the European Commission, notably the number of Commissioners and the appointment process: With rising numbers of members it becomes unwieldy to allocate one Commissioner per country (and two for the large countries), to be appointed largely through the political process of the Member State they represent. A second concerns the fear of small Member States being overwhelmed by the large members or, alternatively, of the large members being overruled by a majority of small States, because of the unequal division of voting rights; this raises the question of the extent to which there should be qualified-majority voting in the Council of Ministers and how such votes should be weighted. Finally, calls for streamlining and strengthening the workings of European institutions have become much more insistent.

As a result, the presumptive agenda of the now ongoing Conference has been expanding in a number of directions (European Commission 1995a, pp. 13-15), making a successful outcome of the Conference much more difficult to achieve, yet at the same time so much more crucial for Europe's future.

5 – Unforeseen Circumstances

Four unforeseen circumstances, because of events since the Maastricht Treaty was agreed upon, stand out. First, when the Treaty was negotiated it had been taken for granted that foreign-exchange markets for most currencies of the Member States would continue to function smoothly and remain fairly stable, at least as far as the rates with respect to each other's currencies were concerned. That expectation was based on more than a decade of monetary cooperation in the context of the exchange-rate mechanism (ERM), which had been quite successful for some period since the mid 1980s; the underpinnings of the EMS and the convergence process toward broadening participation in the

ERM; and the gradual shift toward phases 1 and 2, and convergence toward phase 3, of monetary union, as I clarify in some detail in Chapter 2.

Nobody seemed to have reckoned at the time with the potential strength of private markets to test the resolve, and indeed the ability, of the EU's Member States, individually and collectively, to stabilize foreign-exchange markets. In retrospect, this is surprising given the intrinsic inconsistency between fixed exchange rates, capital mobility, autonomous fiscal policy, and only partly coordinated monetary policy with limited resources for intervention purposes. Given the inevitable credibility problems of maintaining fixed exchange rates without removing this inconsistency, it was precisely such a challenge by private financial markets to the determination and capacity of policy makers to maintain fixed exchange rates that erupted in the fall of 1992 and again in the summer of 1993. Consequently, the ERM as originally conceived (see Chapter 3) – a zone of exchange-rate stability with central parities and narrow bands for fluctuation backed up with credit lines for central intervention for as many currencies of the Member States as possible – had to be abandoned for all practical purposes.

The center of Europe's intervention mechanism to keep together some kind of monetary system worthy of that designation was thus extensively undermined. The so-called core countries of the original ERM (those with a narrow band – 2.25 percent around central parity – for reciprocal exchange-rate fluctuations) have in fact since returned roughly to exchange-rate stability within the bands of phase 1 of the ERM, but not to the earlier form of cooperation among central banks, except in the case of Germany and the Netherlands (Pisani-Ferry 1995, p. 449). The much wider permitted margins of 15 percent around parity remain officially in place, although they were inaugurated as a "temporary measure," and this poses a problem when deciding whether to move toward phase 3 of EMU, because one of the convergence criteria refers to the degree of stability in exchange rates within the ERM context (see Chapter 3).

Second, after the euphoria which followed the collapse of the Berlin wall the European economies in 1992-1994 moved into a severe recession with a substantial rise in unemployment, to around 12 percent on average of the EU's labor force. The recession was deep and lasted longer than had been anticipated. Although the recovery strengthened in 1994, it faltered prematurely in late 1995 and a return to levels of unemployment of, say, the late 1980s is still nowhere in sight. Just over 18 million people were reported unemployed in the EU in December 1995, an average unemployment rate of nearly 11 percent (but worse for women and much worse for people under age 25), the same as in December 1994. Whereas in the course of 1995 some countries (notably Denmark and Spain) improved their performance on the labor front, elsewhere and notably in Germany it worsened; in fact with 11.1 percent of the labor force out of work in February 1996, Germany reached its highest level of unemployment since postwar reconstruction.

In virtually every single Member State there has been increasing political opposition against subordinating national priorities, notably on unemployment and/or welfare provisions, to regional, let alone supranational, objectives. There is therefore considerable pressure to include explicit provisions on employment in the revised Treaty, and thus in the evolving agenda of the present Conference. In fact, the various issues around unemployment impinging on the policy debate have been very much stressed notably by French and German policy makers. It has also been advanced as a crucial objective for forging ahead with integration issues at the Conference by both the European Parliament and the European Commission in recent months. It forms now part of the mandate (see Chapter 2).

Third, the optimistic expectations of the mid 1980s that surrounded discussions of the future European architecture, seemingly justified by actual implementation of most of the provisions of the Single European Market, gave way to increasing skepticism. This has been focused especially on issues of democracy, efficiency, subsidiarity, transparency, and accountability in the workings of the European institutions and the comportment of policy makers. Apprehensions about further integration, as well as genuine fears that yielding hard-won national priorities to EU mandates would jeopardize welfare at home, have come to the fore in public debate all too often, albeit frequently in a rather disingenuous manner. The prevailing popular concerns and doubts about creating a common currency (since the Madrid Council of December 1995 rebaptized from the 'ecu' identified in the Maastricht Treaty to the 'euro') are symptomatic of these wider anxieties about 'deepening.'

Finally, as part and parcel of the optimism regarding the 'construction' of Europe in the late 1980s, it had been taken for granted that the political changes since 1989 in the countries of the eastern part of Europe would be irreversible, that their economic transformation would proceed much more smoothly than in fact it has, and that with the first steps toward political union taken at Maastricht it would be fairly easy to move ahead with stabilizing and reinforcing the second and third pillars of the European architecture. The drawn-out crisis in the former Yugoslavia and the difficulties encountered in pooling even national Interpol organizations into Europol, a European policing organ, underline how hard it has been to make progress in these directions. Relations with the CIS, especially Russia and Ukraine, and the difficulties of integrating the smaller economies in transition into a broader framework of European security, also demonstrate how complex it has become to extend integration beyond the spheres in which the earliest efforts in the EU were successful, namely, the elimination of intragroup tariffs, the harmonization of the external tariff, and a few trade-related policies (such as those for agriculture, fisheries, transportation, sectoral restructuring, and regional issues).

Conclusions

The foregoing discussion has provided a compact *tour d'horizon* of the antecedents of the ongoing Conference and the main types of policy issues that must inform the debates over a protracted period of time. It is in the nature of such an IGC that important solutions to deep-seated institutional and governance problems are anticipated. Without them it will be all but impossible to cling to the precepts on Europe's *finalité politique*, as set forth in the Rome Treaty and stressed in so many Council deliberations since then, and enlarge the Union notably in the eastern direction. Too many obstacles would be in their way to make such a fifth accession and beyond feasible without there being major changes in the manner in which the Union is run.

As a result, the current Conference must without hyperbole be considered a make-it-or-break-it meeting at the highest policy-making level. That such crucial issues need to be tackled at a time when the pronounced sentiment for 'Europe' is not particularly favorable, when several major countries are falling into another recession so shortly after the end of the previous one, and when several Member States appear to be adamant in their opposition to contemplating anything more than a mild consolidation of past achievements is unfortunate. But, individually and together, they provide tough challenges ahead. Will 'Europe' be able to live up to its own expectations? Or will it falter again for several decades of stagnation because of lacking political will and a strategic vision of how Europe could be remade with many of the economies in transition as full partners?

This backdrop now needs to be filled out with details that pertain to the policy climate in which the further accession of countries to the Union, notably the economies in transition, will be negotiated.

2

The Conference: Agenda and Policy Dilemmas

Thus far the EU Member States do not seem to have agreed upon an official agenda of the 1996 Conference – at any rate none has been disclosed to date. The opening ceremony of the IGC in Turin conferred a mandate for the deliberations to be held by the Council of Ministers of Foreign Affairs and their assistants (European Commission 1996d). Presumably an agenda will be formulated and approved once that Council begins its deliberations in earnest, after the preparatory meetings of their assistants which started almost immediately after the Turin Council. Initial rumors had it that such a meeting would take place by late April 1996 as per the agreement reached at the Turin meeting. The calendar of meetings scheduled for April-June 1996 by the EU, however, suggested that the deputies of the Ministers of Foreign Affairs would devote first several weeks of deliberations per basic topic of the mandate (see Section 2), report regularly to whatever Council of Ministers of Foreign Affairs is convened, not necessarily especially on IGC matters, and then prepare an agenda for the Council, perhaps in time for the next European Council in June 1996. In April-June, three broad issues are scheduled: a citizen-friendly Union, firming up the EU's external dimension, and institutional reform (European Commission 1996e, l). This is likely to occupy deliberations for some time before a concrete agenda on the issues to be negotiated, at least in terms of modifying the Maastricht Treaty, will become available.

The aim of this chapter, in the absence of a clear-cut agenda, is to detail the likely areas of policy debate that are bound to inform the Conference. From the various documents that have already been prepared and from the wide-ranging debate that has been under way since the conclusions of the 1990-1991 IGCs at Maastricht it is reasonable to suppose that the most important agenda items will revolve around five broad problem areas. I detail them in the first section. Next I briefly refer to the Westendorp Report and the issues tabled in Turin for the Council of Ministers of Foreign Affairs and their assistants, including the European Commission. Then I argue the case for viewing matters more broadly, and I develop a functional catalogue of issues that are bound to form the backdrop of the deliberations of the Conference, even though they may well fail to be formally on the agenda. I opted for this approach because, in my view, such a broad source of guidance is required to build up a more comprehensive picture of the policy issues that affect the Conference, whether or not they will be explicitly debated. I conclude the chapter with some pointers to the widening issues that emerge from considerations of the deepening that the Conference's outcome is presumably intended to ensure. Whether it will is, of course, anybody's guess at this stage.

1 – Broad Policy Areas on the Agenda

From the backdrop sketched in Chapter 1, five broad policy areas informing the deliberations of the current Conference can be discerned: (1) widening versus deepening with the accent initially on deepening as a precondition for making widening practically feasible and politically acceptable; (2) forging ahead with monetary unification and the completion of the single market in practice as opposed to the legal environment circumscribing it, though even in that area more work needs to be done to ensure a level playing field for all Member States; (3) institutional and decision-making reforms; (4) reform of the transfer programs to permit enlargement of the EU's geographical remit toward the selected twelve countries and perhaps other potential candidates; and (5) reviewing the various preferential arrangements that the EU has developed over the years.

First, there is bound to be a discussion of finding ways and means to overcome the lethargy about moving ahead with integration – 'deepening' in other words – that set in soon after endorsement of the Maastricht Treaty. The shaping of Europe's *finalité politique*, or its envisaged final constitutional arrangements, deserves to be a priority. At the very least, a clear recommitment by Member States to the goals set earlier will be needed to restore momentum to the integration process. Continuing with the drift of the past several years can only undermine relations within the EU. If instead of a final constitutional arrangement only a recommitment to the vaguer ambitions of the Rome Treaty can be engineered, as seems likely, such an outcome would leave the final shape of the Union as a topic to be decided upon at some future point in time, perhaps another IGC, following further experience and the gingerly concertation of political will. In the meantime, however, it could ensure progress with some 'deepening,' even if it were to fall far short, in speed as well as in the breadth of the movement, in comparison to what the more federalist proponents of European union would have wanted to see emerge, certainly at this 'late' juncture.

Second, the IGC will need to make progress with EMU in spite of the fluctuations in policy commitment, the intermittent turmoil in currency markets since late 1992, and the current slowdown in the pace of economic activity in key Member States, including among the core of those constituting a critical minimum of any functionable monetary union. After all, this was the only firmly agreed commitment enshrined in the Maastricht Treaty. It is unlikely that all countries, or even all those whose membership at least in the 'core' is held to be desirable, will meet the strict convergence criteria by the set date, but there is room for maneuver within the Treaty on proceeding with monetary union among at least a core of Member States (see Chapter 3).

 Third, satisfactory solutions to Europe's multiple issues of governance (democracy, subsidiarity, efficiency, transparency, accountability, and so on) need to be found for a Union whose membership and diversity are expanding. This calls for institutional reforms to ensure that there is a more streamlined division of powers among the four core institutions of the EU. It also is predicated on agreeing on reform in decision-making rules and in representing both the Member States and the citizenship at large in the various institutions. Straightforward majority decision making, even if it were to be politically acceptable, notably by the small Member States, would simply not fit within the *sui generis* character of integration in the EU.

Fourth, the various transfer programs need to be refashioned in order to permit other countries, particularly some of the transition economies, to join the Union as full members, and also to keep the EU budget manageable in spite of fiscal stringency in most Member States. But budgetary matters *per se* are not supposed to be on the political agenda of the European Council until 1999, as per the decisions of the Edinburgh Council of December 1992. By that time, budgetary pressures from within the Union are likely to mandate a review of the most costly common programs, notably the CAP and the structural funds to enhance 'cohesiveness' within the EU (Begg, Gudgin, and Morris 1995).

Finally, a coherent assistance and cooperation program for other economies in transition, and indeed for nonmember countries more generally, needs to be formulated, perhaps by reexamining the EU's multi-tier preference system. This too is not an issue that is explicitly on the debating table set in Turin. But most observers believe that the questions involved cannot be completely ignored at the Conference. For one thing, any further enlargement of the EU will affect in an asymmetric fashion the existing members of the Union, the new members, as well as other countries that enjoy some preferential arrangement with the Union. Furthermore, most if not all of these preferential arrangements could usefully be reviewed and updated to ensure greater coherence and efficiency. Moreover, in a world that is no longer the one prevailing when these assistance programs were first formulated, the Union's current and prospective interests, economic as well as others, could be better served by fine-tuning these preferential arrangements accordingly.

These five areas of broad economic and other concerns undoubtedly offer a very complex set of issues from which a concrete agenda will need to be extracted. The Member States and the European institutions hold widely diverging views on what the most central agenda topics should be. Some are underlining their commitment to forging ahead with the integration process by moving toward political union, and perhaps other objectives, within a reasonably coherent economic union. At the same time they are aware of the political imperative of expanding membership, despite the practical problems of accommodating more and more diverse members and indeed the obstacles that will remain for years to come in order to ensure the smooth functioning of most economies in transition within the context of the Union's single market. Some Member States, the United Kingdom in particular, are emphasizing the need to review the Treaty and to achieve "sensible amendments in the areas which have been identified for review" (United Kingdom 1996a, para. 12); it has accordingly structured its preferred agenda in accordance with the strictest remit of governance reforms (United Kingdom 1996a, para. 18). Other Member States, while emphasizing the desirability of confining the Conference's purview chiefly to the review of the Treaty, are evidently prepared to look at the agenda from the wider point of view of the tasks ahead for European integration. This is notably the case for France (1996b), but also for Germany (1995, 1996) and indeed the Benelux (1996) countries.

The juxtaposition of widening and deepening among the priorities of the EU's agenda is not an easy mixture; it has never been – indeed it could not have been otherwise. Matters have become more intricate over time, with the weight given to deepening being reduced in favor of widening almost from the moment the Maastricht Treaty was signed (Giscard d'Estaing 1995). The extent of this shift has led some key policy makers to warn of the danger of the Union's existing achievements being eroded if a decisive step forward with deepening is not accommodated during the present Conference. Their concern is that a weaker commitment of the membership to deepening integration could result in the dilution of the Union into a free-trading area, perhaps only for industrial goods, and with some broader issues dealt with primarily at the intergovernmental level. Although some Member States would welcome such an evolution, a larger number would see it as a reversal of most of the goals of integration which they have been pursuing, however gradually and fitfully, for the past forty-six years.

2 – The Westendorp Report

The EU Informal Foreign Affairs Council of 27 March 1994 agreed to set up a working group, usually referred to as the Reflection Group, composed of senior officials and policy makers from all Member States, one from the Commission, and two from the European Parliament, to prepare for the new IGC. Its mandate, defined at the Corfu Council meeting (24-25 June 1994), was to examine and elaborate ideas relating to: (1) provisions that the Maastricht Treaty identified as subject to review; (2) other possible improvements in democracy and openness, based on an assessment of the results obtained during the implementation of the Treaty; (3) options on institutional questions relating to the prospective enlargement of the Union, and focusing, among other matters, on the weighting of votes, the threshold for qualified-majority decisions, and the number of Commissioners and their selection; and (4) any other measures deemed necessary. The Group was called upon to submit a report in time for the Madrid Council meeting (15-16 December 1995).

At the same time the European Commission was requested to submit to the group by mid 1995 a report on its views regarding the agenda of the new IGC (European Commission 1995a). That report set out three broad topics for the Conference. The first encompasses the four specific areas mentioned in the Maastricht Treaty: (1) the scope of codecision procedures (largely between the Council and the European Parliament); (2) security and defense (or the CFSP); (3) energy, tourism, and civil protection (in part to specify the CJHA); and (4) the hierarchy of Community acts.

In addition, the Council added two sets of issues: (1) the number of Commission members, the weighting of voting in the Council, and the measures required to facilitate the work of the institutions and ensure their efficient operation in reaction to the problems that surfaced with the fourth enlargement; and (2) the institutional arrangements required to ensure that the Union can function smoothly in the event of any further enlargement.

Finally, the European Parliament, the Council, and the Commission agreed to place two other subjects on the agenda: (1) the operation of budgetary procedures, notably as regards the classification of expenditures; and (2) the arrangements for exercising the executive powers conferred on the Commission to implement legislation adopted under the codecision procedure.

From July until December 1995, the so-called Reflection Group constituted as indicated above under the chairmanship of Mr. Carlos Westendorp y Cabeza, then Spain's State Secretary for European Affairs, met to identify the issues to be dealt with at the IGC96, to assess the extent of prior agreement, and to clarify the areas of disagreement among the members. This group delivered its report (Reflection Group 1995) to the Madrid European Council in December 1995, at which it was decided to open the IGC on 29 March 1996 in Turin. That report contains four main agenda topics: (1) the citizen and the Union, (2) collaboration in justice and home affairs, internal security, and free movement, (3) foreign and security policy; and (4) the institutional system.

The report's suggestions are mainly concerned with the spirit of the mandate and, by and large, simply register the existing disagreement among EU members about virtually all the problems to be tackled (Davidson 1996a). It is a lengthy catalogue of issues that the eighteen members deliberated about with a broad representation of the various points of view held in the various European organizations and the Member States. Commentary on the report has not been particularly favorable.

Whatever one may think about or however one may wish to read the above report, three features seem to be its hallmark. First, it does provide an overview in easily accessible language of most of the obstacles facing further integration, and it discusses institutional and policy matters with a view to making the EU far more transparent, citizen-friendly, and democratic. Second, it provides a catalogue of critical integration hurdles, questions for incisive reform on which consensus ought to be gained. That could not be reached in the course of elaborating the report, however, which notes virtually at every twist and turn the prevailing dissent. Finally, unlike earlier IGC, the Westendorp Report does not offer a ready-made text for negotiations. That is not now expected before early 1997, following the October and December Dublin Councils (European Commission 1996q, pp. 1-2).

This means that such a negotiable text or texts will have to be prepared by the assistants of the Ministers of Foreign Affairs and the European Commission, even though they, as well as two representatives from the European Parliament, were the principal participants in the preparation of the Westendorp Report! In fact seven of the fifteen national assistant-representatives in the IGC (European Commission 1996h) were also members of the Reflection Group.

On a final note, it is worth observing that the Westendorp Report does not consider the important matter of enlargement, except insofar as the institutional and decision-making reforms that are required anyway are also crucial for accommodating new members. In fact, the report strongly favors, although by no means unanimously, "the separation of the Conference exercise from the study of the impact of enlargement in relation to future development of common policies" (Reflection Group 1995, para. 21 of the Annotated Agenda). The grounds invoked for this choice are solid but neither particularly compelling nor persuasive. Nevertheless, although some elements of the 'widening' issue can perhaps be better addressed in other fora than the present IGC, the decision to enlarge membership and move ahead with it soon after the conclusion of the Conference was taken at the Essen Council session (9-10 December 1994), and it is therefore difficult to see how 'widening' cannot inform the debate and outcome of a number of issues that are explicitly on the Conference's agenda.

3 – On the Conference's Mandate

By way of the "Presidency's Conclusions," in a rather oblique manner, the Turin Extraordinary European Council on 29 March 1996 issued a sort of mandate. Unfortunately, the released *communiqué* (European Commission 1996d) is not particularly informative. This is a pity for if that reflects the IGC's state of affairs at end March 1996, it suggests that the Heads of State and Government have left the specification of the concrete agenda for deliberations up to the Council of Ministers and their assistants; so far their deliberations have remained carefully shrouded. After the Florence Council (21-22 June 1996), major progress will probably not become public until the Extraordinary Council scheduled for Dublin, 19-20 October 1996.

From the above document issued by the extraordinary Turin Council meeting (European Commission 1996d) and the scheduled activities through June 1996 (European Commission 1996e, l), the envisaged procedures appeared to be as follows. The assistants of the Ministers of Foreign Affairs, six of who are their country's permanent representative (ambassador to the EU) in Brussels (European Commission 1996h), met on almost a weekly basis. There were ten such meetings before the European Council in Florence. Two rounds of first two and then one meeting were devoted to the three main mandated tasks: (1)

bringing the Union closer to the citizens, (2) making the institutions more democratic and efficient, and (3) strengthening the capacity for external action. Originally, it had been planned (European Commission 1996i, p. 3) to have sufficient material for a 17 May 1996 round of negotiations on drafting a preliminary report for the Florence Council. That schedule slipped as meetings on the external dimension were held well into June 1996 (European Commission 1996l). Even the aim to have an interim or progress report ready by 17 June for a special session of the Council of Ministers of Foreign Affairs, in time for the Florence Council (European Commission 1996o, p. 1) had to be abandoned. Indeed, only a Presidency's report by Silvio Fagiolo on a review of the deliberations rather than an interim IGC report (European Commission 1996p, p. 1) was tabled in Florence, the substantive negotiations having been deferred to the Irish Presidency, which follows in the second half of 1996. At that stage, it might be appropriate to draw up a concrete agenda that the Council of Ministers can approve for negotiations on substantive issues to commence. That is not expected before later in 1996. A major impetus will probably emanate from the Extraordinary Dublin Council scheduled for 19-20 October 1996. Negotiators count on having sufficient material to report back to the European Council in Dublin (December 1996), which can then issue further instructions for the Council of Ministers to reach for a rump agreement sometime by mid 1997 (European Commission 1996q, pp. 1-2).

The confusion and lack of progress about the negotiations to date is illustrated by the discrepancies between the Commission's published calendar (European Commission 1996e, l), which does not envisage IGC meetings by the Ministers of Foreign Affairs, and its affirmation (European Commission 1996i) that there will be monthly meetings of that Council to evaluate and guide the further preparatory work of their assistants and the Commission's President. Indeed, such sessions did take place on 22 April and 10 June in Luxembourg, and then 17 June in Florence, but apparently the concern with the IGC was more on the margin of other foreign-policy matters (European Commission 1996n, p. 10; 1996p, pp. 1-2; 1996q, pp. 1-2).

The overriding instruction to the negotiators at the IGC96 is that "[i]t is essential to sustain the very nature of European construction, which has to preserve and develop its features of democracy, effi-

ciency, solidarity, cohesion, transparency and subsidiarity" and to finalize its work by adopting "a general and consistent vision throughout its
work" so as "to meet the needs and expectations of our citizens, while
advancing the process of European construction and preparing the
Union for its future enlargement" (European Commission 1996d). The
concrete steps mentioned in the rather general mandate rely on the
Reflection Group's report "without prejudice to other questions which
might be raised during the Conference." This is indeed all too vague for
remaking Europe!

As regards bringing the Union closer to its citizens, respect for non-
discrimination, democratic values, human rights, and equality should
inform the Conference and urge the participants to deliberate about
how best to "strengthen these fundamental rights and improve the
safeguarding of them." The Conference has been asked to produce on
these issues better methods and instruments; to ensure better protection
of the Union's citizens against international crime, especially drug
trafficking and terrorism; develop coherent and effective asylum, immigration, and visa policies; and remove divergent views on jurisdictional
and parliamentary control of EU decisions in CJHA.

The second topic under this heading is unemployment. The IGC is
requested to examine how the Union could provide the basis for improving cooperation and coordination in order to strengthen national policies with a view to reaching a high level of employment while ensuring
social protection. Next on this part of the agenda is the compatibility
between competition and the principle of universal access to essential
services in the citizen's interest. In addition, the IGC should examine
the status of outermost regions, of overseas territories, and of island
regions of the Union. Moreover, it is asked to ensure a better environment by making environmental protection more effective and coherent
at the level of the Union. Finally, it should ensure a better application
and enforcement of the principle of subsidiarity to provide transparency
and openness in the Union's activities, and "to consider whether it
would be possible to simplify and consolidate the Treaties."

On institutional issues, the overriding task of the IGC is to look for
the best means to ensure that the core institutions function with greater
efficiency, coherence, and legitimacy. In that context, the Conference
is called upon to examine the most effective means of simplifying legis-

lative procedures, making them clearer and more transparent; widen the scope of codecision in "truly legislative matters"; and look into the role of the European Parliament other than its legislative powers, as well as its composition and a uniform procedure for its election.

In addition, under this topic, the IGC will examine how national parliaments can be better involved with the Union. It must improve the functioning of the Council, including by looking at the extent of majority voting, the weighting of votes, and the threshold for qualified-majority decisions. As regards the Commission, the IGC will contemplate means by which its fundamental functioning can be accomplished more efficiently, including by having regard to its composition and its representativeness. Whether and how to improve the role and functioning of the European Court of Justice and the Court of Auditors is also part of the mandate. Particular emphasis will be given to achieving greater clarity and quality of legislation and the ways and means of putting up a more effective fight against fraud. Finally, the IGC is asked to study whether and how to introduce rules "to enable a certain number of Member States to develop a strengthened cooperation, open to all, compatible with the Union's objectives, while preserving the acquis communautaire, avoiding discrimination and distortions of competition and respecting the single institutional framework."

The third heading concerns strengthening the capacity for external action to ensure that the EU's political weight will be commensurate with its economic strength. To accomplish the CFSP, the IGC has been invited to identify the principles and the areas of common foreign policy, to define the actions needed to promote the Union's interests in these areas and according to these principles, to set up procedures and structures designed to improve the effectiveness and timeliness of decisions in a spirit of loyalty and solidarity, and to agree on suitable budgetary provisions. In that context, the IGC will study whether and how a post for a super Mr. CFSP will be created. Moreover, the IGC has been called upon "to better assert the European identity in matters of security and defence," paying particular regard to the future of the WEU. In that context the operational capacity of the Union to discharge the so-called Petersberg tasks (military participation mainly in humanitarian and peace-keeping missions) and the desirability of greater cooperation in armaments are emphasized.

This offers quite a wide range of controversial matters on which the Member States have exhibited widely diverging views now for years. The question of enlargement is behind every single statement made, though it is mentioned only in passing, if at all. Since I am in any case far more interested in the economic obstacles to enlargement, particularly towards eastern Europe, rather than in matters concerning CSFP and CJHA (but see Ludlow 1996b, c), I deem it more useful to look at the issues slightly differently. Before doing so, however, I should like to recall that having an agenda in place and ensuring that the negotiations stick to the agreed-upon schedule are by no means trivial matters, as the experience with earlier IGCs has amply demonstrated. Niels Ersbøll, who has been at the center of these deliberations either as representative or a highly placed EU official (he was Secretary General of the Council of Ministers for a very long time indeed and a key member of the Reflection Group), has underlined this in unmistakable terms: Managing the agreed-upon agenda, once put in place, ranks "amongst the most important and most difficult tasks of the presidencies concerned" (Ludlow and Ersbøll 1996, p. 11).

4 – A Functional Catalogue

Combining the elements that can be extracted from the sources discussed above with the other areas of concern that have emerged in the recent policy debates on furthering integration, the issues for the IGC96 can be more usefully grouped under several functional headings. Note that these are not necessarily the topics that will be explicitly debated during the IGC, as the agenda is still unknown. But the entries selected here provide a plausible checklist against which the achievements or failures of the IGC96 are likely to be judged.

1 – Economic and Monetary Union (EMU)

This is the core of the Maastricht Treaty and the only firm instance in which explicit commitments were made on timetables for moving ahead with and the conditions to be met for the establishment of and participation in monetary union. The latter was deemed to evolve gradually toward EMU in three phases, leading in the end to a single, rather than a composite and notional, European currency – the 'ecu,' but since the Madrid Council (December 1995) rechristened the 'euro' – by the late 1990s (but now deferred to 2002, as lucidly clarified in Silguy 1996). In turn, this would be a stepping stone for moving beyond economic integration into other domains, which would increase the cohesiveness of the EU. Phases 1 and 2 of the progression toward EMU were precisely determined. Phase 3, however, was made conditional upon meeting certain criteria.

In Phase 1, to ensure the smooth transition from the Single European Market toward the start-up of monetary union, and thus complete the EMU, apart from drafting the relevant components on monetary union of EMU as specified in the Maastricht Treaty and passing that Treaty, Member States were to coordinate their macroeconomic policies better than previously, and thus lower inflation and the variability of exchange rates. Exchange-rate stability and convergence were in any case viewed as important policy objectives, given the EU-wide mandatory liberalization of capital markets by mid 1990 (except for the newer entrants into the Union who received some extra time for compliance). In Phase 2, to begin with the entry into force of the Treaty, pursuit of the convergence criteria was to become the guiding beacon of macroeconomic-policy stances. Also the European Monetary Institute (EMI) was created in January 1994. Phase 3 will inaugurate the monetary union.

Phase 1 was accomplished and phase 2 was started according to the terms of reference in the Treaty, subject to the ramifications of the currency-market turmoil in September 1992 and July-August 1993 (for details, see Caporale, Hassapis, and Pittis 1995). In the third phase, monetary union should be inaugurated no later than early 1999, with only Member States able to meet the strict criteria of convergence qualifying for membership. It could have been done no earlier than January 1997 provided a majority of the Member States met the convergence criteria. It has now been decided that this will not be the case, and so monetary union is to start in early 1999, when the Maastricht Treaty calls for the automatic start-up of monetary union as per article 109j(4): "If by the end of 1997 the date for the beginning of the third stage has not been set, the third stage shall start on 1 January 1999"

(European Commission 1993, p. 238). In addition, the new common currency – now the 'euro' instead of the ecu mentioned in the Maastricht Treaty – should be adopted within three years of the inauguration of monetary union, that is, now by 2002 at the latest. All of the matters concerning phase 3 of monetary union were supposed to be settled at the present IGC, unless this task had been accomplished already earlier in the European Council.

The specification of the Treaty to the effect that "the third stage shall start on January 1999" has traditionally been interpreted, including by successive sessions of the European Council, to mean that if no decision on starting monetary integration before 1999 was taken, meaning that at the latest by end 1997 a decision to inaugurate monetary union in 1998 at the earliest could have been taken, monetary union would begin automatically in early 1999. But the first part of the specification (a decision on "the third stage by the end of 1997") has recently been interpreted in some legal circles as permitting the Member States to select a different date, including later than 1999, before the end of 1997. This purely legal interpretation may very well be beyond legal dispute. But it is unlikely to be one of the more credible options for flexible policy making discussed in Chapter 3, at least in the view of Cees Maas, who is the chairman of the Committee of Experts on Transition to the Common Currency established by the European Commission to advise on the creation of the common currency and monetary union. He has labeled the legalistic way out of the bind as a "figment of malicious spirits" (Maas 1995, pp. 39-40).

It is useful in this connection to make a clear distinction between the politics and economics of monetary integration, and of integration more generally. The dates set for monetary unification were selected largely for reasons of political expediency rather than economic logic. To adhere to them in a completely inflexible manner is not likely to constitute constructive policy making. Nor does it make for a viable monetary union in 1999. To strengthen the latter and ensure that it will not become subject to unwieldy imbalances almost from its first inception, constructive policy making will in any case be required. Some flexibility can therefore best be considered already at this stage. This issue is so important in the current policy context, including in making arrangements for enlarging the Union without jeopardizing the core aims of integration as stated in the quasi-constitutional acts of the Union, that I deal with it separately in Chapter 3, after I will have explained the other crucial policy and institutional matters that, in my view, form the backdrop to the core topics of the ongoing Conference.

As a final comment on EMU at this stage, a word needs to be said on its first component. That is to say, the more concrete assessment of the functioning of the single market and related matters are to be dealt with at the Conference as well. The monitoring of economic policies in Member States and efforts to foster better policy concertation will need more concrete and effective content, if only to impart greater credibility to financial and other markets. The logic of EMU calls for a coordination of macroeconomic policies that is far broader than monetary affairs in the strict sense (Ghymers 1995). Unfortunately, there is as yet no binding commitment to enact such broader coordination with perhaps the assistance of the European Commission. Once again, the Member States remain quite jealous of their sovereignty in those other domains of economic policy making.

2 – Institutional and Decision-making Improvements

Deepening can occur only if the integration process is and remains governable. For a number of reasons, the possibility of achieving this stage of maturity has been increasingly questioned not only in EU policy circles but also by the public at large in a number of Member States. In several countries, popular support for European integration, after its resurgence in the second half of the 1980s with the enthusiasm about the creation of the single market and the welcome improvements in economic performance (on growth, productivity, and employment accounts), has declined again and the broader public is often indifferent or cynical about it. Many interest groups outside the narrow circle of EU cognoscenti are concerned about the lack of adequate information, openness, democracy, transparency, and accountability of Union actions and programs. In many cases this attitude is quite in order. But in others it stems simply from the apathy of broad layers of the population regarding the integration enterprise, which prevents them from being induced to inform themselves appropriately. After all, there *is* considerable information available about the Union's activities!

Meeting these objections involves more than a hasty exercise in repairing public relations. The EU institutions tend to project an aura of technocratic superiority and élitism, a sort of club where fundamental matters affecting the citizenship at large are decided behind closed doors and with a minimum of justification and clarification. Both alienate the citizen. This is particularly so for major decisions affecting citizens' rights and national sovereignty. Whatever the foundations of this perception, popular disaffection can only undermine support for the EU and reflect negatively upon the credibility of its activities. Widespread fears about losing a national currency, which is perhaps the most conspicuous symbol of national sovereignty, is a case in point. Trust in a new common currency will have to be earned the hard way, by deeds in financial and other markets, not simply by technocratic imposition.

But apart from this external dimension of governance, arguably the most pressing challenge in governing internal affairs is how best to reach decisions for and by the present fifteen Member States, essentially on the basis of rules and regulations originally designed for the six founder members, without adopting straight majority voting. As a minimum, the weighting system will have to be made more democratic, in a sense more "equal." This can be seen immediately, for example, from the fundamental asymmetry in representation: Germany with 10 votes in the Council now has one vote per about 8 million inhabitants, while Luxembourg with two has one per about 0.2 million inhabitants. That could hardly be viewed as democratic representation!

Also the "qualified majority" rules (requiring about 71 percent of Council votes for passage of a tabled item dealing essentially with other than constitutional matters) will have to be redesigned, if only because of the controversy that arose with the fourth enlargement on how to protect the 'small members' without impeding the 'large members' from being as fully heard as they deem it necessary. It was the so-called Ioannina Compromise. This refers to the "temporary" solution reached in connection with the fourth enlargement of the EU at the Ioannina Informal Foreign Affairs Council of 27 March 1994. After Norway decided not to join, the Ioannina Compromise qualifies the qualified-majority voting system with 87 votes for the Council of Fifteen: If 23 to 25 votes in the Council intend to oppose a Council decision adopted by qualified majority, the Council will do its utmost to obtain a satisfactory solution; the latter is to be adopted with at least 65 votes in favor within a reasonable period of time (European Commission 1995d). Introduction of such a Council decision will be delayed for a month, and possibly for a second one; thereafter it will be introduced (for a detailed explanation, see Vignes 1994, p. 562) like any decision passed with less than 23 votes against.

The above compromise, just like the critical so-called Luxembourg Compromise of 1966 (as detailed in Brabant 1995a, pp. 183-4), which requires that negotiations be continued indefinitely on issues about which any one Member State feels it has a fundamental interest, and thus deems them to be "very important" (see Camps 1966, pp. 111-12; Henig 1983), was just that. Just like the Luxembourg Compromise cannot be maintained indefinitely, the Ioannina Compromise must at some point be refashioned as a result of a revision of decision-making rules. Otherwise it will be impossible to reach and implement effective decisions. In fact, part and parcel of the latter Compromise was to reexamine it at the current IGC (European Commission 1995d, p. 2), unlike the Luxembourg Compromise, which will remain in force until the Member States will voluntarily relinquish their right to veto. That is not yet in sight as many of the larger Member States remain opposed to relinquishing this ultimate power of sovereignty.

Perhaps the only solution consists in a constitutional arrangement to enact several levels of decision making and of qualified majorities, possibly a representational and membership majority. There will probably remain exceptionally important constitutional matters, very limited in number, such as on new accessions, for which consensus will continue to rule. Hard choices will need to be made for the unanimity rule can quickly become counterproductive with fifteen members, let alone with the prospect of thirty or even more members. On all other issues, however, decisions will have to be reached through some "qualified majority," but not necessarily with the present ceiling of about 71 percent of the votes. Yet some kind of qualified majority that protects the interests of small countries without granting them a blocking minority, will have to be worked out. With more and more small members, safeguarding this may become all but impossible.

True, such rules will further complicate decision making. However, it will be a level of complexity that differs in important respects from that impeding progress at this juncture. This issue is bound to be rekindled, and indeed aggravated, with the negotiations after the Conference for accession of the EU's eastern and southern neighbors. It will therefore have to be resolved in a more durable manner one way or the other, but preferably along constitutional lines.

In this connection an important investigation of the European Parliament has recommended that if the Conference were "unable to reach a positive conclusion owing to failure to reach a unanimous decision," it should consider "proceeding without the minority and, possibly, providing for instruments to enable a Member State to leave the EU, subject to meeting certain criteria" (Bourlanges and Martin 1995, para. 17, p. 11). Without it, the future negotiations for accession of mostly small eastern and southern neighbors are likely to become very cumbersome rather quickly, threatening to complicate, possibly even paralyze, decision making in the EU.

Even more controversial will be the division of powers in the EU among chiefly the European Commission, the European Parliament, the European Council (and Council of Ministers), and the European Court of Justice, on the one hand, and the member Governments and regional Councils, on the other. The EU is expected to arrive at a *modus vivendi* in responding to the public's perception to the effect that there exists a "democratic deficit" in the EU and embrace constructive pragmatism on "subsidiarity" through purposeful dialogue. At the same time, Member States, once agreement is reached, must allow the European institutions to function within the context of a longer-term vision of Europe. European citizens expect the EU institutions to be able to discharge their assigned functions effectively, transparently, reasonably democratically, and with full citizen representation and accountability. In that perspective, the machinery and procedures of governance ought to be refashioned in a comprehensive manner.

The governance and financing of common endeavors also figure prominently on the Conference's presumed working agenda, whether officially acknowledged or not. Formally, the foundations of the EU's budget are not subject to policy debates until 1999, as the Edinburgh Council in December 1992 determined budget priorities and limits until the end of the decade. But revisions will almost certainly be introduced beginning with the year 2000. There are several reasons for this position. One is that the EU cannot afford to continue to allocate the bulk of its funds to support agriculture and cohesion. Another is that without reforms, particularly in the latter two programs, enlargement toward the economies in transition will become impossible. Finally, agricultural subsidies are due to be discussed again at the global level in the context of the World Trade Organization (WTO) in 1999, as agreed to during the Uruguay Round.

The nature, scope, and objectives of most of the current transfer programs administered by the European Commission – such as for agricultural support, and the cohesion, social purposes, and structural funds – will have to be reexamined as the financial resources required to discharge fully their mandated tasks are likely to far exceed the available sums. This is all the more likely insofar as the agricultural and structural funds in the 1993 budget claimed 54 and 32 percent, respectively, or no less than 86 percent of the overall budget (Dutheil de la Rochère 1995, pp. 101-2) and is roughly expected to remain at that level throughout the remainder of the decade, as per the rules agreed upon at the Edinburgh Council (see Thomas 1994, p. 475). It should, then, be clear that if the Union is to address the vital communautarian issues through financial support, it cannot do so while the vast bulk of its resources continue to be appropriated for agricultural supports and cohesion purposes. Claims on such resources can only escalate with the eventual accession of the EU's southern and eastern neighbors, given their levels of development and population size.

Perhaps the most daunting problem of governance, one that cannot be avoided at the ongoing Conference, but which is unlikely to be resolved either there or soon after, concerns the nature of the EU and its *finalité politique*. Regardless of whether policy makers agree to strive for some type of federal, confederal, or simply intergovernmental way of running the Union in the years ahead, decisions will have to be reached about the fundamentals of cooperation in areas other than free trading or the coordination of selected economic policies. Member States will have to define the core elements of EU integration to which all present and future Member States must necessarily subscribe and conform, possibly after some mutually-agreed transition period. This involves the identification of Member States able – and willing – to fulfill the *acquis communautaire et politique*, those willing but not yet able to do so, and others that are looking for a form of regional economic cooperation that essentially diverges from the EU's very nature. Under such circumstances there may well emerge a core group of countries whose objectives will differ permanently from those held by other Member States. Valéry Giscard d'Estaing (1995), for example, argues strongly that the current integration path, now more and more being focused on widening, is bound to deteriorate into a continent-wide free-trading zone and that it is therefore imperative to start up a new organization among the core countries devoted to more ambitious goals, such as those that led to the Paris and Rome Treaties but made more explicit in the envisioned constitutional arrangement.

This problem cannot be avoided by resorting to some form of variable geometry with staggered levels of increasingly closer integration. The reason is simple: Because there cannot be independence in most endeavors between what, say, core countries do and what the next tier or tiers may wish to subscribe to, it will be virtually impossible to maintain coherent coordination among and within those groups. This is clear for monetary union, for example: Those joining the union will not tolerate wanton exchange-rate movements of the Member States that cannot join the union or do not wish to do so (see Chapter 3). That is to say, if the EU's ambitions are to be preserved, an EMU of core countries, for example, would be incompatible with its location within a larger free-trading area, precisely because the latter's commitment to anything but the features of at most a customs union would offer them free-riding opportunities not available to those constituting the core. One such example is that the "outs," as current EU-speak has it, would find themselves in a position to gain advantages in trade through competitive currency realignments, which their core partners would, legitimately, consider 'unfair.' But there are other opportunities for free riding that would be intolerable to those constituting the core.

Finally, the convoluted problems of "widening versus deepening" can in reality be tackled only jointly, as the debate on integration since the deliberations at Maastricht has amply underlined. Although it is conceivable to consider moving ahead with deepening at the express expense of widening, the reverse option is only feasible at the cost of losing the EU's very *raison d'être*: It would almost certainly destroy core elements of the *acquis* and in time probably turn the EU into a free-trading area. To stabilize relations in the EU, the essential elements of its achievements over the postwar period and its constitutional structure, as it presently exists, will have to be strengthened and utilized as a platform to forge ahead in new endeavors. The guidelines for doing so will have to be based on fundamental elements of the *acquis communautaire* and the principles of solidarity, subsidiarity, cohesiveness, a shared destiny, and gradual federalization of core governance tasks eventually to be enshrined in a constitutional charter. Of course, a more focused distinction needs to be made, with a judicious use of an appropriate subsidiarity rule, between the essentials of EU unification as envisioned in the organization's treaties and more voluntary areas of multi-country cooperation. Consequently, widening and deepening will have to be pursued simultaneously with a delicate balance being maintained over time.

In this context it is useful to raise the issues underlying the variable-geometry, concentric circles, or *à la carte* debates on the future organization of the EU, such as I understand them. I have avoided this terminology for quite specific reasons. Various configurations thereof have figured prominently in the post-Maastricht debates and in the discussions around the preparations and the early discussions of the current IGC (Brabant 1995a, pp. 516-19). None has offered a compelling alternative to EU practices since 1950. The reason for this is that more often than not the precise meaning of the particular piece of variable geometry, as well as the other configurations, invoked is left unspecified. Incidentally, the same criticism applies to the "flexibility" now urged upon the Conference as a core constitutional principle (see below). If variable geometry, and I confine myself to this figure of speech as the other proposals are even less credible, means gradualism in accession, both for existing members and new entrants; the spreading of costs and benefits of integration over time; or enabling some Member States to join in some particular program (such as Eureka) that is not part of the core of EU integration, then calling for variable geometry (or another such faddish catchword) as a constitutional issue is superfluous, indeed a needless complication of the debate on vital matters.

It is redundant, indeed sheer tautology, to insist upon such a configuration of variable geometry as providing a potential solution to the future governance of the Union: Gradualism and flexibility in adjusting toward the common core measures have been the practice of the EU from its very inception. There is no reason why this should not be continued, notably in smoothing the accession of new members (as detailed in Chapter 5) and in allowing some Member States to move faster and farther with their integration than others in matters that are not at the heart of European integration. The latter has been explicitly acknowledged, including by the European Commission (1996a, p. 16). If on the other hand variable geometry means that there will be permanent differences on core issues among the participants of the Member States, such as on monetary union, that would seem to be irreconcilable with the EU's essential ambitions as enshrined in the quasi-constitutional documents underlying the EU.

The IGC96 might contribute to elucidating this issue by making a more pointed distinction between the essential parts of European unification as broadly envisioned in the Rome Treaty but that may need further specification, as discussed earlier, and other common areas of interest. The focus should be on competition in open markets based solely (at least primarily) on genuine productivity performances, while ensuring the appropriate scope for raising productivity levels and prosperity throughout the union. This includes without exception *all* aspects of the single market, notably EMU. Although not all members will have to move at the same pace, there can be no permanent exemption from that fundamental commitment without altering the very ambition of the Rome Treaty. The EU's future cannot be about intergovernmentalism or free trading as such; that would *de facto* refer to another organization, one that is not envisioned by most EU members.

More voluntary areas of regional cooperation in economic and other matters can be entertained, as indeed they have been in EU activities in the past. Examples are legion: Eureka, the technology-cooperation program, or the European space program. They need not involve all members. Judicious use of an appropriate subsidiarity rule can pragmatically validate this division of labor in these and many other conceivable areas. Conflicts in other cases will then need to be resolved through pragmatic political compromise

With much the same logic, I refute some of the current interpretations about the allegedly "new willingness" of the EU founders to explore "flexibility." Ian Davidson (1996b), for example, has interpreted the European Commission's (1996a, p. 11) express invitation to the Conference to work toward greater "flexibility" as a vindication of the call made by Mr. John Major (1994) in a speech delivered at Leyde (The Netherlands) on 7 September 1994, for allowing some Member States to "integrate more closely or more quickly in certain areas" and that "conformity can never be right as an automatic principle." That interpretation reads too much into the European Commission's statement, which emphasizes quite explicitly that any such measure should not be "against the general interests of the Union." It also explicitly rejects the "pickandchoose Europe" approach of the Social Protocol (see European Commission 1996a, p. 16). In other words, it is very difficult to read an endorsement of "variable geometry," let alone of "an *à la carte* Europe," into the Commission's position, which admittedly waffles on the issue for how can one combine flexibility on core integration matters without jeopardizing the *acquis*?

Of course, the French-German position on "flexibility" is quite something else (see Howe 1996, p. 14). The latest buzzword is "reinforced cooperation" between "countries willing and able to go further and faster than others in certain fields"; but that excludes virtually all of EMU (European Commission 1996o, pp. 2-3). My reading of the entire debate is that flexibility in the sense of permitting some Member States able and willing to move ahead with some aspects of integration while others will abstain from new areas or follow suit in areas already committed to at a later date is something worth taking at face value. But there can be no permanent deviation from the very essentials of the Treaty of Rome without irretrievably altering the EU's ambitions. I am not aware that there is presently a consensus, or even a majority, on working toward such an incisive constitutional modification in the EU.

In the above light, while the debates have perhaps not yet fully exhausted the usefulness of deliberating about and considering the more plausible variable-geometry arrangements, they have nonetheless, in my view, lost most of their appeal in the face of these policy challenges. That does *not* mean that all integration endeavors at all times will have to be fully supported by all members. But a Europe *à la carte* or with a permanently differing geometry or multi-paths, let alone a pick-and-choose Europe, without a convergence being in sight in essential areas of the *acquis*, in my view, simply cannot be reconciled with the EU's prime purposes.

3 – Deepening Union Endeavors

The second and third pillars of the Maastricht Treaty, as mentioned earlier, are treated at the intergovernmental level; and the fourth group of concerns around social issues was never enshrined in the Treaty because the United Kingdom claimed and received exemption from any common social policy, even for issues that directly affect the competitive position of Member States (European Commission 1995a, pp. 47-8). The latter has proved to be a very unsatisfactory arrangement. The experiences with the second and third pillars since they were first worked out in 1991, it is widely noted by leading policy makers as well as observers of the EU scene, have been quite disappointing. Although there have been a few positive achievements they have trailed far behind the expectations that prevailed at the beginning of the decade.

The Maastricht Treaty provided in any case for a reexamination of these two other pillars with a view to moving closer toward EPU as part and parcel of the *finalité politique* and of perhaps an examination of some social issues, particularly those revolving around the other three pillars. In view of the experiences gathered since 1991, such a review and reconsideration will be more than necessary to consolidate integration achievements and move ahead with deepening integration. The goal is not necessarily to transfer national responsibilities to supranational decision-making levels; but sharing them, in a constructive manner with member Governments, the regions, and citizens according to a properly interpreted subsidiarity rule, is widely considered necessary if the EU is to regain its élan and make progress. More concrete contents beyond simple consultations will have to be agreed upon to foster the CFSP and to promote core ambitions of the CJHA.

A number of important topics that should have been resolved with the official completion of the single European market by end 1992 have yet to be addressed in full, as the European Commission (1996f) has recently underlined. For some of them, only the implementation of rules and regulations needs to be reinforced. For others, their very foundation as components of the Single European Market are yet to be completed, some even at the Union level. There are also several disconcerting variations between the nearly 280 items of the Single European Market that were completed roughly by late 1992, on the one hand, and those actually adopted in the respective national legislatures, and even more the number that is actually enforced, by Member States, on the other hand (European Commission 1996f, k). Particular problems at the Union level have arisen notably with fiscal harmonization, the common migration policy for aliens residing in a Member State and for those residing outside the EU, the European company statute, cross-border financial services, and divergences in social policies that tend to distort market-based competition. Certainly, the contentious social agenda derives, among other considerations, from political calculations as well.

In other words, the "widening versus deepening" debate has frequently been less than genuinely concerned about the real, at times delicate, technical and political issues at stake. The earlier experiences with widening, and the difficulties of some countries and the lack of will displayed by others to adhere to their treaty obligations, at least to a minimal degree, provide little guidance to finding constructive solutions to the many governance problems facing the EU at present. The prevailing hindrances can be overcome only in a *sui generis* fashion construed around real policy choices and decisions. That reflects the fact that deepening constrains widening and *vice versa*, not only by design but also by the very nature of the conflicts that may arise between the two policy priorities. This is certainly the case when it comes to dealing with the challenges of enlargement and beyond.

Forging ahead with integration, even toward the contentious objective of political union, does *not* imply that all facets of policy making, regulation, and administration need to be increasingly centralized at the Union level. However, a sensible, federal-like structure set up specifically to cope with the core issues of integration and constructive subsidiarity will have to be erected eventually if greater democracy, efficiency, transparency, and accountability in Union matters are to be attained. The *finalité politique* also implies progressing with the restructuring of the EU's "weaker pillars." These are all subject to intergovernmental deliberations and frequently stalled there precisely for inadequate decision-making ability.

Deepening also means that Member States implement in good faith the rules governing integration. The *finalité politique* may have to be reexamined in a more realistic and pragmatic manner than has been the case in recent years. New or incremental elements of national economic, political, and social sovereignty will have to be shared at least with member Governments if the EU is to progress beyond EMU.

4 – Accession of the Transition Economies and Beyond

At the Essen European Council of December 1994, it was decided that, following the conclusion of the Conference scheduled for 1996, accession negotiations could be initiated in principle with some ten eastern European countries, identified in Chapter 1, all of which have formally requested accession, beginning with Hungary on 1 April 1994 and ending with Slovenia on 10 June 1996; and with at least two southern European countries (Cyprus and Malta), both of which had already applied in 1990, as did Turkey in 1987; Turkey is not, however, being included among the countries whose applications will be considered by the European Commission before a negotiating mandate can be worked out by the European Council (as examined in Chapter 1). By the time these negotiations start, more recently viewed as happening only after "successful conclusion" of the Conference, several other countries are likely to have lodged entry applications.

It should be noted that the meaning of a "successful" conclusion to the Conference is not self-evident, and will probably emerge only from the deliberations themselves. However, the prevailing sentiment is that, barring really adverse circumstances, the negotiations for accession will begin in late 1997 or early 1998 with Cyprus and Malta (for which the Madrid Council of December 1995 decided to commence negotiations within six months following the Conference's successful conclusion) and, roughly at the same time, with the economies in transition, in the first instance probably those that are more advanced in their economic and political transformation; note, however, that the European Commission has been mandated to proceed with the preliminary evaluation of the applications from the transition economies. Indeed, in the words of the European Council, it "hopes that preliminary accession negotiations with the [economies in transition] will coincide with the start of membership negotiations with Cyprus and Malta" (European Commission 1996g). A similar sentiment was expressed in the concluding document of the Madrid Council (European Commission 1995e, chapter 3, p. 2). There would, however, seem to have been some backtracking on this promise since then, as discussed in Chapter 5.

In this connection one should be clear about the economies in transition that have applied and for which the European Commission has been requested to prepare one composite, overall recommendation to the European Council on how best to approach the accession negotiations in parallel with those for Cyprus and Malta. So far the EU has not yet selected any subgroup of the ten transition economies with which negotiations will first be conducted. At one point, however, there was broad agreement that as a minimum the Czech Republic, Hungary, Poland, and Slovenia would be among the first transition economies to negotiate for the first wave of entry, perhaps in parallel with Cyprus and Malta. Otherwise the process would be unnecessarily protracted for the countries that are generally recognized to be more advanced in the implementation of their transformation policies, including notably with market-based resource allocation and the creation of a pluralistic democracy.

This earlier consensus on splitting up the ten potential entrants from among the transition economies into meaningful subgroups, as discussed in Chapter 5, is now in doubt. For one thing, the Commission has received a mandate to look simultaneously at all requests for accession and to prepare one composite recommendation document for the Council. Also the European Parliament has become more vocal on that point, arguing that the Commission should deal with the ten economies in transition simultaneously and accord them at best minimal derogations from the *acquis* at the start of the transition phase upon entry. If so, the procedure is bound to have major implications for the length of the negotiations and the more likely date of entry of this group of countries, as detailed in Chapter 5.

The key issues are essentially twofold. One set revolves around ascertaining the various dimensions of pluralistic democracy and viable market-based economies. The other concerns the costs and benefits of widening, their level and their distribution, both among the present Member States and the new entrants, as well as over time. Whereas the first set of issues can pose tricky problems, with some good will pragmatic solutions can no doubt be elaborated and implemented, as detailed in Chapter 5. That will not necessarily be so for the second set of problems, however, given the population size (over 100 million people in total) of the likely ten applicants among the economies in transition and their average level of development, which is bound to remain well below the lowest levels in the EU for some time to come, and almost certainly when serious negotiations begin. Moreover, it is difficult to envision pragmatic solutions to problems arising in the first group of issues that affect directly the costs and benefits of accession. For example, if a potential applicant is not in a position to adhere to essential elements of the *acquis* (such as ensuring effective competition), it is not easy to see how a compromise to facilitate membership can be struck without explicitly hurting the interests of the present Union membership. The adverse experiences with some earlier accessions to the EU, notably Greece, that were primarily politically motivated should not be ignored at this juncture.

Without a comprehensive change in the purposes and instruments of the EU's redistribution programs, the claims on the resources of the EU budget are bound to escalate by a multiple of their current level. The present EU membership, or the electorate in most Member States for that matter, is unlikely to be willing to raise their contributions to the EU budget to anything like the level required to apply the present transfer programs of the *acquis communautaire* to the transition economies, even when rapid growth in the years ahead, as is now widely hoped, will have reduced their potential net claims on the EU budget. I return to the details of these propositions in Chapter 5.

As already noted, if the EU's objectives are not to be severely undermined, it must be clear that a country is either a member of the Union or it is not. Once a member, a country must subscribe fully to the *acquis*, although transitional derogations will be required and as a rule agreed to in order to allow full assimilation of the regulatory framework at a gradual pace. But proposals to exclude newcomers from the two most expensive EU transfer programs – agriculture and structural support – are not viable; the same applies to proposals to withhold some of the EU's freedoms (especially labor mobility) from newcomers, at least for some extended period of time.

Given present policies, scenarios that incorporate a fundamental reform of these expensive programs in the near future, certainly before the end of this decade, are simply not credible. As such proposals violate the special nature of the EU, they could not be realized without a major revision of the EU's basic ambitions, for which enthusiasm among the majority of the present Fifteen is lukewarm at best. Unless the chief beneficiaries among the present membership are willing to drastically reform these programs, newcomers will have to be given access to those parts of the *acquis* as they presently exist. So other solutions will have to be found if the EU's viability and ambitions are to be preserved, as detailed in Chapter 5.

It would be fundamentally wrong, however, to read into the above analysis any suggestion that for as long as the economies in transition remain 'poor,' they cannot become members of the EU. In fact, as argued earlier (see second subsection above), by the time the budgetary issues are due for thorough review later in the decade, pressures from within the EU for the reform of the CAP and of the structural supports will probably have mounted. A gradual reduction of these expenditures relative to the overall budget and a better focusing of the appropriations will in all likelihood occur before the negotiations for the accession of any transition economy can be completed.

5 – Preferential Arrangements with Nonmembers

The EU has elaborated over a long period at least eight grades of preferential arrangements with nonmembers: (1) the General System of Preferences (GSP) with respect to developing countries and, temporarily, for some transition economies; (2) the European Economic Area (EEA) with the pre-1995 EFTA members except Switzerland (for Liechtenstein the EEA became applicable only in early 1995); (3) the twelve 'other' Mediterranean countries; (4) the developing countries grouped in the so-called Lomé Convention (with a number of Asian, Caribbean, and Pacific States); (5) the Europe Agreement with ten eastern European countries; (6) partnership arrangements with some of the successor States of the Soviet Union; (7) an assortment of trade and cooperation agreements with a variety of countries; and (8) the customs union with Turkey since 1996. Other negotiations, such as with the Asian group and another form of the association agreement with Albania and some of the successor States of Yugoslavia, are under way (European Commission 1996o, p. 17).

There is a recognized need to review, revise, and streamline many of these arrangements, if not during the present Conference then at least on the basis of positions to be agreed upon at that meeting. The controversies that arose in 1995 about, on the one hand, the mid-term review of the Lomé Convention (Islam 1995, p. 13) and, on the other, the longer-term financing of assistance to the transition economies and the countries provided for under the Mediterranean agreements, under-lined the complex political economy and the weight of the many issues at stake. The Essen Council in December 1994 proposed the formation of a Euro-Mediterranean Partnership that in time (probably by the year 2010) should lead to a free-trading area between the EU and selected Mediterranean countries, in particular those that cannot expect to become full members because they are not European. Since then consi-derable attention has been devoted to that region, particularly by the southern tier of the Union, which has few countries of direct interest among the Lomé Convention. The details are yet to be worked out, however (see Hoekman and Djankov 1995). The process seems, how-ever, to have been started with the association agreement concluded in July 1995 with Tunisia (IMF 1996b).

The need for initiating an early and comprehensive review of these preferential arrangements derives in part from the substantial changes in the make-up of Europe after the presumed end of the Cold War, and indeed in the rest of the world, since these agreements were first con-ceived. It also derives from the potential for coordinating or harmon-izing more effectively the EU's global relations in economic, political, social, and other areas in the light of the Uruguay Round, the establish-ment of the WTO, and other developments. If and when the Union will be able to proceed with the solidification of its other pillars, it *must* revise its foreign economic relations in the light of its broader interests than the commercial ones that were largely at the origin of the prefer-ential arrangements when they were first negotiated. This is especially important in the case of economies in transition that are unlikely to be in the first wave of new entrants to the EU or that may never join it for reasons examined in the last three chapters.

Conclusions

Just about all of the cited problems are highly controversial issues, particularly among the larger EU members. Some have been debated for decades. Others have gained a new lease on life with the approaching target date for monetary union. They cannot be ignored, nor could they conceivably be papered over, if market credibility is to be sustained. Tackling them head on and embracing constructive solutions justified by current and prospective circumstances would be a positive act of statecraft at this stage and impart a new impetus to the EU's integration movement, in spite of the recent setbacks and the prevailing rather gloomy outlook on growth in the years ahead, particularly for adjudicating the founders of the monetary union.

There can thus be little doubt that the Conference is being held under a cloudy environment with a degree of policy complexity that has arguably never before been known. The issues range over a wide field. This will almost certainly lead to very difficult negotiations even if all participants were to be fully imbued with the mission of forging ahead with integration in an effective, transparent, accountable, and democratic manner. That, unfortunately, is not quite the case for reasons of national electoral calculations. But also because some policy makers do not really share the core ambitions of the Treaty of Rome as reworked for the convoluted Maastricht Treaty.

Key among the solutions to be reached is a more flexible EU. As I have argued, that cannot mean moving from inclusive quasi-supranationalism to "concentric circles," "variable geometry," or an "*à la carte* Europe," if the latter were to imply a *permanent* differentiation among members on core issues of the *acquis*. Flexibility can apply only gradualism in catching up, if necessary through solidaristic measures; otherwise it implies eventual exclusion from the EU of those unwilling to commit themselves.

Even if the latter were to constitute the alpha and omega of what will guide the deliberations and determine the outcome of the Conference, policy makers would have a tough time. The complexity is notched up several degrees by the comparative lack of success with assistance programs in favor of the economies in transition, as measured by the delivery of support to a speedy turnaround in the eastern part of

Europe. They also confront the obstacles of bringing into the Union some ten countries, and later even more, whose institutions and policies in the postwar period were truly inimical to supporting a vibrant market economy. These countries therefore face special problems of merging themselves into the EU. Chapters 4 and 5 are designed to clarify those issues before I consider plausible alternative assistance formats in the final chapter.

3

The Dilemma About Monetary Union

There has arguably been no more controversy and widely diverse commentary over the past decade concerning any other aspect of EU integration than about monetary union, its necessity in the context of the EU, its advantages and drawbacks, how best to prepare the Member States for monetary union, what needs to be done to ensure stability in the union, and how best to arrange for stability in a monetary union that encompasses fewer than the whole membership of the Union, either temporarily or quasi permanently for the countries that do not wish to join the monetary union (in the case at hand notably Denmark and the United Kingdom).

The official prescriptions on monetary union are contained in the Maastricht Treaty and a special protocol in which the so-called convergence criteria are detailed to strict quantitative yardsticks as compared to the more qualitative assessments called for in the Maastricht Treaty itself. Note that some of the issues revolving around EMU are at times needlessly confounded. As argued in Chapter 2, EMU consists of at least two wings: the single European market and monetary union. These are admittedly inextricably intertwined (Ghymers 1995). But it is the second component – monetary union – that is principally at stake in this context. As argued in Chapter 2, however, further improvements in the single market in law and in practice are also required, as the European Commission (1996k) has recently underlined once again, but these issues belong to a separate discourse.

This chapter amplifies on the policy dilemmas that have arisen around monetary union, that is, the completion of the EMU's fundamentals. I first look at the convergence criteria and their place in the monetary-integration effort. Next I explain why pursuit of the convergence criteria is presently confronting policy makers with several painful policy dilemmas and hard choices. Thereafter I speculate on the likely impact of not starting up monetary integration in 1999, if such a choice were to be made, perhaps in the context of the Conference. Then I look at the issues around monetary union for a group of countries that do not form an optimum currency area. This is followed by a brief note on the emerging rules for countries that do not wish to or cannot participate immediately in monetary union. The policy options available at this stage are taken up in the final section, after a bird eye's review of monetary cooperation in the EU, chiefly since 1979.

1 – On the Convergence Criteria

This is not the place to examine whether the convergence criteria in and of themselves make good economic sense (see Labhard 1996a, b for a lucid review of the core issues). That must mean, in this context, whether they provide a reasonable guarantee that the monetary union can be formed without causing severe policy problems in moving toward this goal and indeed in operating the union once established. Suffice it to point out that the criteria as constituted are neither necessary nor sufficient to ensure stability in the monetary union (Bilger 1993; Buiter, Corsetti, and Roubini 1993; Eichengreen 1993; Eichengreen and Wyplosz 1993). This has major implications for proceeding with the implementation of the EMU part of the Maastricht Treaty, as I show below.

1 – The Convergence Criteria

One can look at them from various angles, and it is important to bear that in mind. In their most rigid format, that is according to the protocol (European Commission 1993, pp. 581-3), not the Treaty as such (European Commission 1993, pp. 236-8), there are four criteria.

• First, price stability is envisaged. This means that the rate of inflation in the candidate for entry during the year preceding the assessment of suitability for joining the monetary union should not be more than 1.5 percentage points above that of the three Member States with the lowest rates.

• Second, fiscal imbalances must be sustainable according to a dual criterion. This is deemed to be within reach when the budget deficit relative to GDP does not exceed 3 percent and the public debt relative to GDP 60 percent in the year preceding verification.

• Third, exchange rates must have participated in the ERM and stayed within the regular margins of fluctuation for at least two years, without devaluation with respect to the currency of any other Member State. Regular in the context of the Maastricht Treaty means with at most 2.25 percent around par but preferably fluctuating within narrower margins in the lead-up to monetary union. The exceptional ones were 6 percent around par, but Member States desirous of entering monetary union were expected to narrow these margins to the regular bands for at least two years. Following the foreign-exchange turbulence of 1992 and 1993, on 2 August 1993 (Labhard 1996a, b) it was decided to adopt "temporary margins" of 15 percent around par to fend off, at least to discourage, further speculative attacks. It is unclear whether this temporary character, which is still in force, can be considered "regular" or not. The Conference will presumably have to resolve this issue, as argued in Chapter 2. The core countries (those that observed "regular bands" in the earlier ERM) have in fact remained within the former "regular" margins, once the currency-market convulsions of 1992-1993 subsided (for further details, see Caporale, Hassapis, and Pittis 1995).

• Finally, long-term interest rates should converge toward the more stable and lower ones prevailing within the EU, in order to sustain expectations of price stability and avoid pressure on exchange rates, and should not be more than 2 percentage points higher than the rates prevailing in the three best-performing Member States in the year before verification.

Note that all of the above have time dimensions. Thus, if T is the year when monetary union is initiated, or later when a Member State wishes to join, the evaluation of suitable candidates will be completed early in $T-1$, while referring to the data for $T-2$ and, in the case of exchange rates, $T-3$ as well. The comparator "best three" requires further precision, as I shall explain in Section 7. These comparisons will presumably be carried out by the EMI, which is the precursor of the ECB, itself to be created with the inception of monetary union. Furthermore, as already hinted at, one should preferably bear in mind that the Maastricht Treaty (European Commission 1993, pp. 236-8) itself takes a more qualitative view of convergence, stressing the dynamics thereof, rather than the exact stage reached by the time verification is due to be completed. The protocol, on the other hand, is rather rigid (European Commission 1993, pp. 581-3).

2 – The Purposes of the Convergence Criteria

As already intimated, the convergence criteria are unlikely to be sufficient for creating a credible and stable monetary union. Some are not even necessary when evaluated against that objective. These matters are usually discussed within the context of the theory of optimum currency areas (Grauwe 1996b), which leads to the finding that the convergence criteria are neither necessary nor sufficient. This can be illustrated with reference to the inflation criterion, for example. Inflation convergence is not necessary because the participating countries in the monetary union prior to its formation may be very similar in economic structure, so that they are not likely to be confronted with asymmetric shocks, even though inflation differentials exist because of different institutional features around monetary policy making. The criterion is not sufficient because two countries may have similar inflation rates but exhibit structural differences that are so large that a monetary union between them would be suboptimal, given the danger of asymmetric shocks. Even so, the low-inflation candidate for monetary union may wish to stave off spillovers from the high-inflation candidate, and thus insist on a considerable degree of price convergence prior to monetary union, particularly if prices are only imperfectly flexible (Bini-Smaghi and Giovane 1996).

That noted, as I shall detail in Section 4, the theory of the optimum currency area is not particularly germane to the EMU, given that the basic political decision to move to monetary union on the way to strengthening productivity-driven competition in the single market has already been taken. Whether this was a wise decision can be adjudicated within the context of evaluating to what degree the EU is an optimum currency area. If the political decision holds, however, the real question is rather a dual one: How best to get to monetary union? and What can be done about asymmetric shocks once union is established?

However, some of the convergence criteria do have some economic underpinning, in the sense that their fulfillment will make it more likely, but they will not guarantee, that price, exchange-rate, and interest-rate stability will be within reach, thus mitigating the potential adjustment costs once monetary union is inaugurated; the potential for coping with subsequent asymmetric shocks is a different matter, however, to be dealt with appropriately in a political-economy framework, as discussed in Section 4. For that very reason, it might have been desirable to set the timetable for the start of monetary unification as the final step in a concerted strategy rather than up front. The start of monetary union could then have been triggered when all or a "critical minimum" of Member States had met the chosen convergence criteria as constituent parts of the strategy, or whatever other adjustments in policies might have been considered necessary.

The above reasoning can be justified also by comparing the economic outlook prevailing in the early 1990s with the views on short- to medium-term economic performance that are widely held at this stage. If expectations of medium- to long-term growth in the EU had been less optimistic than they were when the Treaty was under negotiation in 1990-1991, the set target dates of, and possibly the chosen convergence criteria for joining, monetary union would probably have been quite different from those actually adopted. Now the EU members are committed to a deadline for meeting the criteria although the economic, let alone the political and social, circumstances for doing so are far from congenial at the present juncture. They are therefore weighing upon the more general policy climate regarding enlargement as well as the debates at the Conference, though EMU is not supposed to be dealt with there (see Chapter 2). This episode suggests useful lessons for setting integration targets in the future, such as are likely to be needed prospectively in upcoming accession negotiations (as examined in the last two chapters).

2 – Merits of the Strict Convergence Criteria

Serious questions have been raised about the merit of holding on to the convergence criteria and the wisdom of risking a delayed start-up of monetary union or of initiating it with only a few, possibly mainly small, Member States (as cogently reviewed in Grauwe 1996a). It bears to stress, though, that several of the large countries, including France and Germany, are presently undertaking determined efforts to meet the convergence criteria by late 1997, in time for the assessment of membership in early 1998.

The issues have not yet been resolved and will, in all probability, be taken up at some point by the Conference, in spite of earlier expectations that monetary matters were settled. The European Commission has been adamant on this issue. Thus in its suggestions for the Reflection Group (European Commission 1995a, p. 7), it specifically advocates the exclusion of the issues around the EMU from the Conference's agenda because in that domain "the path has been mapped out and there should be no renewed discussion on the provisions agreed. The recent turbulence on the currency markets merely serves to underline how vital this is." It should be clear, however, that as crucial an issue as EMU, which is, after all, the core of the western European integration achievement, could not possibly have been excluded from the debates at the IGC (Ludlow and Ersbøll 1996, pp. 16ff.).

There are many reasons that could be adduced by way of justifying the above assertion. Let me cite only one: The process of monetary unification in western Europe has since the signing of the Maastricht Treaty run into an array of daunting policy and institutional problems for which some solution must be hammered out preferably soonest. The current debate on the fiscal convergence criteria (the ratios of the budget imbalance to GDP and of the government debt to GDP) deals with only one set of issues. Another is the rising disaffection among policy makers about the implications of the Treaty: At least in terms of monetary policy and the repercussions on other variables, such as exchange rates, to be anticipated, it would split Union membership into a so-called hard core and one or more other layers of members and potential members that may or may not be expected to comply with the EMU's admission criteria at some future point in time.

Not only that, the likelihood at this stage that the initiation of monetary union in 1999 will occur with only a small number of small members – such as Denmark, Ireland, and Luxembourg – is growing; in any case, Denmark's compliance with monetary union is by no means assured, given its special status as defined in protocol No. 12 of the Maastricht Treaty (European Commission 1993, pp. 607-10); the Government does not seem to have altered its stance on this issue.

From a purely formal point of view, one could in principle inaugurate a monetary union with no members. The EU Member States would then gravitate toward admission into that club, perhaps with a concerted strategy to meet the convergence criteria or any other strategy deemed necessary and economically justified, as argued below. It is inconceivable, however, that such a formal start-up would be read as 'progress' by financial-market participants in particular. It would in all likelihood exert negative pressures on the latter's expectations, thus adversely impacting on investment decisions over the longer term until monetary-union matters become more transparent. But those effects, real as they are, should not be blown out of proportion.

3 – Would Failing Monetary Union in 1999 Be a Tragedy?

Adhering to the strict convergence criteria and to the dates stipulated in the Maastricht Treaty is now creating dilemmas for policy makers. One may well ask whether the dramas one reads about, if monetary union were not to take off in 1999, reflect realities. And here a sharp distinction should be drawn between prevailing realities and expectations about forging ahead with integration held by policy makers and many participants in financial and real markets. In my view, there can be little doubt that missing the target date of 1999 for EMU is unlikely to constitute a tragedy in *economic* terms. Much of the rhetoric voiced in journalistic and political circles that monetary union would make or break the postwar integration mold, thus fragmenting the interlacing of the EU's economies achieved to date, depending upon whether monetary union is initiated in 1999 or not, does not mirror the present realities of Europe. The degree of interdependence of most of the economies of the Member States is now so great that the disintegration of the Union's single market is a very remote possibility indeed. Nor would the absence of monetary union forcibly overturn the broader achievements of the EU. But the full benefits of monetary union would not, of course, be available to prop up growth in the Union for the duration.

However, the transition economies in particular could suffer from such a check to European integration, a danger that few observers appear to be willing to admit (Ludlow 1996a, p. 73 is a refreshing exception). For one thing failure to start up monetary union as foreseen is likely to affect their still relatively fragile trade relations with the Union and complicate the process of merging into intra-industry trade relations. With a weaker commitment to deepening integration in the EU, which is what economic agents would read into a failure to start up monetary union on schedule, the prospects for strengthening expectations about the EU's future economic development not only with the eastern part of Europe but also within the EU itself are likely to be adversely affected as well. Within the Union, this will essentially surface through modifications of the investment horizon and the positive interest-rate premium for greater uncertainty levied over what would prevail with monetary union.

However, the latter adversity for transition economies has a much broader base. Indeed the next *political* opportunity to revisit the issue of monetary integration would probably only occur after a protracted interval during which the movement for extending European integration would be set back in several respects. The history of the EU since 1962, when the first attempt at monetary union was made, is replete with evidence to the effect that dissent about monetary union is largely a veneer for disagreement about a much wider array of issues pertaining to further integration – in other words, once again about deepening the EU's integration endeavors (Brabant 1995a, pp. 292-312; Ludlow 1982). That is likely to be the perception of market participants, as well as some policy makers, if the target date for monetary union were to be missed or if the Union were to be inaugurated as an empty shell.

One final point before proceeding with the examination of the policy tasks ahead in western Europe. Much has recently been made in journalistic and related circles about the fact that EMU, and specifically the start-up of monetary union in 1999, "could unhinge the Atlantic alliance and leave Central Europe out in the cold" (Passell 1996, p. D2). The former Prime Minister of Poland, Mr. Jan Krzystof Bielecki, is quoted in the same source as having asserted that if monetary union were to be launched in 1999 "it will touch off a chain reaction that will halt integration." In all of this rhetoric, the one key point seems to be overlooked: Monetary union suppresses the exchange rate as a policy instrument for fostering structural adjustment. Just like a uniform currency in any single but diverse country may relegate some regions to a backward status, unless other policy instruments are activated, although even then there is no guaranteed success, monetary union in the EU may trap some Member States in that status as well. I return to this issue below.

One further thought will set the stage for the discussion in the final half of the volume: If the candidates for accession were to be compelled into joining monetary union at an early stage with entry, they might well fail to embark on the productivity-driven trajectory for catching up with western European levels of development, technology, and wealth. This is not a trivial matter for the transition economies in particular. The crucial issue now is: What can conceivably be done to forestall such an eventuality from taking shape? This is the topic for Chapter 6.

4 – Monetary Union and the Policy Tasks

Concern about establishing a monetary union for a group of countries that do not, in fact, constitute an optimum currency area (that is, one in which factor mobility is sufficiently flexible to substitute for the leeway for structural adjustment otherwise provided by exchange-rate modifications, as examined at greater length in Brabant 1995a, pp. 313-17) has become more intense with the recent slowdown in economic activity and the continuing high rates of unemployment in western Europe. In this connection it is particularly shocking to have Mr. Nicolas Moussis (1996, p. 16), a high-level EU counselor, simply assert that the EU's envisaged monetary union comes close to being an optimum currency area! Of course, this view must be erroneous for otherwise there would be no problem in moving to such a union and maintaining it without being compelled to adopt strenuous policy efforts associated with potentially considerable costs in terms of growth forgone.

The debate on monetary union has been propelled in part by popular disaffection about social-welfare cutbacks at a time of a slowdown in economic activity with already very sizable levels of unemployment. The latter do not stem from EMU, of course. However, the lackluster economic performance in combination with the limited room for social-policy flexibility has been inhibiting some countries from bringing their macroeconomic balances in line with the convergence criteria set forth in the Maastricht Treaty, notably on the budget and debt fronts. But in and of itself those budgetary priorities, except the coincident timing, have next to nothing to do with EMU, since the prevailing policy sentiment is to downsize government and close budget deficits. Moreover, considerable apprehensions have been raised by the nature of a common monetary-policy stance with a focus especially on monetary stability as the overriding goal, something very similar to the policy that the German *Bundesbank* has been practicing with almost unbending rectitude now for quite some time.

Currency revaluations cannot lower unemployment over the long run and can only interfere with the proper performance of productivity-driven competition, which constitutes the very essence of the EU's *economic* integration. Nevertheless, they can ease the adjustment of economies to changes in their economic environment. In the short run, and despite the large share of intra-Union trade in each Member's overall commerce, a devaluation of the currency of one Member State when there exists demand outside the Union for its products would not necessarily harm its integration partners, particularly if such gains were for products for which the latter are not readily able to substitute. The United Kingdom in particular has benefited from this in extra-EU trade since the pound exited from the ERM in the fall of 1992.

But this policy flexibility will no longer be available with monetary union for those who join and the leeway for other Member States to resort to devaluations for adjustment purposes will be much confined if any of the current proposals for ERM II (see Section 5) will in the end be endorsed. But something of the kind must come about in due course. The French Prime Minister, Mr. Alain Juppé, has recently stressed this in unambiguous terms: "It is not possible to have a large single market function with currencies that play the full stability game and currencies that practice so-called competitive devaluations" (France 1996c, p. 11). The crux of the matter is not just competitive devaluations, however. Discrete adjustments in exchange rates in response to a build-up of pressures stemming from lax stances on basic macro-economic aggregates, and indeed on how policy can influence them, can be equally divisive and disruptive of productivity-driven competition in a single market in which the participating countries transact the bulk of their trade. Clearly, the "small-country assumption" that usually is tacitly assumed in praising the benefits of the exchange rate as a policy instrument for adjustment, such as in the EU context, is manifestly inappropriate under the prevailing conditions in western Europe, even for the "economically small" Member States. This is a fundamental proposition that needs to be fully grasped in order to understand the controversies about moving toward monetary union in the EU.

As indicated, the policy flexibility afforded by a currency realignment will no longer be available with monetary union. Asymmetric shocks previously amenable through exchange-rate changes (Erkel-Rousse 1995, p. 190) will now have to be weathered primarily through wages and prices, for which downward flexibility may be limited, even with regulatory reform. In order to stave off regional imbalances, especially in labor markets where unemployment is already deemed to be excessive, other policy instruments will have to be activated to bring about structural adjustment. A prime candidate for this is some form of so-called fiscal federalism (Begg, Gudgin, and Morris, pp. 11-13), although a number of academics have rejected fiscal federalism as needless centralization (Berthold 1995). Those who confine the role of the state to that of caretaker of the minimal framework for the market economy see, of course, little merit in modulating fiscal policy. I disagree with the extreme views, however: Fiscal redistribution, if enacted credibly without overly blunting incentives and creating a dependency clientele, can indeed play some useful role in fostering adjustment.

Unfortunately, there is very little fiscal-policy coordination in the EU because the share of the EU's budget in overall GDP of the membership is small (presently just over 1 percent), fiscal matters remain by and large a prerogative of the national parliaments, and there is as yet no agreement on even a minimal coordination of fiscal policies among the Member States (Eatwell 1992a, b) at least to take care of unavoidable spillovers of national policy stances.

Fiscal federalism does not, of course, necessarily require a high degree of centralization of fiscal authority. With monetary union and decentralized fiscal powers, there is, however, a coordination problem to be satisfactorily resolved: Decentralized fiscal policy may undermine the successful conduct of a low-inflation monetary policy by the ECB (for details, see Heinemann 1995; Krichel, Levine, and Pearlman 1996). That policy task – coordination not necessarily centralization – is the heart of the matter. Hence at least a minimal degree of concertation among national, or even lower-level, fiscal authorities will be required to correct imbalances or forestall their emergence. Decentralized fiscal authorities may do too little stabilization as compared with the credible cooperative alternative for the group of members in the monetary union, primarily because intercountry or interregional spillover effects are not internalized. Some observers have argued that there will be a tendency in a decentralized system for regionally specific shocks to be adequately taken care of or even overstabilized, while the system is understabilized against common shocks (for an elaboration on this point, see Alsopp, Davies, and Vines 1995).

The upshot of the academic debate, then, is that a monetary union needs stabilization properties specifically designed for the union even though the underlying policies could, in principle, be implemented in a decentralized manner by lower-tier authorities. In such a decentralized arrangement, credibility is likely to be lower than with a more centralized solution of fiscal federalism, however.

Nevertheless, in spite of all these complications and other obstacles that spur on skepticism about the stability of monetary union, and by implication the absence of political and economic tensions in the EU deriving from disparities among the Member States, the core issues of monetary integration, which are integral to the *acquis communautaire*, are by no means obsolete. They are at this juncture certainly not less relevant than they were when the Maastricht Treaty was drafted and signed; or, for that matter, when tentative steps toward monetary union were first discussed in 1962.

The critical issue, the litmus test of economic integration within the EU's objectives, derives from the argument that competition within the Union should be based primarily on market-driven criteria, comparative advantages being determined by real-productivity differences. That is to say, economic agents in Member States should not be able to gain a competitive edge within the Union, and by implication even outside the

Union with respect to other Member States, even if only in the medium run, by changing their exchange rate *vis-à-vis* those of other members, regardless of whether unilateral or concerted exchange-rate realignments are envisaged. On this issue, the room for political compromise must be very narrow, if indeed there is any at all. Any compromise would only concern the *process* leading up to monetary unification, such as in the case of a monetary union of core countries in 1999 with the others joining somewhat later (currently projected within three years, as discussed in Section 5 below), not unification itself.

In this connection, observers frequently question whether the EU, or whatever subgroup of the Member States will proceed toward meaningful monetary unification, forms an optimum currency area. The answer is: "Almost certainly not." Those who find comfort in this technicality by way of arguing against monetary union in the EU should at the same time recognize that this particular issue is nearly completely irrelevant in the context of ensuring real competition within the EU. By virtue of the EU's maxim on establishing and strengthening a unified market characterized by productivity-driven competition, compromise on the final goal of monetary union is not possible as monetary unification forms an integral part of reaching economic union pure and simple.

The problem of monetary union, that is, reaching the objective of a unified market is, of course, an acute one when it comes to considering the implications of forming such a monetary union in terms of both the preconditions to be met (which is precisely the origin of the convergence criteria in the Maastricht Treaty) and the guidelines to be observed in order to maintain cohesion once the union is formed, when adjustment problems need to be addressed without having resort to the benefit of an exchange-rate devaluation.

Unfortunately, the debate, even in the academic literature, has confounded these three areas of concerns (that is, whether or not the EU is an optimum currency area, the conditions to be fulfilled in order to move to a monetary union with minimal credibility and stability, and the policies to be embraced to ensure timely adjustment in the monetary union) that, at least when discussing policy matters, could usefully have been dealt with separately. It seems also to have conflated the pre-union conditions – the convergence criteria such as they stand recorded as contractual commitments – with what would ideally be required to minimize the risk of imbalances arising from moving toward this end, and even during the transition period leading to monetary union, because of the need for transfers in the first case and of weathering credibility problems in the second case.

But the crucial point is that if competition in the EU is to be based on a single currency, either *de jure* or *de facto* in order to purify competitive forces, then policy makers will have to come to terms with the need to shift the adjustment process to internal price and volume variables rather than through exchange rates. Given the limited downward flexibility of these variables, even if substantial regulatory reform – notably in labor markets – were feasible in the near term, the extent of redistribution of fiscal revenues for stabilization purposes, as noted above in connection with so-called fiscal federalism, will have to be expanded well beyond what presently prevails in the EU. Several Member States, and even some candidates for accession, are adamant about the prerogatives of national parliaments when it comes to fiscal powers and fulfilling recognized societal priorities, however.

5 – A Monetary Rule for Nonparticipants

A re-creation of the ERM is by some commentators referred to as EMS II. That would seem to be wrong (European Commission 1996m, p. 1), as discussed in Section 6. Any ERM II set up roughly along the lines in which the first version was established in 1979, is currently being mooted (European Commission 1996m). It was the subject of discussions of the Council of Ministers of Finance and Governors of Central Banks in Verona (12-13 April 1996), after the central banks of the Member States had already worked out, and apparently agreed upon among themselves, a detailed proposal (Fisher and Norman 1996a, b). Only Portugal has so far committed itself to joining such an arrangement if, as seems likely, it were not to be able to join the monetary union in 1999. Great Britain and Sweden have aired serious reservations, the first doubting the usefulness of any ERM II and the second, while appreciating its potential, not willing to commit itself early.

The full details of the new ERM that will be inaugurated together with monetary union in early 1999 are still to be worked out. In broad

outline, however, the ERM II would be based on the principles observed in its predecessor (see Section 6) and these would have to be gradually reinforced to enable the latecomers to enter the monetary union,
according to Jacques Santer, by the year 2002 at the latest (Krimm
1996, p. 15). Details, however, are yet to be worked out. But Hans
Tietmeyer, the powerful President of the *Bundesbank*, has indicated
that the purpose would be to place the ERM II under surveillance of
the ECB's chairman, who would see to a "more efficient, less politi-
cised way of changing parities of non-Emu members" (Fisher and
Norman 1991a, p. 2) with a view to spurring on the asymmetric functioning of the monetary systems in Europe toward convergence. In
other words, the goal would be to ensure that those not in the monetary union would move toward this standard, and will therefore have to
pursue, in relative terms, stricter stability rules than those inside the
monetary union until reasonably smooth accession can be completed.
The ECB itself would not be responsible for the stability of the exchange rates for Member States' currencies that are not part of the
monetary union, although the behavior of those currencies "will have to
be especially carefully guided [*begleiten*]" (Tietmeyer 1996, p. 3) in the
sense of surveillance and policy concertation indicated earlier.

In an uncharacteristic editorial attack, the *Financial Times* has
adjudicated such measures as "illegal, unnecessary, counterproductive
and unworkable" (FT 1996, p. 9). One may harbor legitimate doubts
that putting in place a convention to ensure that the "outs" will eventually make it into the monetary union as well, at least *de facto* such as by
shadowing the policies of the monetary union, would be illegal or
unnecessary. I also think it would be productive to subject the "outs"
to some discipline. Whether any arrangement to be agreed upon would
be workable depends entirely on the degree to which proper macroeconomic-policy stances in the countries that stay out of the monetary
union can be expected to prevail or can be enforced, at least to some
degree and whether the ECB can come to prevail in harmonizing the
policies of the "ins," the "ERM II outs," and the real "outs." The potential danger for the second group is very considerable (Grauwe
1996b). Inasmuch as they are to observe greater rectitude than members of the union, ERM II participants may be more prone to exposure
to speculative attacks and higher interest rates, both of which may

render convergence even more cumbersome (see Daniel Gros quoted at length in IMF 1996a, p. 138; Grauwe 1996a, b).

At the Verona meeting, with the exceptions of Sweden and the United Kingdom, the Ministers of Finance and Governors of Central Banks agreed to the creation of ERM II by 1999 (Buerkle 1996, Krimm 1996, NZZ 1996a, Tell 1996, Tell and Hill 1996). It would provide for the broad margins currently applying on a "temporary basis," but those presumably will have to be narrowed over time, at least *de facto*, precisely by pursuing low inflation and indeed observing budget discipline. But it is now almost a foregone conclusion that the ECB's president will have a powerful, decisive voice in overseeing and assessing the economic and monetary policies of the "outs," whether or not they are part of the ERM II. This point has raised some controversy (see IMF 1996a, p. 138) in that those staying out, unlike participants in the ERM II, would allegedly not be exposed to the danger of speculative attacks and higher interest-rate premiums. To the extent that monetary convergence is imposed by some deadline, such as the year 2002, and the Maastricht Treaty requirement of having been in the "regular" ERM for two years jettisoned, provided the country has observed the required exchange-rate stability on its own, whether countries are in the ERM II or not does not seem to make much difference.

The point is that from 1999 on there will have to be greater all-around coordination among the monetary authorities of the "ins," the "outs," and the "semi-ins" via the ERM II, and this cannot be achieved credibly by enforcing a near-fixed link between the euro and the currencies of the Member States that do not join the monetary union (Persson and Tabellini 1996). Precisely because this has given rise to problems in the past, within limits, the president of the ECB would be entitled to stabilize through interventions the exchange rates in case of speculative attacks; but would otherwise engineer technically warranted devaluations. The member countries will be held to respect the convergence programs at the risk of being exposed to sanctions, though agreement on the latter is yet to be reached. Other details too will now be worked out over the next six months or so by the EMI and the EU's monetary committee, it is hoped, in time for the Dublin Council in December 1996, certainly for the countries that hope to join the euro regime fairly soon. Furthermore, preliminary, but detailed reports on the exchange-rate and budget regimes were already presented to the Florence Council (21-22 June 1996), which presumably issued further instructions on how to finalize the proposals by the end of the year.

It is also of some significance that at the Verona meeting it was decided, in addition to the convergence criteria, to adopt in principle a "stability pact" that would aim at even lower inflation, budget imbalances, and debt, at least for the participants in the monetary union, than the strict convergence criteria in principle allow. Germany has been particularly adamant on holding its partners in the monetary union to very strict rectitude on the inflation and budget scores, perhaps because the monetary authorities there have been facing obstacles in holding the fiscal authorities to their commitments.

6 – Experiences with Monetary Cooperation

In the absence of details on ERM II, it might be instructive to recall the salient features of ERM I and the earlier EMS (the new one presumably being the euro regime to which the ERM II will be linked) and distill from that overview a few fairly obvious lessons that could, and should, be drawn in designing the successor regime.

1 – Rationale for Monetary Cooperation in the EU

Monetary problems in the context of the EU's integration format arise for several reasons, all fundamentally harking back to the perceived need to create a level playing field on which economic agents can compete for market access chiefly on the basis of their intrinsic economic strengths. One can discuss them under three entries (Brabant 1995a, pp. 186-92). One is the question of monetary accounting in a common regional organization such as the EU and related transactions when members have their own separately managed currencies. Another is how to ensure that the accounting is executed as fairly as technical details permit for all countries working presumably toward a common goal, whichever it may be. Finally, given the ambitions of the single market with productivity-driven competition, a number of monetary problems must eventually be tackled by creating a single currency. This can take the shape of a *de facto* union, such as by irrevocably locking exchange rates for all currencies in the union in conjunction with far-reaching concertation of macroeconomic policies. It could also be engineered *de jure*, such as by creating a single currency for the entire area of the EU managed through a uniform monetary system with appropriately dovetailed or uniform flanking policies, notably in the fiscal and regional-policy domains.

Attaining a coherent monetary system poses essentially the question of the minimal format of monetary integration, comprising at least fairly tight, credible policy coordination. This constitutes a logical component of the aim to construct a single market with the four freedoms guaranteed and their realization safeguarded to their full logical extent. Unlike what strict economic theory and logic might suggest, political-economy considerations – and these are the only ones that should count in rationalizing the decisions of European policy makers (not the extraneous political economy marshaled, for example, in Eichengreen 1993, Eichengreen and Wyplosz 1993, or Grauwe 1993, 1996b) – simply place beyond argument the proposition that beggar-thy-neighbor policies can be pursued by various means other than commercial policy. Once the latter's instruments are no longer available in the arsenal at the disposal of policy makers in individual Member States, the temptation to discriminate between 'local' economic agents and those from other Union members by other means than tariff barriers is hard to resist when enforceable coordination instruments are absent or inadequate. Hence the need to ensure conformity in monetary, especially exchange-rate, policies.

2 – The Origin of the EMS

The EMS was created in 1979 in part to replace the earlier 'currency snake' (see Brabant 1995a, pp. 306ff.). Both had as objective "obtaining a zone of monetary stability" by preserving fixed but adjustable exchange-rate parities among several European currencies with at best narrow bands for movement of exchange rates around central parities and a varying commitment of monetary authorities to defend relative exchange-rate stability, thus trying by other means to maintain for the EU some semblance of the Bretton Woods regime (Tew 1967), though with wider margins for fluctuation. Those objectives led in the end to the IGC on EMU (see Chapter 1).

Technically the problem was the following. With the Smithsonian Agreement of December 1971, following the suspension of gold convertibility for the U.S. dollar (henceforth, simply dollar), the band for fluctuation in the Bretton Woods regime was widened to 2.25 percent around the newly agreed parities. This implied that the exchange rate between any two EU currencies could fluctuate by as much as 9 percent if they were to switch position between the ceiling and the floor of their respective margins against the dollar. This degree of variability was then deemed to be excessive (Gros 1989, Gros and Thygesen 1992, Ludlow 1982, Padoa-Schioppa 1985, Thygesen 1993, Thygesen and Gros 1990). With the subsequent abolition of fixed parities in favor of generalized floating, the EU Member States felt that they should try to put each other's currencies on a par with the dollar in terms of predictability. The solution was the snake.

The chosen band width was to be ensured in principle through appropriate stabilization policies. When any currency threatened to fall outside the band, the members agreed to intervene with reciprocal support. Loans with a term of two to five years could be extended with considerable conditionality on how to adjust to the discipline of the snake. Very often, however, countries shunned this conditionality and simply left the snake temporarily or for good. Unfortunately, following the breakdown of the Bretton Woods system, turbulence in financial markets, currency markets in particular, exacerbated the width and frequency of exchange-rate fluctuations. As a result, several countries could not attain the goal set for the snake, which eventually degenerated into a *Deutschmark* regime to which three currencies (the Belgian franc, the Dutch guilder, and the Danish krone) were pegged.

With fixed parities abandoned, also the very practical need arose in the context of the EC to fix a common currency unit, or at least a surrogate. One such necessity emanated from the way in which the Union had failed to ensure uniform support prices for agriculture, hence the development of the so-called 'green dollar,' with the exchange-rate adjustments of the late 1960s (see Brabant 1995a, pp. 117-18). A second reason was very much an in-house requirement: Accounting in the various EU institutions had to be conducted in some comparable unit to ensure that every member was appropriately assessed with exchange risks borne by each Member State. Eventually, with the creation of a single currency in a credible format there would no longer be such monetary risk to be borne; but the underlying economic danger could manifest itself in other forms.

Even with this deterioration the rationale that the erosion of a country's currency can affect its competitive position, hence that of any other Member State, in the single market in particular, held as before. Currency variations may thus take the place of earlier customs duties, at least in some respect. For that reason a new, more comprehensive and better-anchored, monetary arrangement – the EMS – was put in place in 1979 with a specific policy on managing exchange rates – the ERM I – adopted by the seven countries (all EC members except Italy and Great Britain at the time) that felt they could and wanted to adhere to the common discipline; Italy was granted a looser status while Britain absented itself for years.

3 – Basic Features of the ERM-EMS Regime

This had four main features. First of all, the ecu was created as a composite of the currencies of the Member States with each currency radially anchored to the ecu. Although one of the aims was exchange-rate stability, from the beginning there was to be no irrevocable commitment to central parities. As a result, exchange-rate parities were reviewed relatively frequently in the earlier years of the ERM, as they were intended to be changed to avoid building up speculative pressures (Corden 1986, p. 141).

Second, the mechanism on containing exchange-rate fluctuations foresaw mandatory intervention when the exchange rate moved outside the 2.25 percent (6 percent in the case of Italy) fluctuation band. Active surveillance and fine-tuning were meant to counteract such an event.

Third, interventions would be possible through mutual loans (Edwards 1985, pp. 327-32). Very short-term credits (up to 1.5 months) would be available in unlimited amounts. As such, exchange rates were to be defended in the short run by much-extended credit facilities, available on more favorable terms as compared to the snake regime, both for the short term, which would be unconditional, and for the medium term, which would be available on a conditional basis; the latter implied that access to such funds was predicated on observing certain macroeconomic-policy commitments. That these facilities were in the end used marginally, save for very short-term financing (up to 45 days), is immaterial in this context (Triffin 1991).

Finally, efforts were instituted to coordinate exchange-rate policies with respect to third countries.

Note that unlike the snake, which was an arrangement among countries mostly associated with the EC, the ERM was without a doubt an EC arrangement, although not all Member States participated. Great Britain shunned it for years and then entered it only with the broad margins at an overvalued exchange rate, and new members (Greece, Portugal, and Spain) could join only much later, after they had been ushered into the EMS (that is, when their currencies became constituent parts of the ecu's evaluation, following the agreed-upon transition phase after entry); only Portugal and Spain eventually joined the ERM in November 1990 and Great Britain in 1991, but they left under onslaught of the currency crises of 1992-1993. Furthermore, countries that were not members of the EMS could not join; at best, they could shadow the EMS by pegging, as did Austria and most of the Nordic countries at some points in time. Moreover, it provided for a great deal more consultation and negotiation among the participants and reconciliation between exchange-rate and macroeconomic policies.

Initially, the fundamental question of how participants could be persuaded to synchronize to some extent their economic and exchange-rate policies remained unsolved until about 1987, when the so-called Basle-Nyborg Agreements on intervention and monetary cooperation came into effect and a period of very successful cooperation with supportive, dovetailed macroeconomic policies was inaugurated (see Gros 1989, Gros and Thygesen 1992; Thygesen 1989, 1993); countries with a wide band regularized their participation; and others that had shunned the ERM joined at least with broad bands for fluctuation. In due course, however, this exercise was terminated.

Together with the introduction of the EMS, the EC created a new reserve currency – the ecu, which will be replaced by the euro before 2002. As indicated earlier, unlike eventually the euro as a *sui generis* currency, the ecu is a composite currency consisting of a combination of the national currencies of the EU Member States, regardless of whether they participate in the ERM. When the ecu was first created, its value was set equal to the IMF's special drawing right (SDR), if only because from its inception the Union's accounting had been effected in a unit with a gold parity equal to the dollar as the central currency of the monetary system. Especially since the mid 1980s, the common currency has gained considerable following in private transactions, particularly by companies and financial institutions bent on having a more stable accounting unit than any one national currency, in spite of intermittent turbulence in foreign-exchange markets. But to date the ecu does not circulate as a fiduciary means of payment, except in the form of some commemorative coins. True these can be used for payment purposes because they are legal tender in the issuing country. In fact, however, they are not used for that purpose at all, if only because they trade well above par.

The ecu's creation and daily management were entrusted to the European Monetary Cooperation Fund (EMCF). Its valuation is determined by daily fluctuations in the exchange rates of the currencies that make up the composite. Issuance is strictly through asset substitution, that is, it is decided upon in terms of monetary reserves acquired from the monetary authorities of the Member States. Each participant in the ERM (but not necessarily in the EMS) is bound to contribute 20 percent of its gold holdings and 20 percent of its gross dollar reserves to the EMCF. Members that do not participate in the ERM are welcome to contribute in the same amounts too, but they are not required to effectuate such transfers.

Emboldened by the comparative stability achieved, after some initial turbulence in exchange rates, from 1987 on policy makers began on the whole to perceive an implicit commitment to exchange-rate fixity as a credible step in progressing toward monetary integration. Perhaps it was felt that by then the degree of empathy among policy makers for heeding regional economic policies sufficed so that countries would not step outside of the bounds called for by implicit coordination of fiscal and monetary policies. Once *de facto* fixed exchange rates became irreconcilable with the degree of policy coordination achieved, the system could no longer be adequately defended. Hence the importance placed at this stage (Fisher and Norman 1996b) on ensuring that the members of ERM II will devalue when fundamentals warrant it rather than when politicians deem it opportune to do so.

4 – Successes and Failures

It is instructive to recall that, at its inception, the EMS (not unlike the monetary union at this stage) was greeted with much skepticism, basically because it was expected to be inflationary: Surplus countries were anticipated to be forced to grant inflationary financing to partner countries unable or unwilling to avoid 'excessive' current-account deficits (McDonald and Zis 1989, p. 186; Triffin 1991, p. 421), rather than to force them to devalue their currency and seek adjustment through this instrument. But the EMS's operation has confounded its critics in this respect. Indeed, until its near-demise in 1992-1993, the ERM was generally perceived to have been a considerable success (Cobham 1989, Glick and Hutchison 1993, McDonald and Zis 1989, Pomfret 1991, Triffin 1991). Its members had reduced their rates of inflation, they had experienced a marked reduction in exchange-rate volatility, and, perhaps foremost, they had managed to avoid prolonged and substantial exchange-rate misalignments, in the sense that exchange rates would otherwise have deviated for a protracted period of time from their long-term equilibrium level. As such, the EMS-ERM arrangements may also have contributed to eroding inflationary expectations and lowering the pace of inflation.

The above achievements cannot, of course, without further ado be unilaterally ascribed to the EMS. But there are good reasons to believe that the latter contributed to them to more than a trivial extent. Those achievements could have been more robust, however, if several of the policy-coordination measures mooted, and in principle agreed upon, in 1979 (Pomfret 1991, p. 623), had been introduced in a credible manner by, in fact, dovetailing macroeconomic policies. One of the lessons to be learned from the earlier experience is that the reluctance to devalue, or enact adjustments, for that is what a devaluation should be all about, in a concertized manner through appropriate policy coordination contributed to unhinging the system. The debacles of 1992-1993 showed clearly the tensions between coordination and centralization of macroeconomic policies in the EMS. That experience should notably inform the incipient common monetary policy of moving toward and enacting monetary integration. It should also persuade participants in monetary union to dovetail to some degree their fiscal-policy stances.

5 – Toward Monetary Union

Almost by definition, a real monetary union features a single currency managed from within a uniform monetary policy entrusted fundamentally to a *de facto* central bank (Lachmann 1993). This may be a unitary bank or it may be constituted in the form of a federal constitution, as in Germany or in the United States. A proper monetary union could also be conceived as one in which exchange rates among currencies of the union members are irrevocably locked, a single monetary policy is formulated in consequence of a far-reaching coordination of monetary policy, and several central banks in control of their country's monetary policy act, in fact, as a single monetary authority. At first glance, one might think that, under the latter condition, one could just as well move immediately to monetary union, and avoid in the process the overhead and transaction costs as well as the lingering lack of credibility about the policy intentions of working with multiple institutions. There is a grain of truth in this.

Nonetheless, it must be clear that there are also substantial differences, such as on the size and distribution of seigniorage (Gros 1993), the psychological impact of 'losing' one's familiar currency, as well as the large transaction costs of operating in multiple currencies, even if the latter are credibly interlinked through presumed fixed exchange rates. Once the latter matters can be settled as part and parcel of the necessary dovetailing, no other room for maneuver remains. Or rather, any other option is liable to lead in due course to some degree of monetary instability. This can be reconciled only by tolerating a realignment of exchange rates, after all, or by combining the unitary monetary policy with considerable fiscal coordination and institutional reform.

The experiences with the EMS since the late 1970s have yielded a mixed picture of the possibilities of monetary integration in the EU context, notably as regards fighting inflation and exchange-rate stability. The rather convoluted state of affairs, particularly the lukewarm attitude of some policy makers toward proceeding expeditiously with genuine monetary integration and the euro regime at this juncture, compounds matters.

Progress with monetary integration in Europe remains fundamentally predicated on achieving a monetary union with an interim ERM II *with* new instruments and procedures, or strengthening of existing ones, to provide an adequate capacity in the Union to cope with regional adjustment problems. That cannot be achieved without new rules on effective Union-wide decision making; qualified-majority voting to safeguard the interests of small countries and prevent the latter from outvoting the large ones would be in order here as well. Such instruments might include a strengthened EU regional policy and fiscal adjustments to be implemented by expanding the budget.

The EMS-ERM experiences suggest several lessons that the euro regime and the management of the ERM II might well heed. Let me draw five. First of all, it is not particularly useful to seek nearly fixed exchange rates when the underlying macroeconomic fundamentals do not support such a policy stance in a credible manner. Second, the power of intervention by monetary authorities is limited even if resources are pooled. Third, when the fundamentals call for a devaluation it should be enacted swiftly rather than deferred until pressures build up and necessitate an overhasty reaction. Fourth, adjustments in economic structures need to be undertaken swiftly, whether or not in conjunction with an exchange-rate realignment. Finally, whatever commitments are made verbally or in writing, short of a monetary union with a uniform, fairly independent monetary policy aiming at stability, there are rather strict limits to the degree of cooperation that can voluntarily be achieved among the participants, particularly given the three classes of EU Member States once monetary union goes into effect.

6 – Potential Benefits

One may well ask, as many academic commentators have done, why progress with monetary integration if only because it may appear to be required to ensure fair, productivity-driven competition? That could be reasonably realized with other means than abandonment of the exchange rate as a policy instrument. This is a legitimate question, and a brief look at the other benefits, and indeed drawbacks, of monetary union may be in order. If all obstacles to monetary integration in Europe could be overcome and stage three of EMU reached in full, the benefits would emanate largely from the greater transparency gained in the EU as well as from the reduction in transaction costs.

As far as the microeconomic effects are concerned, the major implication derives from the further reduction of uncertainty about exchange rates following monetary union, not only as observed in markets but also as it influences the behavior of economic agents through their altered expectations about exchange rates and prices. But the size of this benefit, one might argue, should not be exaggerated if only because substantial savings from the compression of exchange-rate volatility in Europe have already been derived from earlier cooperation, as discussed. Even so, particularly at this stage, when currency peace appears to have been restored in Europe, nonnegligible interest-rate differentials remain, suggesting that 'markets' still fear the possibility of realignments. If only for that reason, the microeconomic effects of EMU could still be quite palpable. To harvest those benefits, however, other policy commitments, notably in the fiscal sphere, than the simple declaration to move toward monetary integration, must credibly be introduced and applied. Only then can the ERM II contain exchange-rate movements and eventually eliminate them altogether.

The real economic benefits could emanate from several channels (Baldwin 1989, 1992). First, firms would be able to reduce spending on hedging instruments to guard against exchange-rate changes. Second, the reduction in uncertainty would narrow the risk premium attached to foreign investment and thus lead to a higher level of capital expenditures. This would entail faster growth in the EU in the medium term. In addition, if this more stable climate also encouraged increased investment in R&D, and notably in the enlargement of the human-capital base, the long-run rate of growth in the EU could be permanently lifted onto a higher trajectory. But this outcome is a function of the initial conditions and the nature of the externalities driving the growth process.

The reduction in exchange-rate uncertainty could also have beneficial effects on competition by reducing the effective magnitude of sunk costs adjusted for risk or the investment needed to enter new markets. As a result, further perfecting of the functioning of the single

market would lead to increased convergence between the real economies of the Member States so that the likelihood of regionally asymmetric shocks would be reduced. This would lessen the macroeconomic
strains on the monetary union, and so improve its credibility. In this
sense, the success of monetary union will be intimately linked to ensuring that the single market remains intact, and is indeed improved over
the next several years, with important effects in the production and
consumption spheres.

Faster growth in the EU could be expected to have beneficial spillover effects on the rest of the world too but the implications for non-
member countries are neither transparent, nor are they likely to be as
significant as other elements of the single market. One potentially
important direct effect emanates from the lowered transaction costs of
EU firms as they begin to formulate their decisions against the backdrop of a single unit of account and indeed increasingly against a single
currency. Their costs would be lower on intra-EU transactions, as
compared to non-EU trading, which would still have to go through the
exchanges. Also indirect benefits could be derived. As a matter of fact,
the presence of a single currency will eliminate the uncertainty associated with adjustable exchange rates, thereby giving a further potential
edge to European-based producers in the single market.

Still, all of these potential effects are of relatively minor importance.
If full monetary union were to be realized, the truly crucial impact
would emanate from the greater adjustment pressures created within
the Union by a single currency and a singular monetary policy. But
some potential drawbacks need to be noted too (Brabant 1995a, pp.
328-31), notably the components invoked in the earlier discussion
about the EU as an optimum currency area (see Section 4 in particular)
and what needs to be done to ensure stability in the monetary union.

As far as the more aggregative economic effects of EMU are concerned, in the analyses of those who view active monetary policy as
potentially influencing economic buoyancy, its full realization could
result in slower growth in the EU and would disadvantage the poorer
members because of loss of control over monetary policy and the
presumed deflationary bias of strict monetary-policy rectitude in the
monetary union (Eatwell 1992a, b). As entering the monetary union
would mean giving up the option of devaluation against members of the

union, the only policy tool remaining for these countries to counteract country-specific shocks would be fiscal policy, as argued in Section 4. Indeed, capital controls and trade policy have been given up as part of the realization of the single European market.

In that respect, one should note that the EMU as a currency union free of controls on trade and without substantial fiscal transfers is without historical precedent. However, in contrast to all existing currency unions without trade barriers, current plans for EMU do not envisage any role for automatic stabilizers on a Union-wide basis, such as the funding of unemployment benefits. Thus, stabilization will be left up largely to national governments, as discussed earlier in connection with fiscal federalism (see Section 4). John Eatwell (1992a), among others, argues, however, that the leakage abroad of much of any fiscal stimulus and problems of high national indebtedness will result in an inadequate commitment to stabilization and higher levels of unemployment. Furthermore, the EU with the EMU in place is unlikely to have an expansionary impact on the world economy any time soon; rather the reverse is more likely to hold, as came to the fore with the early stages of Germany's EMU and subsequent unification.

7 – Policy Options

On present policy positions, a major dilemma now arises from having conceived of monetary union as a pre-set policy target with a fixed date. On the one hand, some policy makers are strongly against *any* relaxation of the convergence criteria come what may, and this was in fact reaffirmed, upon Germany's insistence, by the Council of Finance Ministers in Valence in September 1995 (Maas 1995, pp. 42-3) and stressed again at the Verona meeting in April 1996 (Buerkle 1996, Tell 1996, Tell and Hill 1996). At the same time, some of those who argue this way are in favor of starting the monetary union, as per the deadline of January 1999 in the Treaty, with more than a trivial membership.

On present expectations, as noted, very few countries would qualify by that date. Other policy makers stress that because of credibility problems the creation of monetary union cannot be deferred. Any decision to postpone its inauguration in 1999 would, in their view, sound the death knell of monetary union for years to come, and thus deliver a significant blow to the prospects not only of economic integration, inasmuch as the logic of the single market cannot possibly be upheld, but also undermine other forms of collaboration in Europe. As argued earlier (notably in Section 3), these fears should not be taken at face value. But that there might be a quick resumption of the political debate on trying yet again for EMU, which would be the fifth attempt, seems rather unlikely.

In the light of all the above, the leaders of the EU now face the dilemma of having to move forward to monetary union but that they can do so only by undertaking strenuous efforts to shrink budget deficits at a time of an economic slowdown. At least four policy options are available to enable them to cope with this dilemma.

• One is to proceed with monetary union as set in the Maastricht Treaty come what may, even if it is set up as an empty shell or it starts with very few participants. While entirely possible, this would not be very credible to market participants and it would probably have negative effects on other components of the integration process.

• Second, the Member States could alter the convergence criteria sufficiently to enable a group of core countries to initiate monetary integration by the target date. This too is unlikely to be very credible, especially to financial markets; it might even introduce an element of undesirable instability into the union from the very beginning. That would almost certainly occur if major deviations from the specified criteria were allowed, especially as the emphasis of policy makers in recent years has been on the vital importance of observing a strict interpretation of the convergence criteria as conditions for admission.

• Third, given the unexpected slowdown in economic activity in key Member States, after a deep and protracted recession, this early into the recovery that started in 1994, which has made it more difficult to meet the deficit criteria, the Fifteen could revise the Treaty, and specify another date for starting up the monetary union. While this might provide a breathing space for policy makers, there is no guarantee that conditions at the time of the new date will be any better for helping most Member States to meet the convergence criteria. Moreover, as already indicated, past efforts at launching monetary integration suggest that slippage in implementing an agreed EMU program invariably sets the movement back by at least a decade. Deferring the date of the inception of monetary union at this juncture, which is the fourth attempt, may make it politically and diplomatically very difficult to revive the agenda for some time to come, perhaps another decade.

This objection could be removed if a genuine revision were to be agreed upon, entailing concurrence on different policies to be observed at least by a critical minimum of Member States before such monetary integration could be initiated. The present Conference itself, however, does not provide the proper venue to accomplish such a revision. And so another platform similar to the 1990-1991 EMU Conference would have to be agreed upon and mounted. The danger of the latter option is, however, grave as past failed efforts at launching monetary integration have amply underlined. The project would be delayed by at least another decade.

• Finally, the Maastricht Treaty itself, although not the particular protocol on the convergence criteria, provides for a measure of flexibility that would permit the monetary union to be inaugurated in 1999 with a larger membership without violating the spirit in which the specific convergence criteria, whatever their intrinsic economic merits, were conceived in the Treaty. Thus article 104c(2a) states explicitly that compliance with budgetary discipline shall be conducted by examining whether, in the case of the deficit-to-GDP ratio, "either the ratio has declined substantially and continuously and reached a level that comes close to the reference value; or, alternatively, the excess over the reference value is only exceptional and temporary and the ratio remains close to the reference value"; article 104c(2b) contains a similar statement on flexibility with regard to debt-to-GDP ratios (European Commission 1993, p. 215). Article 109j(1, indent 2), which refers specifically to the convergence criteria for admission to monetary union, also stresses this flexibility (see European Commission 1993, p. 236).

Now, none of the supplementary criteria are precisely defined in the Treaty, and they could thus be suitably interpreted at the present IGC without necessarily jeopardizing the other aims of monetary union. (It could in theory be done also at another level, notably in the Council, but to date policy makers have not succeeded in that forum with making progress toward a political compromise. It might therefore be more appropriate to envision such a compromise as part and parcel of a broader package of measures, such as might emerge from the ongoing Conference.) Interpretation will in any case be necessary even for the specifications of the protocol, if only because it is as yet unclear whether the evaluation of compliance, which will determine for the first time in 1998 eligible members for entry into the union in 1999, will be against the average or one of the extremes of the range, and which one, of the three best-performing Member States. The same applies to the 'regular' bands for exchange-rate stability, as indicated earlier in the discussion of the monetary turmoil of 1992-1993 (Erkel-Rousse 1995, pp. 182ff.).

In this context, reference to the progress made toward convergence in a number of Member States could usefully be acknowledged, as could the cyclical situation in Member States, which has aggravated the slippage in economic convergence. Thus it might be useful to underline the progress made, for example, with the reduction of the structural budget deficit, even though the conjunctural component of the budget may have risen, owing to the unforeseen economic slowdown, whose duration and strength is still unknown.

What the above discussion leads up to, in other words, is the finding that hiding behind the presumed impossibility that core large countries will meet the fiscal criteria as *the* argument for postponing monetary union is simply an excuse, and a feeble one at that, for not moving ahead at all with monetary integration, given the available room for policy flexibility. This is reinforced by evidence to the effect that monetary unions, even in the absence of binding fiscal constraints, such as on government debt and deficit levels, generate their own fiscal discipline (see Glick and Hutchison 1993).

If the Treaty cannot be renegotiated and there is little point in forming a monetary union with just a few, chiefly small, countries, the sole room for flexibility would seem to lie in reinterpreting some of the convergence criteria, notably in the fiscal domain, no matter how reluctant some policy makers may be to set such a step in the direction of political compromise. Actually, as noted, the Treaty provides precisely for such a process to take place, possibly at the current Conference, as already indicated. The Member States may well wish to consider this fourth option, if only as a fallback to ensure the start of monetary union in 1999. If a strong economic recovery were to occur in the second half of 1996 and strengthen in 1997, it could permit a larger membership of the monetary union, which would be important to forestall exchange-rate instability in countries that do not or cannot join it until later, before the year 2002 on present expectations held by EU insiders, as reported earlier (Section 5). The rhetoric about adhering rigidly to the protocol convergence criteria could then be relaxed in favor of reasonably flexible policy making, in the light of unanticipated circumstances.

Conclusions

Directly or indirectly, then, the Conference will have to tackle important issues and reach decisions on the nature of EMU, on the strategy for reaching it, on the governance of a common monetary policy, on ensuring that Member States that cannot or do not wish to join the monetary union observe monetary and exchange-rate discipline, and on balancing the monetary objectives with other areas of economic and social policy. But prevailing levels of unemployment simply cannot be ignored in charting the future course of European integration. Several national policy makers and even the European Parliament, while advocating that the timetable should be kept without modifying the convergence criteria, have already called for "reinforced economic policy coordination" to establish "a more balanced EMU" (see Bourlanges and Martin 1995, para. 5, p. 7).

A determined and firm stance on the convergence criteria interpreted within the full letter of the Treaty, but not limited solely to the explicit quantitative targets, would go a long way toward affirming the determination of at least the core countries to forge ahead with integration. (Christian de Boissieu [1995, pp. 6-7] has made an argument along the same lines, but Cees Maas [1995, p. 43] is less sanguine that this will be possible.) Finally, procedures and incentives for countries outside the core to eventually join the monetary union, or at least to espouse its basic spirit, would further buttress the credibility of integration policies. Alexandre Lamfalussy (1995, p. 13), the Chairman of the EMI and thus a key decision maker on implementing and safeguarding EMU, has described such a compact as "a matter of capital importance."

4

The Economies in Transition and the EU: The Experience to Date

Almost as soon as the 'revolutions' of 1989 erupted in the eastern part of Europe, beginning with Hungary and Poland, the smaller and more western of these countries aired their strong desire "to return to Europe." This expression has meant many things, of course, and it would have been more constructive if observers could keep the "idea of Europe," however elusive, separate from what the "European Union" has embodied (Havel 1996). Confounding the two is definitely not very helpful. For the purposes at hand, however, I take the expression to mean, as emphasized by one after another policy makers in particular of the smaller economies in transition, the ambition to seek, as quickly as possible, close economic, political, and security ties with the then EC. Their express aim was to become members of that organization, and join the 'spirit' in which they believed the EU still to be functioning, at the earliest possible moment, in part to integrate themselves fully into the large common market and extricate themselves from the CMEA 'markets.' It bears to recall that the latter, and the institutional arrangements within the CMEA context, were then being avidly spurned, especially by the central European countries. They did so for economic, ideological, political, security, and undoubtedly an entire array of convoluted other reasons (see Brabant 1990, 1991), whose foundations are at times difficult to grasp, and perhaps for that reason very often glossed over by the impatient newfangled advisers, including the many assistance providers, of these countries.

This and the following chapters are designed to trace the evolution of what in the end should be a more constructive relationship between the EU and the transition economies. In the first place, I envisage here the accommodation of the ambitions of the ten transition economies that have since signed a Europe Agreement (though it bears to recall that only six have been ratified; the four other agreements are still in the process of ratification (since the Slovenian agreement was signed only on 10 June 1996, after a protracted delay pending the removal of political obstacles around postwar expropriations on the part of Italy, the ratification process can only now be initiated). With the Slovenian *démarche* on 10 June 1996, as noted, all have now submitted their requests for full accession. Recall that this process began on 1 April 1994 when Hungary followed by Poland just a week later submitted their applications. The others followed suit later on, Slovenia being the most recent, following the settlement of the dispute with Italy. Though these countries merit particular attention, I also wish to deal with other economies in transition because most, if perhaps not all, desire to be treated as an intrinsic part of the European architecture, almost regardless of how Europe's eastern frontiers will eventually be traced.

This chapter considers the evolving relationship between the EU and the eastern part of Europe prior to concrete discussions about accession, which have yet to be initiated. I first briefly summarize where matters stood on the eve of the momentous economic, political, and social shifts in the economies in transition. Next I look at western Europe's reaction to this unprecedented opportunity. Then I provide a rationale for the assistance rendered by the international community in general, but especially by the EU. In a fourth section, I trace the assistance efforts western Europe in particular engaged in. Then I discuss in more detail the Europe Agreement and what it may mean for the economies in transition. In the final section I ask the question whether the interactions between the EU and the economies in transition have emerged from, or given rise to, some well-defined strategy on the basis of which a constructive relationship leading in time to full membership in the EU could be built up; and in the event of a negative answer what could reasonably be entertained by way of an alternative path toward fashioning such a constructive strategy.

1 – On the Eve of the Transformations

Until the felicitous eruption of the *annus mirabilis*, overt contacts between the EU and the former planned economies had been highly limited, direct encounters usually crystallizing as part and parcel of negotiations in other fora, such as the General Agreement on Tariffs and Trade (GATT) or the UNO, and for some the IMF and World Bank. This had multiple origins. One was that the CMEA authorities, with the Soviets in the lead, were opposed to any of the 'fraternal' countries (excepting the former Yugoslavia, which was only an associate CMEA member, and, to a lesser degree, Romania as a CMEA maverick) reaching out to the then EC and concluding anything like comprehensive trade, let alone trade and cooperation, agreements with it. The CMEA authorities insisted adamantly that such a course could be envisioned only after putting into place a comprehensive bilateral framework agreement with the EC.

The EC opposed that view for its own reasons for many years. Formally, the objection to hammering out such a framework arrangement was that the CMEA as an institution really had little of stature as a counterpart negotiator, since by its nature it was little more than a regional secretariat, and a very weak one at that. This contrasted notably with the European Commission's authoritative role in the common commercial policy. Many of the Member States preferred in any case to manage their trading relations with the individual eastern countries themselves as part of their foreign policy, even though trade *per se* was part and parcel of the then EC's common commercial policy. Germany's *Ostpolitik* was perhaps the most conspicuous of those stances. But other Member States too, notably France and Italy, envisioned to be able to promote their own interests by proceeding in this bilateral manner, including by arranging various loan-guarantee formats, a financing path that remained fully subordinated to national decision makers at the governmental level, hence a matter of 'national security,' rather than subject to the quasi-supranational authority of the EC.

After years of on-off negotiations, an entirely innocuous Joint Declaration on establishing direct relations was reached only on 25 June 1988, really far too late to make much of a dent in the relationship between the EU and the planned economies, though some cooperation agreements, which had already been under consideration for some time, were quickly concluded, largely for political reasons (for Hungary, see Balázs 1996). The European Commission, as distinct from some of the Member States, as a result, had little interest in the eastern part of Europe and had built up a very limited range of capabilities, which were even then rather shallowly developed, to deal with these countries. These features came especially to bear on the sudden involvement of the European Commission in particular in assisting the economies in transition barely a year after signing the EC-CMEA agreement, partly on request of the international community but also because of its own determination to play a much larger role in foreign-policy matters, sort of the first feelers under the heading of the emerging CFSP as Mr. Jacques Delors envisioned it at the time.

The second reason, of course, was that the planned economies were tightly drawn together in the CMEA framework. This included the real sphere based on planning and market segmentation. That was also true in more financial aspects for the CMEA had developed over time very special – by international standards indeed rather peculiar – pricing, payment, and settlement arrangements as appendages of comprehensive bilateral trade and payment agreements, which remained the real anchor of CMEA economic cooperation almost up to the very demise of the organization. Not only was the CMEA characterized by peculiar relations when compared with the multilateral liberalization that had transformed most of the western world, the 'free-market' global economy in particular, after World War II, also the bulk of the trade of the members was conducted among themselves almost till the very outbreak of the political transitions. Making allowance for exchange-rate and price distortions would not materially alter this picture.

In this context, allow me to underline once again, without going into the details, that it is historically incorrect to charge only, or even mainly, Soviet policy makers, Mr. Mikhail S. Gorbachev in particular, with responsibility for the CMEA's collapse, hence for the external shock to which the transition economies without exception – a logical impossibility, in any case – became exposed. Because of their intransigent political stance around the end of 1989 and early 1990, the central European policy makers bear as much responsibility, relatively speaking, of course, for the precipitous collapse of the CMEA as the Soviet Union. Constructive pricing, trading, settlement, payment, and other reforms that then seemed entirely feasible (Brabant 1990), at least from a technical point of view, could have been instituted, based on solid economic incentives (for some of the arguments, see Brabant 1990,

1991). They were spurned for ideological, political, and strategic reasons, by far not all of which were well founded.

Paradoxically, now that these countries are on their way to economic recovery and have forged a much stronger relationship with the EU, the above-cited arguments for strengthening intragroup cooperation based on economic rationality have been slowly reemerging these past two years or so, but particularly since 1995 (UNECE 1996a, pp. 106ff.). I do not want to be misunderstood, of course: This is a most welcome, if quite belated, development, as clarified in Chapter 6.

Just a few words about the implications of CMEA involvement for the subsequent problems of the transition whose nature, if perhaps not quite their full extent, were entirely foreseeable, given the trade, pricing, and payment regimes anchored to the transferable ruble. Their essence was four-fold: (1) market separation through the state monopoly of foreign trade and payments adhered to by each planned country but administered according to its own rules; (2) artificial trading prices; (3) rather rigid equalization among domestic, transferable-ruble, and east-west pricing so that trade and other economic decisions would remain the exclusive preserve of each country's policy makers; and (4) comprehensive interstate bilateral trade and payment agreements arranged around some odd rules, notably regarding pricing, payment, and settlement. All of these features were maintained separately from the links of these countries with the outside world, especially those based on more or less normal trading conditions; that is, chiefly with the industrial countries since the bulk of trade with developing countries was managed through special bilateral arrangements with a few privileged partners.

The resulting patterns of trade were on the whole in support of maintaining economies that were by design without competition from within and sheltered against external competition; that engaged in widespread redistribution of incomes throughout their own economy, but were reluctant to do likewise on a regional level, even among like-minded CMEA partners; and that had their economic priorities selected by the political and bureaucratic powers in place, rather than through a pre-set framework from within which economic agents could formulate their own strategies in pursuit of their own profit motives; the overwhelming share of state property in production only reinforced these features, setting the planned economies into a special category in the global economic context.

Part of the calamity into which the transition economies fell after 1989 was caused by the collapse of the CMEA, of course. However, as argued, the CMEA's foundering was not entirely an external shock nor can the bulk of the domestic economic decline in the members be attributed in the large to the steep reduction in intra-CMEA trade. Both are usually ascribed to Gorbachev's posturing in early 1990, but that provides almost too convenient, indeed much too facile, an explanation of events. Some investigators have claimed to have detected a justified link, attributing nearly all of the domestic impact on output and employment of transformation policies to the CMEA trade shock (Rodrik 1992a, b). I find those sciolistic cause-and-effect stories, even if based on purported factual evidence, just not very persuasive.

The CMEA's collapse, that is, the putative external shock, could not possibly have constituted the alpha and omega of the transition rout in the CMEA members, given the autonomy that had been preserved within each of these economies. Indeed, their considerable autarky had earlier been held responsible for much of the failures of inward-orientated central planning in small economies! And, as argued, it could not completely be considered an external shock even for the central European countries for their policy makers in 1989-1990 insisted quite vocally, come what may, on changing these intragroup relations very quickly, and dramatically so. When Gorbachev in mid 1990 decided to enact 'world market conditions' in the CMEA as of 1991, that constituted only the rancid icing on the already thoroughly spoiled cake.

Recall that the expression 'world market conditions' referred to many things, but especially to four features: (1) transactions were to be negotiated by microeconomic agents on their own account; (2) market-clearing prices of a sort, given that there were really not yet genuine, let alone mature, markets in the eastern part of Europe, were the terms at which transactions were to be concluded; (3) imbalances were to be settled in convertible currency on a current basis or, in the case of clearing, periodically; and (4) the usances of world trading, notably on payment conditions (that is, immediate payment for raw materials and fuels and up to 90 to 120 days supplier credit for many manufactured goods), needed henceforth to be observed rather closely.

Instituting these features in intragroup trade, something that the central European countries had been avidly coveting, should in the end have helped to improve rationality in these commercial relations. This would notably have been the case for those members that were then bent on organizing their domestic economies so that microeconomic agents could soon play a critical role in resource allocation within an overall arena cordoned off by the institutions and rules of the new political and economic frameworks. But the implications of abandoning the former regimes in favor of moving to world conditions should be spelled out clearly in terms of a volume shock from real demand and supply factors, both at home and from other CMEA countries; of a terms-of-trade shock; of the shock stemming from the deflationary effect of building up convertible-currency reserves for both precautionary and transaction motives; and of the shock bound to ensue from the disarray during hastily-arranged transformation policies, something that could not have been entirely avoided for some period of time in consequence of the absence or poor functioning of the quintessential institutions supporting foreign transactions (such as for conducting payments, for arranging supplier loans or export credits, for acquiring convertible currency, for issuing insurance and engaging in rediscounting, and for other services required to expedite foreign economic relations). This crucial issue has frequently been misunderstood (when not deliberately fudged), notably in the western advisory assistance rendered to the transition economies, for lack of an elementary acquaintance with the postwar institutions of these eastern European economies.

2 – Confronting the Eastern Part of Europe

Since 1989, eastern Europe has presented the EU with the opportunity to recast its working horizon in terms of 'all-Europe,' a possibility that had been very remote from European thinking for well over four decades, although article 2 of the Treaty of Rome makes it clear that accession to the EU is in principle open to all European countries. Such a broadening of perspective was deemed necessary in these countries to strengthen both the political transitions in eastern Europe as well as the foundations of their economies as they move toward fully-fledged, market-based resource allocation. One pillar was slated to be through sizable western assistance to be delivered effectively as a prop to the transformation policies innovated by the economies in transition. Since then, from the first intimations of these desires, western European policy makers have been preoccupied with the reconceptualization of Europe as a more cohesive area, not only in economic but also in political and security matters, now that the Cold War is widely held to be history. Yet, when all is said and done, this challenge has not so far been squarely met head-on.

The very complexity of any serious attempt to reconfigure the continent would have warranted the formulation of a coherent, long-term strategy leading up to this 'new Europe.' This has, however, proved to be a daunting assignment. Initial reactions by EU policy makers to the events in eastern Europe and to the requests for a rapid, comprehensive rapprochement by the economies in transition were singularly qualified by the perceived need to strengthen the depth and scope of integration policies – deepening integration, in other words – among the (then) twelve members of the Union, rather than to enlarge its membership to eastern Europe. Faced with such a diversity of potential partners, it was feared that the very idea of 'Europe' as a common economic area and, increasingly, as an integrated political space might get lost in the process of enlargement, a development that would serve neither present nor potential members.

Under pressure of circumstances, and after improvised attempts to assist the economies in transition while holding them at bay outside the sphere of potential membership, including by offering them the so-called Europe Agreement as an alternative, the Twelve at the latest at the Essen Council in December 1994 resolved that, once the present IGC "successfully concluded," accession negotiations could be initiated with the ten identified economies in transition, as well as others, if they decided to apply. No specific time frame for the inception of such negotiations has as yet been set, unlike in the cases of Cyprus and Malta, as reported earlier.

At the inception of the transformations in the eastern part of Europe, it was widely assumed by the international community, and indeed by the reform leadership in the transition economies, that the net results of these systemic changes would not only be positive and sizable for the transition societies, and in due course for their outside partners as well, but that these benefits could be obtained quickly and without provoking major social or political upheavals. Western assistance, aside from resources allocated to humanitarian and emergency purposes, was meant to alleviate some of the socioeconomic costs of transition and to provide financial resources and technical knowhow to accelerate the process of change. It was taken for granted that, after a fairly brief period, these societies would embark on a self-sustainable growth path yielding substantial gains in per capita income over a fairly long period of time, thereby starting to close the pronounced gap between their levels of wealth, technology, productive capacity, productivity, and income and those of western Europe.

Note that it was always clear that such a large-scale transformation would have to be accomplished largely on the strength of the efforts mobilized by the economies in transition themselves. It was widely conjectured that a more efficient allocation of available resources, in the allocative as well as technical senses, together with a catch-up with western levels of technology through imports and foreign direct investment (FDI), would permit this scenario to be enacted rather smoothly and with broad popular support. The rapid assimilation of up-to-date western technology would be spurred on via large private capital inflows, though initially stimulated by official transfers, which would lubricate the adaptation and catch-up processes to bolster the credibility of transformation policies.

Little thought was given at the time to the need to prepare these economies in any foreseeable future for inclusion in the EU framework, in spite of the widespread rhetoric of the "return to Europe" in which many policy makers and a broad cohort of pundits and assistance providers, whether official or not, indulged with scarcely any restraints. In EU circles, it was generally assumed that, if such an expansion were ever to occur, it would become topical, at best, only after these countries had been embarked for some time on a rapid and endogenous growth path opened up by the liberalization of their societies. It was taken as axiomatic that the transition economies would eventually come to resemble the western European democracies, albeit at the lower end of the scale of wealth in the EU, but nonetheless they would in due course be vibrant market-based economies with a solid democracy and a lively civil society. Their integration into the EU framework, if requested, would *then* be arranged in much the same way as the measures embraced in earlier enlargements. True, such an entry would almost certainly have had to be engineered at the lower end of the EU's level of development, thus giving rise to all kinds of claims on assistance from the EU because of the then given, and still prevailing, common policy stances. But that would have been in the realm of the feasible, handled from within existing policies.

Most of these basic assumptions underlying the initial standoffish attitude taken by the EU, the justification of the early forms and quantities of assistance (other than humanitarian and emergency aid), the expectations of a quick revamping of the eastern economies and societies with a swift economic recovery, and other anticipations of the trajectory of the transformation have not really been borne out in practice. The transition process has been much more cumbersome and confounding than initially assumed, in terms of the depth and breadth of its complexity as well as of the time required to assimilate all the required changes and innovations. In many ways, this is still the case today. All this complicates the accession of the economies in transition to the EU, even those with a Europe Agreement.

Nonetheless, it is no exaggeration to assert that the remaking of Europe is an unprecedented historical event. Forging ahead quickly and in an orderly fashion, rather than letting matters take shape haphazardly, deserves a high ranking on the agenda of EU policy makers. Focusing squarely on the remaking of pan-Europe, however its eastern borders in particular may be defined (for an historical perspective, see Besançon 1995), while proceeding with the realization of the Maastricht Treaty and moving even beyond that agenda, is clearly one task that is incumbent on the current IGC. It would also be desirable to underpin a more comprehensive, strategic, and longer-term framework to permit a broader coordination of the EU's policies with respect to the economies in transition (see Chapter 6), even if early accession for some would be feasible, which I frankly doubt (see Chapter 5).

Such a strategy should preferably avoid excessive bilateralism, move well beyond providing financial or technical assistance on an *ad hoc* basis, insist upon effective surveillance, and promote a revival of economic ties among the economies in transition themselves. It should also aim at imparting credibility to the transformation agendas as well as at bolstering security in other domains, and have a longer-term horizon with, for most transition economies, membership of the EU or, for others, a well thought-out preferential arrangement as the end target. Such a strategy should not, of course, be seen as an attempt to stall further enlargement. Rather, it should be looked upon for what it truly is and intrinsically hopes to accomplish: a set of guidelines for mobilizing with maximum dispatch available resources to assist the process of enlargement. The very credibility of such a program with the full commitment and involvement – moral, financial, as well as enthusiastic substantive participation of the EU – would avert such an impression. In that process, a crucial consideration is to avoid upsetting the sociopolitical support for the process and objectives of transformation; in many cases, that support continues to be quite fragile. Elements of such a reasonable strategy, without amounting to a fully-fledged preemptive proposal, are discussed in Chapter 6.

3 – Rationale for Assisting the Eastern Countries

It is no exaggeration to assert that the transformation of the eastern part of Europe foreshadowed by the unanticipated political mutations of 1989-1990 has constituted a millennial event, whose full dimensions are yet to come to the fore. Although its actual and potential benefits are likely to be quite considerable in the longer run, even if confined to materialistic accounting, one cannot gloss over the fact that the magnitude of the adjustment costs involved has been staggering, and climbing, regardless of how they are computed, how quickly they will have to – and can – be absorbed, or how equitably they can be distributed over the various layers of society.

Soon after the political changes crystallized in the eastern part of Europe, the international community was asked to provide – and indeed magnanimously volunteered – various kinds of assistance to the transition economies. Initially, western governments and regional and international organizations offered to provide financial, technical, humanitarian, and other assistance to speed up the transition process and, where possible, to help work off part of the adjustment cost faster than these economies would have been able to support on the strength of the resources available to them. The core assumption at the time was that a successful economic, political, and social turnaround in the eastern part of the continent could be engineered fairly quickly and smoothly. We now know that this was a false premise. The transitions can be seen through neither quickly nor without sociopolitically destabilizing costs; nor can outside financial assistance ease its vagaries meaningfully, except perhaps on the margin of what were earlier deemed to be the moral and political imperatives; and there is bound to be path dependency.

In the wake of these and related disappointments, the process of assistance delivery and of making new commitments began to slow down markedly already in 1991, except where policy expediency, as for Russia and for some other CIS States, dictated proceeding otherwise. Many questions arise in this connection: Could more have been done and in a different manner, given the volume and diversity of the appropriated resources and the apparent needs of the transition economies? Indeed, why should the international community feel compelled to assist these countries and for how long? What is the desirable degree of governance that should be available in, or that should quickly be built up by, regional and international organizations, particularly with a view to facilitating the process of fusing the two parts of Europe eventually into a continent remade?

Many reasons could be cited in support of providing a helping hand and dollar (or ecu) to the economies in transition, including altruism, compassion, and guilt. Certainly of equal weight is the proposition that it is ultimately in the genuine self-interest of the global community to compress the acuity and length of the period of adversity in the eastern part of Europe. That can be argued on the basis of a wide range of economic, humanitarian, political, and strategic features. Whereas these factors prevailed from the transitions' inception, they have arguably gained in pertinence as a result of the rocky progress with implementing the transformation agenda up to the present. The realities of the transitions have amply negated the simplistic assumptions on built-in stabilizers and automatic adjustments. Many observers had earlier facilely asserted the latter as uncontestable verities in the sense that they would guarantee smooth corrections of imbalances in the transition economies soon after launching a credible commitment to establishing a pluralistic political setting and building functioning markets.

The particular configuration of the magnitude, timing, and composition of the assistance delivery, and by whom, should preferably have been decided against the backdrop of the envisaged transformation policies. It may be useful to briefly recall the salient features for the issues will crop up again in the last two chapters. Whatever meaningful economic restructuring these countries could have envisioned, sizable adjustment costs would have had to be borne no matter what. These were bound to result from the predictable economic slowdown, and an all but unavoidable real contraction in levels of economic activity. That was predicated on the inertia on the supply side, which was bound to inhibit a quick reallocation of intrinsically still-valuable resources and appropriation of new means to finance economic restructuring from domestic sources, which in any case could be expected to be highly limited during the initial phases of the transformation. Real demand in official and other markets would in all likelihood, on balance, have decreased, regardless of the particular policy stances adopted, in part because of the erosion in wealth, of the drop in real incomes, and of the desire to rebuild precautionary savings. Adjustment costs would also have emanated from the drastic change in the distribution of wealth, owing to rapid adaptations of absolute and relative domestic prices and exchange rates. Moreover, substantial inflation was resorted to, perhaps deliberately, in all transition economies to confiscate most of the monetary overhang, where that was considered a serious policy problem. In some cases, the emergence of hyperinflation until the authorities succeed in regaining control over the money supply should have been reckoned with, rather than its dangers underplayed, from the beginning.

There has been much discussion about whether the transitional recession was necessary and what could have been done to alleviate it. I am prepared to argue that the transition would necessarily have lowered sustainable levels of activity, at least from two to six quarters, even with appropriate policies and timely policy responses.

The critical policy questions are four-fold.

• One set addressed almost exclusively to domestic managers revolved around the determination of the precise size of the adjustment burden (say, the percentage drop in levels of living and of wealth, as well as their distribution over time and over various social layers or interest groups) that they thought could be inflicted upon their societies, bearing in mind the specific features of each country, without generating dysfunctional sociopolitical disaffection with the overall drift of the transformation.

• Second, once the magnitude of the acceptable adjustment burden was selected and outside agencies and governments expressed their willingness to assist in alleviating the burden, the key issue for both domestic policy makers and others was whether such foreign assistance could have mitigated the adjustment burden, while perhaps speeding up the transition.

• Third, directly related are questions, primarily addressed to assistance providers, on who best to entrust with the task and which governance regime to choose for the envisaged action, given prevailing realities.

• Finally, because spare capacities for delivering new assistance from the global community and the political will to earmark incremental resources in the context of national budgets, be it for bilateral or multilateral assistance, are confined at best, the question arose primarily for assistance providers whether resources could be diverted from traditional clients without harming the interests of donors, recipients, or the global community at large.

The first two sets of questions, though interesting and challenging, are not really the proper issue of this volume (see Brabant 1990, 1991, 1992, 1993). But they are not completely irrelevant in the determination of who should be entrusted with the task of coordinating assistance, of how best to ensure that this process remains governable and be best governed in the light of available capacities and other resources, of who would be harmed by the potential diversion of resources, and of the degree to which the worst adverse effects of this reallocation could be alleviated.

The second reason for providing assistance is self-interest. This has various facets. One certainly is the potential for retreat with reform in the transition economies and its implications for other countries. Of course, in most economies in transition the question is manifestly *not* whether there is a chance for political forces to swing back to communism or for economic organization to degenerate again into administrative planning. Rather, the point is that policy reforms anchored to a sharp devaluation of the exchange rate and far-reaching price and trade liberalization usually generate sociopolitical resistance. As a rule, the population immediately feels the costs of extensive, interrelated changes more clearly than it perceives the size, nature, and distribution of benefits accruing over the longer haul. This is especially so for the transition economies, which have been moving, albeit at widely diverging speeds, literally from one socioeconomic system into the veritable *terra incognita* of another, thereby replacing the safety and certainty of the old with the quite palpable hazards of an emerging society new in so many respects.

In many cases, these countries have neither the market to provide shock absorbers nor the democratic and legal institutions to respond orderly to such abrupt simultaneous disturbances. The minimal critical shock required to respond favorably to the economic, political, and social aspirations of those advocating positive changes may well exceed the magnitude of the transition's burden that the electorate at large is willing to support – and prepared to continue to tolerate and indeed actively prop up – irrespective of whether it gets exacerbated as the transformation process unfolds.

Related to this, also in the self-interest mode, is that western governments and multilateral organizations had predicated their initial stance in part on the potential impetus to overall demand that the transition economies could impart to global growth. Following a comparatively brief adjustment period, these countries were expected – and indeed encouraged – to reroute their commercial interests to the west, particularly for the importation of capital goods to shore up their industrial conversion and in time to buttress the new growth path that would enable them to catch up with average levels of wealth in western Europe. This expectation has in the meantime been frustrated in a number of respects. Whereas the prospects for economic recovery in some eastern countries are improving at this stage, at least on average, after a protracted and deep recession, the welcome upturn in the pace of economic activity, notably of some central European countries and Slovenia, or a slowing down of the contraction, notably in some of the CIS States, should be treated with considerable caution. Indeed, it is as yet unclear whether these signs may be harbingers of a sustainable path of economic recovery leading directly, or with minimal interruption, to catch-up growth that will be accessible in the near term. There is no ground for complacency.

The horizon for irreversible recovery may be near or distant. Constraints on external payments in a number of transition economies for reasons of both supply as well as domestic and external demand, large inflow of capital in some countries that may or may not be sustainable but is creating problems of monetary control in some, and continuing difficulties with lowering inflation and with restoring balanced budgets in most suggest that policy makers of these countries would be well advised to persist in their efforts to enact the transformation agenda in various dimensions. Unless domestic absorption can be shored up by modernizing capital expenditures financed largely from domestic savings, retained earning in the first place, of course, it is difficult to see how the economies in transition could jump onto the virtuous bandwagon of intra-industry trade (see Chapter 5) for that constitutes *the* determinant of an economy's capacity to compete in the EU's single market.

Until such a basic consensus on a long-term strategy for transformations without precedent in recent memory can be found and sustained, credible economic stabilization can be enforced, and decisive measures put in train to accelerate the restructuring of these, in some respects footloose, economies, a sharp reversal in their economic fortunes is unlikely to materialize any time soon. Disappointing the expectations that are now running surprisingly high once again could be self-fulfilling in this respect.

The transitions as they have been charted to date exhibit major differences in scope, depth, and range. Even so, the time frame of even the most modest blueprint on desirable transition policies, including institutional modifications, is now widely recognized to stretch far into the future, its duration ranging from one to several decades. Even in the most optimistic case, attaining a functioning polity around a reasonably-behaved market economy is much farther off than it had erroneously been assumed to be 'within reach' at the inception of the transitions by those advocates of the market framework who thought that markets would emerge spontaneously and all necessary adjustments would take their cue from there on. In the process, it was fundamentally forgotten that what we call a 'market' is not in fact a ready-made institution. Rather, it is no more than a reification of a set of behavioral and cultural relations that exist at a given point in time among economic agents, as a rule after having crystallized from protracted interactions in the course of which durable ties become knit. Furthermore, the transitions are likely to last far longer for most of the successor States of the Soviet Union than, say, for the central European countries. While many arduous tasks still lie ahead, the latter countries have nonetheless already set important steps in the direction of macroeconomic stabilization and of enacting policy measures that will in time result in significant structural change.

Much remains to be done, however, before any of these economies will be able to embark on a solid path of self-sustainable economic growth. *A fortiori*, the tasks ahead in those countries where the transition policies remain a subject of acute sociopolitical debate, such as in many of the successor States of the Soviet Union and the former Yugoslavia, are even more daunting. It would be unrealistic to expect that these complicated matters will be resolved quickly or that the transition processes of these countries can be completed any time sooner than now appears to be the case for, say, most central European countries and Slovenia.

Given the salience of successfully engineering the turning point from recovery based mostly on mobilizing previously idled resources to sustainable catch-up, many justifications can be adduced to argue that propping up recovery or ensuring that recovery will be around the corner fairly soon would be wise policy making, particularly in the international community. A resumption of growth, albeit from a much lowered base, will stabilize the sociopolitical situation in the transition economies and, by extension, possibly throughout the European continent. Also, a solid and widely spread economic recovery in the eastern part of Europe will impart a positive growth impulse to the world economy as a whole by opening up opportunities for trade, financial links, as well as factor mobility, notably of capital, based on standard criteria of competition in global markets. It is, therefore, of paramount importance that available assistance resources be properly targeted in harmony with agreed-upon transformation policies. Finally, the transition economies that are in all but name developing countries (at least Albania, Bosnia and Herzegovina, Macedonia, and the Caucasian and Central Asian successor States of the Soviet Union) deserve international assistance on the same grounds as those underpinning the traditional rationale for development assistance; at least what is left of this doctrine, given the pervasive sentiment of aid fatigue.

In tackling the many tangents of providing international assistance to the transition economies, it would be exceedingly and unconscionably myopic to disregard the special role of Europe and its institutions – indeed the unique obligation incumbent upon them. Once the transition economies reach a firm democratic base for decision making and transform their economies so that they can be steered primarily through market-based decisions, there can no longer be any justification for treating these countries differently from other credible applicants for accession to the European Union, for funding from the European financial institutions, or from participating, including eventually as fully-fledged members of the EU, in the emerging all-European economic and monetary regimes. That has been the paramount challenge since 1989.

4 – Europe's Early Assistance Approach

Before inquiring into the desirability of casting a new assistance program under the EU's aegis, it is useful to review briefly the EU's efforts in that respect since 1989. I shall do so primarily with a view to ascertaining whether the experiences since 1989 constitute a reasonably coherent, strategic, and truly forward-looking program of action. For if such a program were already in place, it would only need to be enlarged. There would then, of course, be no justification for innovating an assistance strategy almost *ab ovo*. In the reverse case, as I contend in Chapter 6, such a strategy should be formulated as quickly as possible. Ascertaining this as objectively as the available evidence permits is by no means a straightforward matter, however.

There can be no quibbling about the fact that western Europe initially responded quickly and magnanimously to the requests for assistance from the economies in transition; in some instances, western European countries even volunteered. The response was largely motivated by the hope of thus consolidating a decisive turn away from communism and administrative planning, and indeed from dependence on the Soviet Union for the smaller countries of eastern Europe, and ensuring that these changes would be irreversible. But the assistance efforts for a long time were largely improvised; in more than one respect they have continued to suffer from this inability – could it have been a lack of political will or of strategic imagination? – to take a longer and more coherent view of what has been at stake in the eastern part of Europe since 1989.

This piecemeal approach was probably unavoidable at the start of the transition, given the sudden and extraordinary turn of events in eastern Europe in 1989, the limited information upon which assistance providers were initially acting, the poor infrastructure for comprehending events in the eastern part of Europe, even at the cerebral level, and the fact that the European Commission was at that time overloaded with its own agenda. This included the completion of the single European market, moving toward a unified currency and a cohesive monetary policy in the EMU mode, the absorption of the adjustments entailed by the second and third expansions in membership, and, beyond all that, plans for a tighter social and political union, the latter in particular influencing stances toward the economies in transition. In the process, substantial resources have been misallocated, some utterly wasted (Kaminski 1996).

1 – Evolution of Assistance

The EU's assistance activities in favor of the economies in transition dates from the Group of Seven (G-7) summit in Versailles in July 1989. It was in consequence of the decision in principle reached there that the G-24 donor countries, then coinciding with the members of the Organisation for Economic Co-operation and Development (OECD), of which later the Czech Republic, Hungary, Korea, and Mexico became members, to be joined by Poland in October 1996 (*OMRI Daily Digest*, 20 May 1996), decided to support the nascent reform efforts, notably of Hungary and Poland; this was subsequently extended to all economies in transition save the CIS States, and to help these countries integrate themselves into the world economy. The European Commission in that context was entrusted with the task of coordinating the efforts of individual donors, the multilateral financial institutions, and its own activities. The latter included the so-called PHARE program (for *Pologne/Hongrie – assistance à la restructuration économique*), lending by the European Investment Bank (EIB), and other types of assistance within the perimeter of EU activities, which depends, of course, on *ad hoc* stances advocated by core Member States.

In early 1992, following the fragmentation of the Soviet Union, the EU established its TACIS (Technical Assistance to the CIS) program to assist the former Soviet Union (other than the Baltic States) in its reform efforts; but it had already earlier, before the country's implosion, extended a helping hand. This too was part and parcel of a broad international effort, this time led by the United States, however. Indeed, as far as the successor States of the Soviet Union other than the three Baltic States are concerned, their needs for assistance come within the so-called 'Washington Conference format,' meaning essentially that they are within the ward of the G-7 industrial countries, and thus the Fund, which serves as the secretariat of the G-7 by default.

The designation 'Washington Conference format' stems from the fact that the disintegration of the Soviet Union in late 1991 provided the impetus for the United States to convene a conference in Washington, DC, 22-23 January 1992, on conceptualizing and streamlining assistance to the successor States of the Soviet Union other than the Baltic States among the principal multilateral agencies and donor countries involved. Since then a second meeting was held in Lisbon (23-24 May 1992) and a third in Tokyo (29-30 October 1992), which was attended by 70 countries and 19 multilateral organizations. Since late 1992, however, the format has turned more and more toward the deliberations within the G-7 and the national coordinating centers.

PHARE and TACIS are essentially grant aid designed to support technical-assistance activities of the most diverse kind. PHARE resources have more recently been reconcentrated on supporting infrastructure and the technical assistance required to facilitate accession to the EU, notably by promoting the rapid assimilation of essential components of the *acquis* (more on this in Section 6). The EU has also participated in delivering emergency and humanitarian aid to the few economies in transition that required it.

At the turn of the 1990s, the EU joined other donor countries in granting GSP privileges to a number of economies in transition, which were subsequently incorporated into the Europe Agreements, and in removing those quantitative restrictions that had specifically been imposed upon so-called 'state-trading countries,' as defined in the context of the GATT at the height of the Cold War. It also granted some of the transition economies privileged access to its markets for sensitive products and tariffs cuts (see European Commission 1995h).

Furthermore, the EU has participated, directly and through the EIB, in providing loans, and some grants, in support of stances on macroeconomic policy in a number of economies in transition, supplementing the resources of the IMF and the World Bank. The latter in particular as well as the European Bank for Reconstruction and Development (EBRD), of which all EU Member States as well as the EU itself and the EIB (and indeed now all economies in transition) are shareholders, have provided sizable loans for the purpose of restructuring, including privatization.

By its own reckoning (European Commission 1995h, 1996g), the EU has granted over the five years 1990-1994 to the ten economies in transition with a Europe Agreement as well as Albania and Macedonia (which are the twelve beneficiaries of PHARE) some ecu 33.8 billion – about$44 billion in early 1996 dollars – or 45 percent of the total assistance these countries received from the international community. Grants constituted some ecu 13 billion. Of that total some ecu 4.3 billion was committed under PHARE, the Union's main technical-assistance program. Another ecu 1.17 billion was appropriated for 1995 (OECD 1996, p. 69). A slightly higher annual average has been budgeted for the second half of the 1990s (ecu 6.69 billion for 1995-1999 according to Vrbetić 1995, p. 7), but only after the EU reached an agreement on assisting the nonmember Mediterranean countries at a higher level of support (to the tune of ecu 4.69 billion for 1995-1999) than the majority of the Member States had earlier aimed at, but less than what the southern EU Member States had been pushing for.

The EU has also provided substantial resources to the CIS States. By its own reckoning (European Commission 1995h), during 1990-1994 the Union provided ecu 59 billion in aid out of a total worldwide of ecu 98.3 or 59 percent. Of the Union's delivery, however, a comparatively small share has been for technical assistance (for the period 1 September 1990 to end 1994, ecu 2.6 billion out of total technical assistance of ecu 5.4 billion). The vast bulk has been in the form of loans and guarantees as well as strategic assistance in facilitating the withdrawal of Soviet troops from the eastern part of Germany in particular.

Keeping track of who has given how much to any individual economy in transition, when, and for which particular purpose is by no means an easy task, and all data, including the above, should be taken with a grain of salt. It would have been desirable for the international community to have such a comprehensive monitoring capacity in place. Alas, this has not figured highly on the agenda of assistance providers; nor has coordination and avoiding duplication for that matter! Nevertheless, without laying claim to exhaustiveness, the flow of financial resources to the transition economies, including official assistance, has been regularly monitored in the two major publications of the ECE (that is, *Economic Survey of Europe* and *Economic Bulletin for Europe*); for the latest review, see UNECE 1996a, pp. 141ff. The cited OECD and European Commission sources help to complete at least parts of the puzzle.

2 – Evaluation of Assistance to Date

There seems to be broad consensus among outside observers and policy makers in the economies in transition (see Altmann and Ochmann 1995, Havel 1996, Richter 1996, Weidenfeld 1995, WERI 1995), as well as in some cases from critical observers from within the assistance-delivering institutions, as detailed below, that western assistance has trailed well behind expectations. A Polish commentator has opined, undoubtedly somewhat irreverently, that it has amounted to little more than "lunch and dinner diplomacy" (WERI 1995, p. 188).

One can usefully assess the disappointments at three levels (for a review of the issues, see Altmann, Andreff, and Fink 1995): (1) the mobilization of adequate assistance from bilateral, regional, and multilateral donors; (2) the precise targeting of that assistance toward the real needs of the economies in transition, as seen from within their own societal context; and (3) more-effective and better-coordinated resource delivery, given resource commitments and recipients' needs. (For an early discussion of the need for a coherent framework for providing western assistance to the transition economies, see UNECE 1990, pp. 5-26; 1991b, pp. 7-9).

Criticism of western assistance programs and strategies have been formulated by a number of outside observers, including myself (see, for example, Brabant 1995a, pp. 414-48). But on occasion also by insiders. In the EU, for example, a number of the programs directed at assisting the economies in transition have come under sharp criticism from the Court of Auditors, among others (see, for example, European Commission 1995b, pp. 8 and 201-228). Its final conclusion is telling: "[O]nly if the Commission analyses and expounds the actual problems it is faced with, together with a transparent and realistic proposal concerning the resources it needs to discharge its responsibilities, will it be able to emerge from the present state of deadlock and uncertainty" (p. 217). The charges have been legion, ranging from wasteful duplication all the way to outright fraud. The so-called Emerson Affair (named after Michael Emerson, the former EU Ambassador to Moscow), which burst into the open in early 1996 (Atkinson 1996, Barber 1996), is only the latest, and quite spectacular, emanation thereof. Improving fraud-fighting capabilities is one IGC agenda item (see Chapter 2).

The delivery of various types of emergency, technical, financial, cultural, and commercial assistance is widely judged to have been carried out in a rather haphazard fashion with much of the resources mobilized being 'captured' either by the delivering institutions' formidable bureaucracies or their associated rent-seeking advisers and consultants, from both sides of the divide alike but vastly more from the latter than from the former (Kaminski 1996), and with limited delivery on the ground, as it were, thus confining the positive impact of assistance for the beneficiary countries. As a result, the record of the past six or seven years has not been particularly encouraging. It has certainly not impressed those who had hoped for a decisive breakthrough in the remodeling of Europe, however its borders may in the end be defined.

The variety of responses quoted above, and more details about the Europe Agreements follow in the next section, has given rise to a complicated structure of relations between the EU and the economies in transition. It now consists of bilateral Europe Agreements with ten central and eastern European countries (and four of the ten have not yet been ratified), bilateral Partnership and Cooperation Agreements with a number of the other successor States of the Soviet Union (at least with Belarus, Georgia, Kazakstan, Kyrgyzstan, Moldova, Russia [for details, see Borko 1996], Ukraine, and Uzbekistan, but ratification has not been completed for most of them (and those with Georgia and Uzbekistan were signed only in late April and June 1996, respectively), and so only the "interim" trade part of the agreement is in effect in only some cases, whereas for most of them even that implementation component is still pending; the agreements with Armenia and Azerbaijan were reportedly being finalized in late April 1996 [*Daily Report – Central Eurasia*, 26 April 1996, document Odrili3037rtqr]), and negotiations on bilateral free-trade or second-generation trade and cooperation agreements with some of the other economies in transition, including Albania. Some of the free-trade agreements, such as with the Baltic States, are still in place because ratification of their Europe Agreements is still pending. Albania has a more limited kind of cooperation agreement. With the normalization of ties with the other successor States of Yugoslavia, a renewal in some form of the trade and cooperation agreement that existed before the break-up of the federation is likely in the course of 1996 or soon thereafter. The process has already started in the case of Macedonia, and will probably be taken up soon with the other Successor States (except Slovenia).

Just one word about the origin of the Partnership and Cooperation Agreement. This came about because most of the CIS Member States will never qualify for full membership and others may not be able to do so for several generations to come. Yet, as detailed in Chapter 6, events in those parts of the world, if only because they happen to occur on the eastern flank of the 'Europe' of principal concern to the EU, could not be left in a state of considerable economic disarray and socio-political instability, let alone prone to adopting a strategic reaction to being 'isolated.' If only because pressures for migration into the EU or the transition economies to the CIS's western borders were bound to become aggravated over time, the Union felt compelled to go beyond the strict economic formats of trade and economic cooperation, and thus suggested the Partnership and Cooperation Agreement. Like the Europe Agreement, this is not solely about trade or broader commercial and economic relations, of course. Indeed, specifications on human rights, on protecting FDI (at least from the EU into these transition economies), and on safeguarding intellectual property rights (again, at least those from the EU introduced into the transition economies) are also included. These elements form currently part of the agreements with the countries cited earlier and are envisaged in agreements with some other CIS Member States. But information on the details and the repercussions of these agreements remains sparse at best (for Russia, see Borko 1996).

In any case, most of the kinds of agreements (as discussed above) that the EU has been working out with the various transition economies have not been particularly innovative (Altmann, Andreff, and Fink 1995; Balázs 1996; Kramer 1993). They have proved insufficient to meet four identified and widely accepted needs: (1) to provide economic, political, and strategic security to the eastern partners; (2) to respond strategically to formal requests for accession lodged since April 1994; (3) to strengthen economic and political relations with the western successor States of the former Soviet Union; and (4) to hold a constructive dialogue on strategic cooperation in economic, political, defense, environmental, health, and other affairs with many other economies in transition.

5 – The Europe Agreement: Hopes and Disappointments

Although it quickly became clear that most of the premises on which assistance had been predicated were shaky, the organs entrusted with the assistance efforts, including notably the European Commission, hesitated for a long time about what could and should be done for the economies in transition beyond a number of programs for humanitarian and emergency purposes. It should be recalled that the vast majority of these assistance formats had been hastily cobbled together in 1989-1990 and gradually extended, particularly following the August 1991 coup in the Soviet Union (Reinicke 1992, p. 94), to other transition economies, except the Soviet Union. Later on, these efforts were sort of rationalized in the Europe Agreement, an instrument that was also extended in time to the Baltic States, largely for political reasons, but not to the other beneficiaries of PHARE.

1 – Origin of the Europe Agreement

Becoming aware that the transformation would be more problematic than originally thought in 1989-1990, that the drive of most of the western economies in transition was for full membership, and that its own efforts at assisting these countries were less than visionary, the European Commission on behalf of the EU innovated a sort of halfway solution by extending to the more developed transition economies an associate status based on the so-called Europe Agreement conceived under article 238 of the Treaty of Rome; this does not confer *associate membership*, however, for that category does not exist in the EU context, or any claim to eventual accession. In fact, the first agreements with the then three central European countries noted only that the partner country had expressed its desire to regard the Europe Agreement as a first step toward eventual membership without any commitment at all from the EU. In later agreements, once the decision to enlarge had been taken in principle at the Copenhagen Council (21-22 June 1993), the expectation that such an evolution would materialize, if the eastern partner so desired, is recorded as part of the Europe Agreement. Later on, other countries were offered yet another status through the so-called Partnership and Cooperation Agreement (extended only to the successor States of the Soviet Union other than the Baltic States), as noted in Section 4.

Until the Copenhagen Council, little thought appears to have been given in EU deliberations to whether and when the economies in transition could eventually be brought into the EU. However, policy makers in many of these economies persisted in arguing their claim for 'Europe' status and eventually managed to persuade the Twelve to change their outlook, including their deeply seated reluctance to contemplate yet another enlargement before other building blocks of the EU's 'home' and its governance could be firmly cemented. They did so in part because of the unanticipated effects of transformation policies throughout the area, with their severe impact on economic activity, especially during the first few years, and on income distribution, with growing inequities, which led to rising social discontent after a short period of 'extraordinary politics.' The economic problems were aggravated, among other factors, by the collapse of the economic links among the transition countries built up during the postwar period (and within defunct federations), the disintegration of the Soviet Union, and the calamitous wars in the former Yugoslavia in 1991-1995.

2 – Toward the Europe Agreement

The agreements reached to date with the ten eastern European countries involve notably the establishment of asynchronous and differential trade liberalization for most manufactures. That is to say, the EU gradually removes its import duties on the products shipped from the partner country, initially foreseen over a five-year period (but after the Copenhagen Council of June 1993, this timetable was advanced in the end to three years, as detailed in European Communities 1995h, p. 10), beginning in 1992 for the central European countries, which signed their Europe Agreement in December 1991; the trade provisions came into effect in March 1992 (for Bulgaria and Romania in February 1994, after several delays for political reasons), pending ratification of the agreement by all national parliaments, which has only recently been concluded (February 1994 for Hungary and Poland and February 1995 for the other four countries); this is sometimes referred to as the Interim Agreement, though there is no such formal document. It is only the decision to apply the trade provisions of the signed, but not yet ratified, Europe Agreement ahead of time. The same applies to the Baltic States once their agreements were signed (in April 1995), though they had already from 1 January 1995 activated a free-trade agreement with the EU; Slovenia's situation is different because its agreement was signed only on 10 June 1996, owing to the dispute with Italy over confiscated property after the last World War, and so only the earlier trade and cooperation agreement is in effect.

The eastern signatory has to reciprocate usually over a similar period of time (original schedule), but chiefly during the second half of the 1990s; here no compression of the time period seems to have been enacted thus far. This means that the partner transition economy temporarily gains a relative competitive edge over EU producers and outside competitors, particularly those that do not benefit from a similar preferential status. Eastern Europe has worked out a similar instrument with the EFTA, naturally chiefly for industrial goods.

It bears to note that EU external tariffs on average amounted to less than 5 percent *ad valorem*. As a result, one should not under any circumstance exaggerate the export-revenue benefits then obtained, particularly in the light of the considerable fluctuations in exchange rates; on the other hand, the eastern partner has been spared outright competition from EU agents for some period of time. Whether this is a useful easement in the end depends on whether policy makers of the transition economies utilize the breathing space to forge ahead with their economic restructuring. Though the trade gains stemming from differential tariff reductions are probably small (WERI 1995, pp. 181ff.), I certainly do not wish to minimize the psychological impact of the attainment by these countries of free access for most of their manufactures in the EU by 1 January 1995 for the Visegrád countries (Czech Republic, Hungary, Poland, and Slovakia) and by 1 January 1996 for Bulgaria and Romania (European Commission 1995h, p. 10).

The Europe Agreement, though a fairly standard instrument for the ten countries now, is nonetheless a very complex, voluminous exercise in commercial diplomacy. The key provisions of the original three treaties, which reflect the EU's strong bent on obtaining markets and production facilities in the eastern part of Europe; on managing access to its markets; and on avoiding serious levels of immigration, are set forth in some detail below. Those for Bulgaria and Romania, the Baltic States, and Slovenia and the successor agreements for the Czech Republic and Slovakia, are quite similar. Exceptions are in the less generous access provisions for some quotas, notably for agriculture, which stalled the entry into force of the interim agreement for quite some time notably for the Balkan States; on the commitment to the enforcement of human rights; and in some the commitment of the EU that the Europe Agreement is, in fact, a prelude to membership if the partner country so desires (for useful details, see European Commission 1995h). Note that the entry into force of the agreements depends on national ratification in both the transition economy and each of the EU Member States. This takes quite some time – over two years in the case of the agreements with Hungary and Poland. As noted, the commercial provisions were introduced at the earliest opportunity – 1 March 1992 for central Europe.

3 – Principal Features of the Europe Agreement

Although there are some differences among the various agreements, usually in the details since they are negotiated bilaterally, they all exhibit a number of common features, of which I should like to underline the eight that I deem to be the most important from the economic point of view.

• First, the transition economies must open their markets for manufactured goods within ten years to products originating in the EU. Tariffs will have to be altogether eliminated over a period stretching from between four and ten years. Quantitative restrictions against EU exports too will have to be abolished but only by the end of the transition. If the transition economies maintain import restrictions thereafter, their commercial policy with respect to the EU will have to be formulated in an explicitly discriminatory fashion so that the EU will not be in a worse position than the most-favored partner(s) as per the preferential arrangement. In principle, no new customs duties or quantitative restrictions can be introduced once the agreement is signed, except in the case of infant industries and sectors undergoing restructuring in the transition economies. However, interpreting 'restructuring' has given rise to some controversy in the Association Councils, whose nature is explained below.

• Second, the EU will open its nonsensitive markets virtually immediately, with tariffs being abolished over a period varying between two and five years (after Copenhagen reduced for most products to between two and three years) for products with at least a 60 percent local-content requirement – a rather restrictive condition, which has since been relaxed by extending the 'local' to include some countries with a Europe Agreement as well as the EEA members (presently only Iceland, Liechtenstein, and Norway). "Local content" is by no means an obvious category, and hence the great difficulty of ascertaining and policing it; and indeed its considerable transaction costs. As a rule this is measured in terms of the last major transformation of the product – essentially a change in the three- or four-digit trade heading (Brabant

1995a, pp. 48-50). But for many products it is operational in terms of the value of imports (Winters 1992, p. 19).

Furthermore, many tariffs for nonsensitive products were abolished upon the introduction of the commercial component of the agreement on 1 March 1992; similarly for the later agreements with Bulgaria and Romania. Quantitative restrictions not governed by international agreements, as in the case of the Multi-fibre Arrangement (MFA), too were abolished upon the entry into force of the commercial part of the agreement. The aim is to abolish all tariffs and other trade barriers, but the agreements maintain rather elaborate antidumping and safeguard clauses – 'contingent protection,' in other words, which can be quite deleterious to investment decisions (WERI 1995, pp. 181ff.), hence exports and growth (Švejnar 1995, p. 14). But the Union denies this and refers critics to the underutilization of quotas, which ranged from 70 percent for Hungary to 33 percent for Bulgaria in 1994 (European Commission 1995h, p. 11) – and in 'sensitive product' sectors they offer only a gradual approach to free trade. For certain metal products, tariffs will be reduced over four years and for sensitive products (including some chemicals, steel products, furniture, leather goods, footwear, glass, and vehicles) tariffs will persist for up to five years. The latter period over which tariffs for sensitive products will be eliminated has more recently, following the Copenhagen Council, been reduced to three years for most products and, as noted, many tariffs were cut already ahead of the original schedule, giving the beneficiary countries free access to major components of the single market.

But for sensitive – by an arguably felicitous *lapsus lingae* turned into "sensible" in Altmann and Ochmann 1995, p. 19 – industrial products (especially textiles, clothing, footwear, some chemicals, and iron and steel products) as well as agriculture the abolition of tariffs and quantitative restrictions will take four to six years; developments here, notably for clothing and textiles, depend in part on the Uruguay-Round Agreement, which will unwind the MFA over a period of ten years. Since the Europe Agreement specifies that the textile regime will be eliminated over a period between five years and one-half of the period agreed in the Uruguay Round (Mayhew 1993, p. 14), the final date for the elimination of the regime for the transition economies will be the end of 1997 (European Commission 1995h, p. 11); but duties on outward-processing trade were abolished immediately. Safeguard clauses are included but there is a guarantee that after ten years (that is, at the latest in early 2002) these products will not be given different treatment than other industrial goods. For iron and steel products, improved transitional 'voluntary export restraints' have been arranged, but all ordinary quantitative restrictions were in principle removed on 1 March 1992. Duties will be abolished over six years. For coal, duties will be abolished over four years and other barriers in one year, except for special restrictions on exports to Germany and Spain.

• Third, the EU offered concessions in agriculture, but nothing like free trade (Tangermann 1993). Previous facilitations for exports of foodstuffs have been consolidated and there will be reciprocal concessions for specific products. These have been restricted to a subset of commodities, and then only for within-quota limits. The latter are set to grow by some 10 percent per year from 1990 levels. Variable levies will fall at most by 60 percent over a period of three years; in some cases by only 30 percent. Outside the quota limits, however, for now full tariffs and levies remain in effect.

• Fourth, the transition economies must adopt EU competition policy within three years, during which GATT, and now WTO, rules will apply. For the first five years the countries will be regarded as 'backward areas' for EU purposes (article 92.3 of the Treaty of Rome, which permits some relaxation of competition rules). The Association Council, on which more below, is empowered to extend this period by another five years. The transition economies must also adopt the EU's policy on intellectual-property rights within five years, converge toward EU standards on environmental protection, and make best endeavors to approximate as closely as possible the other legal elements of the *acquis*. The chief negotiator for the EU of these agreements, Mr. Pablo Benavides, has characterized (quoted in Portes 1992, p. 4) achievement of the latter the equivalent of EU membership, save for the CAP. This is obviously political hyperbole. Given the complexity of the EU and the advantages of being a full insider as compared to being on the whole an outsider, as earlier amply demonstrated during the negotiations of the EEA agreement and the subsequent desire of key EFTA members to seek full entry into the EU, abiding by legal prescriptions *per se* can at best be one component of accession, not necessarily the most attractive one. I return to this important issue in the next two chapters.

- Fifth, products from the transition economies will remain subject to key provisions of the EU's protection policy. As noted, many anti-dumping and safeguard clauses have been retained in the agreements even for products that have been or soon will be completely liberalized. Moreover, the EU appears to be using a criterion for assessing the imposition of punitive measures that is not quite appropriate. Rather than referring to the purported foreign-price undercutting, a more acceptable rule could and should be utilized (for details, see Vanden-bussche 1996). Even if a more appropriate rule were utilized, it would still be quite unfortunate that these clauses are rather vague, hinging as they do on 'serious deterioration' in the economic situation of an 'EU region,' whose extent itself is left undefined. These escape rules are perhaps most ominous for 'orthodox sensitive' products, as enumer-ated earlier. But there is nothing in principle to prevent the EU from denominating other goods as 'sensitive' if it deems that 'its market' in some region has been seriously impaired. I am not inferring that the EU will in fact be deliberately restrictive. But having reserved for itself the right to invoke this option at any time and under any pretext of its own choosing, an unnecessarily large element of uncertainty pertains to the contingent protectionism embedded in the Europe Agreement and more generally in the relationship between the EU and transition economies. This unfortunate feature of the new relationship between the EU and the transition economies could – and should – have been forestalled from the outset. It should now be removed soonest (see Chapter 6).

- Sixth, no special provisions for labor mobility are included, other than that 'essential' personnel (managers, supervisors, staff personnel, highly qualified workers, and professionals) in case of outward FDI from the eastern part of Europe can be mobile. But individual EU Member States can contract bilaterally, particularly for skilled workers from transition economies. This provision, together with the rules embodied in the agreements in case of inward FDI into the EU from the transition economies, may encourage brain drain. Of course, it also permits the EU to ward off export of the factor – unskilled, manual, and related 'unessential' labor – in which the transition economies have a surfeit. This provision needs probably to be seen fully within the context of the EU's struggle with severe unemployment problems as well as resentment against the rapid influx of aliens more generally.

• Seventh, the agreements contain strong provisions to encourage and protect FDI from EU members in the transition economies. As regards financial cooperation in official flows, the agreements do not incorporate special stipulations, but they potentially provide the framework within which the assistance programmed under the PHARE program will be conceived and executed (see Chapter 6 for some suggestions on how this clause might be exploited more fruitfully). There is also some promise to the effect that the EU may favorably consider further assistance, if necessary, to support currency convertibility or to buttress economic restructuring or prop up the balance of payments (Chavagnac 1993, Slim 1993).

• Finally, instruments are put in place to maintain a "structured political dialogue" between the Community and each transition economy, chiefly through the so-called Association Council, a bilateral organ between the EU and each 'associated' transition economy. This will reevaluate the agreements after five years' experience. Because these Councils are not particularly structured, the transition economies could usefully propose that they be transformed into a uniform organ if only to mount more cohesive and positive agitation for meaningful reform of the Europe Agreement, looking toward the future of membership rather than the past hazardous approach to rendering assistance.

But for that to make sense, the transition economies will evidently have to come to grips more constructively with their joint problems, mobilizing political will and foresight, so that they can act credibly together, in spite of the historical legacies of "internationalism" under communism and of romantic notions about who is more advanced with democracy and market building, and can thus the sooner lodge a more credible claim for full Union membership. Perhaps some agitation on the part of the European Union to work toward this organ as a vehicle for promoting intragroup cooperation among the transition economies themselves could be highly constructive as well (Bempt 1993), in spite of general apathy on the part of some decision makers from economies in transition. That sentiment was very pronounced at the start of the transitions, and it has only slowly been receding under the weight of the transformation's burdens (see Chapter 6).

4 – Beyond the Europe Agreement

Rather than simply bemoaning the 'withholding' of outright member-ship, however regrettable that may be when seen from a political or narrowly-defined strategic perspective, it would be useful to take the Europe Agreement as a given for now and look ahead toward the future by assembling positive proposals on what can reasonably be done with the instruments, including financial transfers, in place. Such a positive stance, in my view, would be far preferable to the cheap carping about being kept out of the EU because the latter is allegedly not ready, or willing, to cope with transition economies. The Associa-tion Council, particularly if multilateralized for most purposes, could, in fact, become the chief mediator between the Union and the transition economies. It would permit the latter to articulate a more constructive commercial policy, and perhaps assistance approach toward working with the Union, instead of pursuing the rather fruitless course of insist-ing on immediate full and almost unconditional membership or attaining access to a free-trading area, let alone a free labor market for Europe-ans, of course! It would also provide a forum within which the EU could dispense its assistance, advice, and surveillance to ensure that intragroup cooperation be meaningfully exploited as a force to *acceler-ate* the stage at which credible accession applications can be lodged and deliberated about. That would be an act of statecraft in spite of the lingering skeptical view (see Chapter 6) that any interim arrangement deters from moving into 'Europe.'

The agreements are now widely expected to lead up to eventual membership in the EU, as first intimated at the Copenhagen Council in June 1993. This really momentous change in political posturing is likely to be enshrined in any revision of the original Europe Agreement. But the criteria regarding if and when the conditions for entry will have been met are as yet quite unclear (see Chapter 5). Membership is in any case a long way off and in the meantime the Europe Agreement offers a means of managed liberalization, not just trade liberalization, perhaps in anticipation of full membership. Whether it reasonably provides the best offer that the EU could have proffered and the transition econo-mies could have legitimately hoped for are two quite different matters, of course.

All things considered, the beneficial economic nature of these agreements, as distinct from the political and psychological gains they undoubtedly impart, should not be exaggerated; neither should it be downplayed, however. Improved access to developed-country markets, in the first instance in western Europe, is pivotal to successful transformation, particularly for the smaller transition economies. In that sense, lowering tariff barriers and removing some quantitative restrictions rank among the most crucial forms of assistance that developed nations can extend to the transition economies; on balance, it is also the least costly (see Chapter 6). However, for a number of key products, as observed, market access, including in the EU and EFTA, is still being regulated through quantitative means, although this has been constrained by much less rigidity over time and all quotas on manufactured products will be eliminated by the end of 1997; clauses amounting to contingent protectionism remain in effect, however. In the case of the EU arrangements, 'sensitive' products, including agriculture and fisheries, but also some of the enumerated sensitive manufactures, are dealt with separately in annexes to the protocols. Now, it so happens that these 'sensitive' products account for a substantial share of the exports of the transition economies to the EU (between one third and one half, as detailed in UNECE 1992, pp. 79-81; there has apparently been little change since in the importance of these products, as detailed in UNECE 1996a, pp. 110-17). They happen to be for now the products in which most transition economies hold a comparative advantage and could quickly raise their export volume.

6 – A Strategic Approach?

Recognizing the shortcomings in its approach to assisting the economies in transition, especially those with a Europe Agreement, the Corfu Council of June 1994 proposed that a "pre-accession strategy" be formulated for these countries (European Commission 1995g), a subject on which work had already been under way in the European Commission from earlier that year (see Vrbetić 1995). It became more urgent following the decision to pursue the extension of the EU toward the ten economies in transition with a Europe Agreement, as well as

Cyprus and Malta, following the conclusions of the ongoing IGC, at the Essen Council in December 1994.

The Essen Council, as a result, called for a broader 'pre-accession strategy' to be elaborated by the European Commission. This proposes a structured multilateral dialogue, including at the ministerial level, between the economies in transition with a Europe Agreement and the EU's institutions in order to deliberate about matters of common interest. The importance of convergence in juridical matters was also underlined. With that in mind the Commission prepared for the Cannes Council (26-27 June 1995) a White Paper on the "minimum alignment" of essential EU legislation (the core parts of the *acquis*) that the applicants for EU membership are advised to have in place soonest and mostly prior to accession, and which they must be able to apply in practice (European Commission 1995f). But the claimants can do so at their own discretion as the White Paper is purely advisory. It is indeed up to potential applicants for membership to respond, including by availing themselves of the special center for technical assistance on the *acquis*, officially Technical Assistance Information Exchange Office, that the Commission set up following the finalization of the White Paper; it became operational in January 1996, though the transition economies seem a bit perplexed as to how best to avail themselves of this service. The pre-accession strategy also suggests measures to enhance trade, chiefly through the promotion of foreign investment, but also through the cumulation of rules of origin. Finally, it addresses a range of related economic and other issues for cooperation (including the environment, nuclear safety, energy, transport, agriculture, regional development, social policy, culture, and science and technology).

The principal purpose of the EU's pre-accession strategy is to create "mutual confidence through a framework ("structured relations") of regular, well-prepared political contacts with the associated countries" (European Commission 1996g). Another European Commission source (1995h, p. 11) has termed it to "consist of progressively integrating the [transition economies] into the internal market ... by harmonizing their legislation to that of the [EU]."

Indeed, the EU's pre-accession strategy in the spring of 1996 officially encompassed eleven sets of actions (European Commission 1996g), the vast majority of which were already put in place as part of

earlier assistance programs (Balázs 1996). I count nine: (1) the structured political dialogue in the context of the Europe Agreement; (2)
short- to medium-term measures preparing for competition in the
internal European market, ranging from reductions in tariffs on clothing
and textiles to adjusting laws and regulatory regimes in the beneficiary
countries; (3) stimulating investment inflows from the EU; (4) cooperation in, and alignment on, some aspects of the CFSP; (5) police cooperation; (6) cooperation in environmental policies and legislation; (7)
planning the coordination of pan-European transportation networks;
(8) strengthening cooperation in education, youth, and cultural affairs;
and (9) stimulating intraregional cooperation among the economies in
transition, including moves toward a free-trading area (for some of the
details as seen by an EU insider, see Cameron 1996a).

But the other two are genuinely new, and are symptomatic for the
evolving climate for relations between the EU and the transition economies: (1) examination by the Commission of the impact of the CAP and
of alternative approaches to integrating their agriculture and (2) use of
PHARE resources to help the economies in transition with their assimilation and implementation of the essential components of the *acquis.*
The current discussion (*Financial Times*, 17 June 1996, p. 18) about
allowing participation in policy debates around the second and third
pillars and about creating some kind of partial-membership status for
transition economies disappointed by the European Commission's
"finding" that the earliest accession date would be the year 2002 perhaps belongs in this 'new' category as well. But there is insufficient
detail to explore this further at this stage

This suggests that this so-called strategy was primarily meant to
pull together various strands of assistance already practiced and focus
them more explicitly on facilitating the accession of the ten economies
with a Europe Agreement. Various matters have already been tabled,
including on the *acquis* and its White Paper with detailed suggestions;
the assessment of the impact of the CAP and its alternatives on the
EU's budget with another enlargement; and an evaluation of the impact
of enlargement on various other Union policies. These documents and
assessments were discussed most recently at the Madrid Council in
December 1995 and the Florence Council in June 1996, and will be
taken up in later Councils too (European Commission 1995e).

Although the initiative to formulate a pre-accession strategy is to be welcomed, the contours and impacts of what has emerged to date are far more limited than what would seem to be desirable and what had been intimated as being the purpose of the decision taken in Essen (Ludlow 1996a, pp. 23ff.). On the strength of the evidence available to me, I have the unmistakable impression that the EU has been more concerned about clarifying for itself what the further enlargement toward the eastern part of Europe may entail than about facilitating such an enlargement for the applicants. This in itself is a welcome development, of course. Yet, at the same time, this narrower focus is a real pity, given the wide range and the complexity of the issues that will have to be considered when real negotiations for accession get under way. Not only that, there is widespread agreement on the fact that the contacts at the highest political level in areas such as foreign policy, finance, agriculture, and transportation have been less than effective and frequently shunned on the part of EU ministers; some of the discussions have been reported as sterile (see Chapter 6), and even in the words of a rather optimistic observer "[t]heir utility is, admittedly, at the moment limited partly because they are still seen as adjuncts to, rather than part of, the main Council meetings, and partly too because ... they are organised more as talking shops" (Ludlow 1996a, p. 23). The European Parliament, among many other observers, in its so-called Oostlander Report (named after the Rapporteur, Arie Oostlander) has recently called upon the European Commission to finally put together a fully-fledged accession strategy (NZZ 1996b, Southey 1996), though the Commission has interpreted this to mean that it has been invited "to set up a minimum criteria [sic!] in respect of the accession and to report regularly on the progress achieved by the candidate countries in individual sectors" (European Commission 1996m, pp. 13-14).

In considering improvements in the EU's assistance stance, particularly in the light of the multiple tasks ahead in expediting new accessions and in forging a more constructive relationship with other countries, the central question is whether the above pre-transition strategy is adequate for assisting the claimants to accession in their efforts to master the difficulties that still lie ahead in the transformation process and whether the Europe Agreements provide adequate support for such a strategy. The answers are not self-evident. While the initiatives have been welcomed, including by most of the leading policy makers in the transition economies, many observers have been disappointed about the continuing absence of, even by way of aspiration, a comprehensive and coherent strategy pursued by the EU (Gautron 1995, p. 109).

With transition and assistance efforts now in their seventh year, such a strategic approach, including the formulation and implementation of a clearly laid-out strategy, has yet to be developed. However, something better still needs to – and can realistically – be worked out in order to really assist the economies in transition, especially those that wish to join the EU, in the near future and to ensure that the reciprocal adjustments of the two parts of the continent in a unified Europe occur at a tolerable cost with a reasonable distribution of the benefits for all concerned. Many other economies in transition (perhaps up to 18 out of 27) will eventually want to join the EU. I arrive at this number as follows: The Central Asian successor States of the Soviet Union will probably not qualify because they are not really in Europe. It is difficult to envision Russia as a member of the EU, and it may not even desire such a position. The Caucasian successor States of the Soviet Union other than Azerbaijan could conceivably qualify if only because of the western Christian heritage of Armenia and Georgia.

The critical question is, however, defining the path leading up to becoming a credible candidate for accession. That should be one of the crucial issue in appreciating and revising the Union's policies toward the transition economies. If such a membership will eventually be accommodated, it is of the utmost importance that EU decision makers already now put in place the conditions to permit another enlargement toward the east (as well as the south), and that will also make it easier for all concerned to consummate such a remaking of Europe.

Conclusions

I readily admit that the preceding provides a rather critical analysis of what the EU has accomplished since 1989 and what it has failed to undertake. I am by far not alone in airing this pessimistic view (for details, see Brabant 1995a, pp. 421ff.). However, I regard these experiences, as well as the tasks ahead when contemplating the entry of the eastern part of Europe into 'Europe,' as providing an impetus for reviewing what is in place and reflecting upon what could prospectively be improved, and how best to undertake this task, by and large at given resource constraints.

Looking carefully at what has been crystallizing in relations between the EU and the countries of the eastern part of Europe since 1989, one can hardly be sanguine about there being a well thought-out strategy in place to facilitate expeditiously and comprehensively the accession of the economies in transition into the EU. That is not to say that the assistance provided since 1989 has been derisory. Quite the contrary: It has been magnanimous and varied. However, had it been conceived from within a more coherent, hands-on, and dovetailed approach toward helping the eastern part of Europe in overcoming the negative effects of the unprecedented transformations under way, even with the funds actually appropriated much better results could have been attained. With additional funding, obviously other transformation matters could have been targeted.

Again, some waste and overlap and errors were unavoidable. But the European Commission should have been in a position to draw useful lessons earlier and forge ahead with a more strategic approach the moment it realized the uniqueness of what was at stake in the eastern part of Europe: an opportunity to remake Europe.

5

Accession of Economies in Transition

The Turin Extraordinary European Council, held on 29 March 1996, in evaluating the future enlargement of the Union, stated that while it represents "a historic mission and a great opportunity for Europe, [it] is also a challenge for the Union in all its dimensions. In this perspective, institutions, as well as their functioning, and procedures have to be improved in order to preserve [the EU's] capacity for action, while maintaining the "acquis communautaire" and developing it, and also respecting the balance between institutions" (European Commission 1996d, p. 1). John Major, however, on reporting to the Commons after his return from that Council stated that the IGC's principal purpose was "to prepare for enlargement" (United Kingdom 1996b, p. 1). This in a nutshell sums up the great chasm about 'Europe' prevailing at this juncture. And again the grand debate on "deepening versus widening," but largely for tactical rather than strategic reasons, is at the very core of the matter at hand.

Accession to the EU is not a simple thing by any means. It most certainly cannot be accommodated automatically in response to a political decision. Views held by leading policy makers and their advisers in the economies in transition to the effect that everything in the EU turns around politics (Inotai 1994) are erroneous and not very helpful in coming to grips with the complexity of functioning on the terms that delineate the arena of the single market and increasingly of other areas of common EU endeavors. Anyone who has spent some time studying the experience gathered with earlier accessions will probably subscribe to this assertion without much further ado. Whereas some concessions may be granted to the most credible applicants among the economies in transition, historical opportunity or moral obligations, if such justifications are more than a band-aid, are unlikely to overcome the nitty-gritty of ascertaining whether and how an applicant can function reasonably well at least within the context of the single market, as the recent debate on the EU's White Paper for the economies in transition (European Commission 1995f) has amply demonstrated.

This chapter clarifies the core issues to be tackled on the road to full membership, while I gather here as much pertinent information as possible pertaining to the eventual deliberations between the Union and one or more transition economies. First, I sketch the essence of integration into Europe's single market. Then I discuss the rationale that might motivate the EU to seek another enlargement at this juncture and why the transition economies would wish to expedite such an overture. Thereafter I entertain the much heated debate about the criteria determining suitability for accession. Next I sketch the parameters of generic accession negotiations, drawing on as much relevant material as possible for the economies in transition. This is followed by some speculation about the economics and politics of accession negotiations, the date of entry, and the key elements of the transition phase. Before concluding, I flag up very briefly the backdrop to the potential shape of a strategy that could be formulated already now, well before the initiation of substantive accession negotiations. The strategy itself I discuss in detail in Chapter 6.

1 – The Essence of the Single Market

Given that most economies in transition are at the present juncture still fledgling democracies, that the rudiments of a well-functioning market economy are not yet complete, and that nearly all of these countries have a level of economic development, as measured by per capita income, that is low not only in comparison with the EU's average but even with the lowest income in the Union, excepting perhaps Slovenia, the prospect of the accession of a number of transition economies gives rise to a wide range of economic and political concerns. Some are very complicated indeed and their dimension cannot be confined to the so-called political economy of accession when that is understood in the narrow sense of how various competing interest groups within the present Union might be affected by newcomers (for a punctuated example, see Bofinger 1995). Neither is it particularly illuminating to portray western Europe's dynamics in terms of competition among governments (see Corbey 1995). For my tastes, that approach itself suffers from the inadequacies of the postulated, rather nebulous, anthropomorphic concept of national government. Integration in the EU, in my view, has been driven by many more competing interest groups (Garret and Tsebelis 1996), however an academic may wish to streamline that experience for the purpose of fitting some *a priori* theory of governmental behavior. Precisely such complexity, rather than academic reductivism, ought to inform the debate around whether and when to admit the economies in transition as full members and how best to proceed with fashioning a constructive relationship in the interim or indeed for those that will never become a member.

In short, then, 'Europe' has never been solely about dollars(or ecus, and soon euros) and cents. Indeed, the EU's greatest achievement is neither free trade nor regional economic cooperation. Rather, it is the interlacing of economic and monetary policies into the single-market concept, to be complemented at a later stage with further interlinkages in the social and political arenas, into a common and coherent civil society that forms the foundation stone of a federative democracy (Woyke 1993, p. 375). Some commentators interested in European integration, particularly those raised in the utilitarian Anglo-American tradition, may find it disconcerting to think in terms of broad-ranging categories, and indeed somewhat ill-defined ambitions (Brown 1993), of which the economic dimension forms but one component. As such what the European Union has been all about, albeit with fits and spurts, and with a European backdrop in particular, does not neatly blend in with their, largely materialistic, approaches to economic integration. But without fully heeding the apparent desire of the vocal part of Europe to emphasize the 'advantages' of European unification in addition to evaluating the presumed gains in terms of incremental value added accruing therefrom one can at best scratch the surface of the variables determining the integration movement, including its setbacks.

The costs and benefits for members, for potential EU entrants, and for nonmembers alike constitute formidable obstacles to a rapid and full accession of the economies in transition. Simply put: Under present governance and transfer mechanisms, the EU cannot afford an early accession of the transition economies, especially the larger, poorer, and more agrarian ones. This is true not only when reference is made to the potential net aggregate claim of these candidates for entry on the EU's resources, but also when the asymmetries, in time as well as across countries, for members and entrants alike, of all the costs and benefits of another enlargement are factored into the accession equation.

Likewise, whether the transition economies are entirely ready to bear the full cost of 'regular accession' at a price that their societies will be prepared to support, and not just limited to the material costs of assimilating the *acquis*, is by no means self-evident. Even if the transition economies are ostensibly inclined to shoulder the cost of EU accession in principle, disregarding access to net transfers from the Union, it is not at all clear whether, on balance, they stand to benefit economically in the short to medium run from full accession at an early date. But the longer-term advantages, even if confined to the economic calculus, are likely to be quite palpable indeed.

In estimating the short run costs and benefits, considerable weight must be given to the fact that these countries are hardly ready for unbridled competition in the European single market subject to the host of regulations that form constituent, indeed essential, parts thereof. The heart of European economic integration is vibrant competition in intra-industry trade with a highly specialized and sophisticated division of labor in the production and distribution of manufactures and, increasingly, of services. Thus far, economies in transition have at best moved rather slowly, with a great deal of hesitation and circumspection, toward participating at the fringes of the core market of the EU. National economic policies do not yet appear to have paid much attention to fostering such a capability of competing for the heart of business in the EU. Indeed, promoting intra-industry trade does not seem to have been high on the policy agenda of the reform leadership up to now. If full competition within the single market, after early accession, were to relegate more and more economic activities in the transition economies toward low-productivity and low value-added manufacturing, let alone toward agriculture and mining, membership of the EU would not be very attractive, either to most of the present EU Member States or to the potential entrants.

Furthermore, the assimilation of some of the EU's regulatory regimes, including those with respect to health, safety, labor, environmental, and social issues, may turn out to be quite costly for the transition economies, especially in the short run, in that their application, once approved, will erode some of the temporarily acquired comparative advantages in EU markets deriving from less stringent regulations than those that generally prevail in western Europe. These comparative advantages, rather than specialization in genuine intra-industry trade, have been behind the export-led domestic economic recovery in most economies (Lengyel 1995; UNECE 1996a, pp. 53ff.). These countries urgently need to sustain their economic recovery and extend it onto a durable, high-level growth path. Only walking along the latter trajectory for a protracted period of time (at least a decade) will enable these countries to catch up with the levels of income, productivity, technological sophistication, and so on, prevailing at least in the relatively less developed Member States of the Union.

Most serious economic observers of the scene in the eastern part of Europe continue to be reluctant to affirm that the recent output and productivity gains in the economies in transition can be interpreted as indicating that any one of these countries is already finding itself on a self-sustainable, catch-up trajectory. In all likelihood such a process of accelerating growth to a high level and sustaining it for years, if successful, will eventually lead to the abandonment of the temporary advantages deriving from low resource and/or labor costs, and less stringent regulatory regimes, as price adjustments are made and EU regulations enforced. New lines of comparative advantage will then need to be already in place. That is to say, to avoid potential marginalization, these new, dynamic comparative advantages must be created while the catch-up process is under way, and preferably as early in the process as possible to generate rents, thus resources to sustain steady growth in the longer term.

However, the economies in transition do not want to join the EU only to reap economic benefits. They also covet it to strengthen their security, to enhance their political credibility, and to support their transformation agendas. Likewise, the EU is not simply interested in accommodating accession in order to extend the economic remit of the single market. Surely, it is motivated by the potential benefits of free trade and capital mobility in intra-industrial activities and, increasingly, in financial markets, in a much wider geographical area; but it also has a major interest in the security and political stability of the eastern part of Europe. In other words, it is appropriate to address the questions of when, how, and at what cost the accessions of the transition economies can realistically be contemplated within a rather broad political-economy framework. That approach needs to encompass many issues other than the impact of accession on trade, on the displacement of workers in the EU, on competition, and so on, however valuable studies in those domains (such as the highly informative collection of sectoral studies in Faini and Portes 1995) may be.

2 – The Rationale for Another Expansion

As earlier indicated, from the very inception of the political transformations of the late 1980s many of the economies in transition have sought to gain entry into the EU at the earliest opportunity. The Member States of the EU, and the European Commission itself, have been proceeding rather cautiously in considering the merits of new accessions ever since, even though the principle of another enlargement, including toward the eastern part of Europe, has been fully accepted since mid 1993, notably at the Copenhagen European Council. This hesitancy suggests that the interests of the EU in enlargement and those of the transition economies are not quite concordant. It is important to be fully aware of these differences for they are bound to influence the tone and conduct of accession negotiations.

Unfortunately these interests, particularly of the EU, are not well defined. They are certainly not clearly spelled out in anything like a strategy for moving forward with integration and enlargement. Moreover, the various interests are spread out over ecological, health, economic, political, security, strategic, and other domains. Attaching a realistic weight to qualitative assessments in order to assess priorities or reach an aggregate benefit-cost calculus is by no means easy.

1 – The View of the Economies in Transition

It is perhaps easier to identify the principal interests of the economies in transition. Quite apart from "rejoining Europe," they have assiduously sought entry into the EU for economic, political, and security reasons; cultural, scientific, educational, and other interests are also at stake, but these I shall leave aside here, without minimizing their intrinsic importance in what has been afoot in Europe since 1989 (see Chapter 6). Given the fragility of the political situation in the area since the dissolution of the Warsaw Pact and the widespread apathy toward any old or new regional economic or security arrangements, even if supported by the EU or other international groupings, the preference of policy makers in eastern Europe for seeking closer affiliation with 'western' institutions appears to be straightforward. If the EU had succeeded in strengthening its second pillar (that is, the CFSP with the elaboration of the WEU as a European defense force for membership in the EU and WEU is not identical), EU affiliation would have been a natural objective of many of the smaller transition economies as an anchor for their security. Without a strong second pillar, however, it is offhand not clear whether the EU can meet such expectations. The EU's experience in the former Yugoslavia offers a stark reminder of what can go awry and how fragile the EU's stance on these foreign policy, defense, and security matters intrinsically remains.

Strengthening the credibility of transformation policies constitutes a second set of preoccupations. Given the considerable costs of transformation, not just in terms of output forgone but also in terms of dislocations, increasing inequalities of income and wealth, and a considerable exacerbation of personal and economic insecurity (*qua* incomes, jobs, pensions, medical care, personal security, access to basic services, and so on), it is at times crucial for policy makers in the transition economies to gain the approval and support of key policy makers in 'successful' market economies. This is all the more important since convergence toward the minimum criteria for EU accession (see below) is bound to inflict further costs, and these will have to be borne mostly before the more tangible benefits of EU accession materialize.

Closer affiliation with the EU provides access to sources of finance for the reconstruction of eastern Europe, with official grants or loans paving the way for the inflow of private capital flows. Because the European Commission was chosen as a critical coordinator and deliverer of assistance to the transition economies, as reported in Chapter 4, building and maintaining good relations with the EU can provide a 'seal of approval' for policies that are domestically unpopular, and are likely to remain so for some time. This shift in popular sentiment can be traced rather well from the opinion surveys that, since the fall of 1990, have been regularly monitored in *Eurobarometer*, a publication sponsored by the European Commission. This has underlined several important developments among the wider layers of these societies, including with respect to the EU but also vacillating appreciation of and support for domestic policies.

Undoubtedly a major interest of the economies in transition at present lies in the broad area of economics. It is here that access to markets in the EU, which does not necessarily require full membership, is a critical factor. Market access in the first place for the present exportables of the economies in transition, never mind how long that comparative advantage will hold up, is crucial for various reasons. It is arguably no more so than in propping up demand for products coming from an area that has been going through a wrenching socioeconomic depression, in terms of both its depth and breadth. The demand from western Europe for products from eastern Europe has been playing an important role, among others, in supporting aggregate demand in virtually all of the more successful transition economies, by imparting a greater degree of confidence in transformation policies; by strengthening the conditions for a resumption of domestic investment, largely on the basis of domestic savings; and by supporting the fledgling private sector. In time these factors will undoubtedly help to mitigate social discontent aroused by the adverse accompanying effects of transformation policies. Successive issues of *Eurobarometer*, now already the sixth released in March 1996 (European Commission 1996j), have shown a close relationship between growth and popular support for further transformation policies. Moreover, easing the relationship with the EU should strengthen the inflow of private capital, though in some countries a too rapid expansion thereof, as in recent months, can be a decidedly mixed blessing. Finally, smooth relations with the EU as an organization forms part and parcel of the integration of the economies in transition into the global economic framework.

Formal accession to the EU, at least in the first few years, will not add too many additional elements to those listed above which, it should be recalled, the transition economies have been benefiting from. More is potentially available with even closer affiliation with the EU, short of membership. The obstacles to market access for some 'sensitive products,' notably in agriculture, would, however, be reduced and the dangers associated with contingent protectionism for other 'sensitive products' (such as textiles, clothing, footwear, iron and steel, automobiles, some chemicals, and so on), for which quotas will be completely abolished at the end of 1997, would end. Labor migration from the economies in transition would in all likelihood become feasible only after a protracted adjustment period. The same applies to accessing the full benefits of the EU's transfer programs (see Section 4).

Perhaps the single largest economic benefit for the transition economies would come from a firm commitment to eventual EU membership: Based on a credible accession strategy, it would hold both the EU and the potential entrant(s) to observing, and meeting, closely-monitored convergence criteria, as explained in Chapter 6, and could inspire much greater confidence on the part of economic agents, including foreign investors. Such a blueprint would contribute to reducing the still pervasive economic, political, and social uncertainty in the transition economies. The prospect of becoming EU rule-bound economies, including in due course the adoption of well-known rules of rectitude in the area of monetary affairs, could only enhance matters. Such a development would enable foreign investors to configure the potential entrants as part and parcel of the 'single market' in their longer-term investment and distribution strategies. There is little doubt, as the recent fillip to growth in some transition economies underlines, that being included within the global strategies of international companies imparts considerable benefits, especially economies of scale and scope, and integration into the mainstream of buoyant intra-industry trade.

A more effective allocation of the resources at hand, and indeed of those prospectively available, across and within sectors and regions in the economies in transition to exploit economies of scale and scope, given the still distorted nature of resource allocation, should provide a significant, positive impetus to growth based on technical and allocative efficiency gains. As explained, it could also strengthen the basis for identifying a catch-up strategy based on dynamic efficiency gains, which will be critical to facilitating access to the EU, if only by compressing membership costs.

Economic recovery and sustainable growth at a rather high rate are desirable in themselves, if only because they help to satisfy widely-held popular expectations of gaining soon improvements in levels of living, particularly if the benefits of economic expansion were shared fairly widely. But it would also ensure steady convergence between the potential entrants and the average level of development in the EU. Such a narrowing of the gap between the EU's capabilities and those of the eastern part of Europe would, then, facilitate the eventual accession of transition economies into the EU. Although the alpha and omega of entry into the EU is not solely about budgetary effects, as I underline later in Section 4 in particular, such a narrowing of the budgetary implications of eastern accession would be most welcome, just the same, if only because the costs of adjustment would be reduced, both for the entrant and the present EU membership.

The potential gains from a rapid expansion of trade are considerable. However, offhand it is not clear whether the recent growth in exports provides a firm basis for predicting further steady economic gains (see UNECE 1996a, pp. 159ff.). There are good reasons to argue that, with some exceptions, the economies in transition do not yet possess the capabilities of inserting themselves smoothly into the dynamic process of intra-industry trade, notably in manufactures, that constitutes the backbone of economic growth in the EU and indeed in nearly all industrial countries. The recent growth obtained in most of the more western economies in transition continues to be fragile. It has been bolstered primarily by labor- and resource-intensive exports and pent-up domestic consumer demand rather than strong gains in productive investments and restructuring. The latter will be required to carve out dynamic comparative advantages, in part by inserting these economies more fully into the international division of labor notably in intra-industry trade.

That dynamic, I submit, will determine the size and distribution of the economic benefits of participating in Europe's single market. But I do not see them solely by the trade creation-diversion calculus nor by other economic benefits (Olson 1984, pp. 118ff.). The contribution to growth of direct net trade gains has historically been assessed as being surprisingly small (Brabant 1995a, pp. 38-46). Far more important, I contend, is the impetus to expansion deriving from the greater certainty imparted by a transparent, rule-bound regime applicable to a vast area with a substantial demand of some 370 million consumers; with eastern accessions the market's size may expand to some 470 million souls.

It is important to bear in mind that accession to the EU entails not only benefits, which may be substantial for successful transition economies, but also costs. It is impossible to list all of them here without assessing them for individual applicants. But it may be useful to look, at least qualitatively, at five such costs.

• First, full adoption of EU competition policies is bound to expose the more fragile and marginal economic entities, especially those in the process of restructuring, to competition that may drive them prematurely out of business. Inasmuch as the economies in transition *must* make significant headway with economic restructuring and with the acquisition of robust capacities to compete in intra-industry trade, particularly in manufactures, there may be need for some degree of protection that would be simply incompatible with the *acquis*. This is one cogent reason for forging ahead as rapidly as possible with industrial restructuring before entry into the EU.

• Second, agriculture throughout the transition economies has been weakened in general by transition policies, and especially by the destruction of the cooperative infrastructure before new distribution networks, for inputs as well as outputs, could be innovated. In some countries, Poland in particular, agriculture suffers from rural overpopulation and low productivity. The transition economies will therefore have to face something quite similar to the painful restructuring of agriculture that took place in parts of western Europe, the Benelux in particular, in the 1950s and 1960s. This will cost money before the productivity gains obtained in wide swaths of the economy will begin to alleviate matters. Fears that agriculture will lose from competition within the EU are widespread (European Commission 1996j).

• Third, converging toward the Maastricht criteria for admission to the monetary union is by no means a costless exercise, as the recent debates in western Europe have underlined. The more advanced transition economies have made significant progress in correcting public-sector deficits, lowering inflation, and ensuring exchange-rate stability and currency convertibility. However, in many countries capital mobility needs to be further liberalized to conform to EU standards, and both interest and inflation rates brought down to much lower levels than would seem to be feasible at the present time without nipping in the bud the recovery of output, still incipient in many cases, and exacerbating the already calamitous employment situation in many countries. In some, Hungary in particular, levels of public-sector debt are too high to be brought down quickly to the convergence criterion.

True, joining monetary union is *not* a precondition for joining the Union; at least not yet. But it is safe to assume that the members of the monetary union will insist upon fairly demanding macroeconomic convergence policies in other Member States, including new entrants, as the discussion in Chapter 3 has underlined. Like the ERM II's provisions currently under debate, new entrants will probably be held to strict performance criteria in order to permit convergence toward the preconditions for monetary union, *de facto* or *de jure*, within a specified period of time. Otherwise distortions to competition in the single market would be introduced, thereby exacerbating tensions between those acting from within the monetary union and others.

• Fourth, introducing the regulatory framework of the *acquis*, notably as regards standards for health, the environment, safety, and social conditions, is bound to be very costly. The present comparative advantages of some of the economies in transition will partly be eroded, as discussed. Whether it is wise to impose such costs on economies whose economic recovery is still fragile, is obviously a matter of judgment for policy makers. But the alternative policy options should be carefully set out and weighed before pointed decisions are taken.

• Finally, membership of the EU will inflict a costly budgetary burden. There will be a loss in customs receipts because of the elimination of tariffs within the new Union and of lowering the external tariff to that of the Union; and the assistance programs in place, PHARE in particular, will be discontinued. These losses may be small in relation to the benefits and other costs mentioned above, but several billion dollars are at stake and that cannot simply be ignored.

2 – *The View of the Member States of the EU*

The interests of the EU in bringing the transition economies into its fold are also spread over a number of economic, political, and security areas. But there are palpable differences. For one thing, the relative weights of these considerations differ markedly between the EU and a potential entrant(s) from eastern Europe. Also, the EU has other interests, such as in environmental, health, cultural diffusion, and foreign policy, that, at least for the present, would seem to carry a much lower priority in the ranking by policy makers of the transition economies.

There is clearly an asymmetry in the relations between the EU and the economies in transition. In marked contrast to the economic weight of the transition economies relative to the EU (the aggregate GDP of the ten transition economies with a Europe Agreement, which is not easily estimated because of severe data problems, may in 1995 have added up to at most some 8 percent of the EU's total GDP), the EU constitutes a vast and wealthy market for the economies in transition. Admittedly, having buoyant markets at the EU's eastern frontier at a time of slow growth within the Union may provide a welcome lift to aggregate demand, but for some time to come its effect on overall activity in the EU can only be marginal.

Much more important than the eventual trade benefits is that, at least initially, another enlargement is likely to impose considerable net costs on the present EU members and, in the first instance, that means on present net contributors to the EU's budget. But enlargement could also affect the present net beneficiaries. Not only would they lose in relative terms (because economies in transition would enter well below the average level of per capita GDP in the Union, even when reconfigured), it is not at all clear that the aggregate volume of transfer payments would be raised sufficiently to compensate losers to a politically acceptable degree.

In this connection, it is important to be clear how the costs and benefits are configured in the EU. Observers frequently confuse alternative ways of assessing GDP levels with the problem of estimating the impact of new members on the EU's transfer programs. The latter are unambiguously defined in terms of either prices (such as for many agricultural supports) or income levels (such as for the cohesion fund) calculated at prevailing commercial exchange rates, which are presumed to be market clearing. Purchasing-power parities, which diverge significantly from prevailing commercial exchange rates for nearly all transition economies, are a useful tool for assessing the size of the income gap to be closed. It is well established in the development literature that the difference between a currency's purchasing-power parity and its commercial exchange rate gradually declines as per capita income rises. For example, the ratio of purchasing-power parity to the market exchange rate in terms of local currency per unit of foreign currency, all normalized to the Austrian measures for 1993, ranges for the ten economies in transition for which point estimates are available (all data as reported in UNECE 1996b, p. 3) between 1.7 for Slovenia and 5.9 for Lithuania as compared to the EU Member States, where the range is between 0.9 for Denmark and 1.6 for Portugal; the comparable range for OECD members is between 0.7 for Japan and 2.2 for Turkey.

Even so, calculations based on purchasing-power parity are not relevant to assessing the potential cost to the EU's transfer programs of an eastern accession, except insofar as they may be justified in forecasting a "more realistic" path of income growth for the potential new entrants expressed in an international currency than the one calculated in the national currency (hopefully including firm estimates of the so-called second economy). The latter may be warranted on expectations that economic recovery and expansion in the economy in transition will impart a positive impetus to real appreciation of the local currency as a result of real productivity gains, thereby strengthening expectations of a faster rate of convergence toward average EU levels of income.

From a strictly *economic* point of view, then, unless there were to be a very rapid rate of convergence by the time of accession, the potential benefits for the EU from another enlargement do not seem to be very pronounced, certainly not in the short to medium term. However, the EU has much stronger interests from the perspective of, for example, environmental, health, political, and security issues. Some Member States are also keen on propagating their language and cultural heritage. Since environmental problems do not respect borders, and because the postwar pattern of industrial development in the former planned economies has left behind considerable ecological damage, the EU is naturally concerned about mitigating spillovers. It also has a vital interest in ensuring stability and predictability on its eastern border; indeed, this interest applies not just to the economies in transition with a Europe Agreement, but extends elsewhere (see Chapter 6). Finally, inasmuch as the EU seeks to project itself much more forcefully in international affairs, its foreign policy, once the CFSP comes fully into its own, can be better informed by having a close relationship with the economies in transition, particularly those that are the leading candidates for accession. If the WEU were to become fully integrated with the CFSP before the treaty's expiration in 1998, then the EU's security interests in the transition economies would rise appreciably.

Since the Copenhagen commitment to bringing into the EU up to ten economies in transition within the foreseeable future, the EU's stance has been, in the words of the decision of the Madrid Council in December 1995 (European Commission, 1995e, part III, p. 1), that "[e]nlargement is both a political necessity and a historic opportunity for Europe. It will ensure the stability and security of the continent and will thus offer both the applicant States and the current members of the Union new prospects for economic growth and general well-being. Enlargement must serve to strengthen the building of Europe in observance of the acquis communautaire which includes the common policies." When compared with the actions of the EU since 1990 (or even since mid 1992), as examined in Chapter 4, and even more with the daunting difficulties ahead, as examined in the next Section, this is sheer rhetorical hyperbole, devoid of a real base upon which the political necessity and the historical opportunity could be solidly grounded.

3 – Criteria for Membership

One of the major bones of contention in building up a firmer relationship between the economies in transition aspiring toward EU membership and the EU concerns the conditions to be met for submitting a serious membership application, which would then in due course lead to accession negotiations. This has been a constant refrain in claims made by the leadership of central Europe in particular. Some of them, notably Polish politicians, have been particularly insistent, sometimes quite forcefully, in demanding that the EU set a date for entry, perhaps in conjunction with detailing the conditions to be fulfilled by then.

I have serious doubts about proceeding in this manner. As discussed in the context of the EMU debate in Chapter 3, setting a firm date for the entry into the Union of any of the transition economies without associating it explicitly with a well-defined strategy on how to reach that deadline is not particularly useful. True, the politics of doing so may look quite different. Likewise, for the purpose of public relations and of inspiring the media, fixing such a date well ahead of time may be quite important. For a while it may even spark some useful energy into the credibility of the policies pursued by the leadership in place. But it hardly changes the nature of the daunting problems to be tackled head-on, and it is only once solutions for those obstacles are found that the entry date becomes a useful target.

This stance has recently found support, though probably for very different reasons than the considerations I have invoked here, in the examination of the White Paper for the transition economies (1995f) by the European Parliament (European Commission 1996m, n) on 17 April 1996 (NZZ 1996b, Southey 1996). Leading members of the Parliament have indeed stressed that one can realistically speak of ushering the more credible transition economies into the EU only after setting a viable strategy for preparing these countries for the open market and assimilating nearly all the existing rules and regulations, and indeed for acquiring the minimum administrative capabilities to do so. I agree with this thesis, though I suspect it was invoked more by way of politicking against those urging early membership for the central European countries in particular than by concerns about safeguarding the single market and averting negative repercussions for the new entrants.

As discussed in greater detail in Chapter 6, instead of spelling out conditions to be met by a certain target date, I deem it far preferable that the EU set forth in operational detail what has to be in place before entry *and* then assist the transition economies in their efforts to comply in as generous a manner as circumstances permit, both those complicating politics in the EU as well as those encumbering the delicate contours of the sovereignty debates in the economies in transition. The precise date of accession would then be determined when the potential entrant can fulfill all the elements of the negotiated strategy and the Union can live up to its end of the bargain as well. Indeed, compliance cannot be restricted to the applicant. As a result, setting forth such a strategy, monitoring it, and fine-tuning it to ensure that the strategy remains relevant can provide a crucial framework for organizing the

EU's activities as well, particularly those that have a bearing on the process of a further extension of the EU's geographical compass. It would provide a more coherent program for proceeding with pre-accession activities than what is now in place (see Chapter 4).

This suggestion for formulating a more productive and reliable strategy is all the more salient because, when all is said and done, there is no clear-cut checklist of entry conditions into the EU. The previous four rounds of widening the membership (in 1973 for Denmark, Ireland, and the United Kingdom; in 1981 for Greece; in 1986 for Portugal and Spain; and in 1995 for Austria, Finland, and Sweden) have clearly underlined this. That is to say, whereas there are some vague preconditions for lodging a credible application and the EU must be able to accommodate the new entrant, what precisely that entails in detail emerges only from the negotiations. By the latter's very nature the *ex post* criteria to be met are an amalgam of what can be specified before the start of the negotiations as well as the administrative, economic, political, security, and other considerations brought to bear during the deliberations, and how precisely members and applicants decide to go about heeding those quite subjective considerations.

Articles 237 of the Treaty of Rome and O of the Maastricht Treaty are clear on three issues: Acceptable candidates must be European, democratic, and have a clean record on human rights. However, this is not enough for lodging a credible application for accession. As demonstrated in earlier widening exercises, the applicant must not only be willing to live up to the *acquis communautaire*, and increasingly the *acquis communautaire et politique*, and demonstrate that the conditions for compliance are fully in place, and not just on the statute book; it must also be in a position to apply this compendium of rules and regulations in a reasonably effective manner. The question touches not only upon political will but also on the institutional, administrative, legal, and other capabilities to act on this effectively.

The Essen Council in December 1994, after lengthy discussions, stated the conditions for accession deriving from the EU's constitutional instruments and their interpretation; the Copenhagen Council had already done so more synoptically in mid 1993, once again demonstrating the evolving nature of the EU's attitude toward the eventual accession of the economies in transition. (The vacillating pronouncements on admission criteria are traced for the record in Økonomiministeriet 1996, pp. 27-31). No wonder they have created considerable confusion on the part of eastern European observers rather than, as EU leaders may have intended, illuminate the most important issues at stake! As an example, for as much as I know, arguably the most vituperative attack by a serious analyst against these stipulations, which he considers as being highly discriminatory, was formulated by Mr. András Inotai (1994, pp. 15-17). Note that he was then writing as Director of the Institute of World Economics of the Hungarian Academy of Sciences, but he is presently also the Hungarian Government's coordinator for preparing all ministries and administrations for accession negotiations with the EU.

At the Essen Council four criteria in particular were explicitly mentioned: stable democratic institutions; a viable market economy; a sufficient capacity to compete within the internal market; and the ability to subscribe fully to the political, economic, and monetary objectives of the Union (Gautron 1995, p. 109). These, as well as the conditions stipulated in the relevant Treaties, are not very precise. No wonder they have led to considerable confusion among observers in particular from the applicant countries. Thus Mr. Inotai believes the above stipulations to be discriminatory precisely because he contends that the only formal accession criterion applied in earlier enlargement exercises was that the applicant must be European. He also believes that virtually all previous accessions have been engineered solely on political grounds (Inotai 1994, pp. 15-17), that is, without any reference whatsoever to economic criteria. I shall try to dispel this notion in what follows. Without a clearer understanding of what precisely is at stake, regardless of the imputed historical or moral obligations incumbent on the EU, the relationship with economies in transition in general, and negotiations for accession in particular, cannot but be needlessly complicated. And this should be avoided at all cost.

It might therefore be instructive to examine more closely the various pronouncements on democracy and on a market-based economy as fundamental preconditions for accession in order to identify more clearly what seems to be at stake. In this context, one could legitimately also speculate about the definition of 'Europe' in the EU context. I have given my view on the most likely eastern border of the EU in Introduction. I shall not further elaborate on that here. But I do want to present views on the official conditions to be met beyond the rather vague stipulations – indeed at times conjectural and subjective evaluations – cited earlier.

To obtain some guidance it is useful to look at the EU's legal foundations, the rules 'revealed' by the four previous rounds of accession, and the obligations that ensue from membership. At least in that sense, the EU can be compared to a rather loose club with a set of formal rules and regulations – the quasi-constitutional treaties and the legislative enactments and related common positions elaborated since then (notably the *acquis*) – and an entire array of more conjectural and subjective considerations.

For the economies in transition, it is useful to divide the issues around accession into two broad categories, qualitative and quantitative costs and benefits. The more qualitative ones concerning the foundations of political democracy and a market-based economy can usefully be broken down into a multiple of those officially stated to clarify matters (Ludlow 1996a, p. 27). I prefer to cite and examine eight criteria (for a broader justification, see Brabant 1995a, pp. 452-68; 1996a): domestic political pluralism, democratic maturity and political stability, good neighborly relations or peaceful coexistence, introduction and effective application of the rule of law, ability to comply with the EU's *acquis*, acceptance of the overall ambitions of EU integration, a European identity, and market-based resource allocation. Convergence on these issues between the applicant and the EU's average must be well advanced.

It is clear that many of these concepts are rather fuzzy in the sense that the assessment of what needs to be done and of whether the minimum for passing the grade has been reached will depend on subjective evaluations by leading EU policy makers. Take, for example, good neighborly relations. For better or worse, the EU has insisted that the potential applicant from the eastern part of Europe explore the room available for regional cooperation, essentially building upon the comparative advantages inherited from the postwar period whenever they are economically justified by current market criteria. This challenge has led to various regional initiatives, including the so-called Visegrád process and a commitment to create a free-trading area during the

1990s among the members (now five in all). Recall that the Visegrád process, which is broader than the Central European Free Trade Agreement (CEFTA), was started by three countries (Czechoslovakia, Hungary, and Poland). By the time the CEFTA came into force in March 1993, there were four countries as a result of the splitting up of Czechoslovakia. Slovenia became a member as of 1996, after it initialed its Europe Agreement. Having achieved the latter, as well as membership in the WTO, would seem to be, still largely tacit, preconditions for further enlargement of the CEFTA.

Some policy makers in eastern Europe reject any 'counseled' form of regional cooperation other than what would spontaneously arise from market forces; they fear that temporary arrangements will almost inevitably tend to become permanent, thus holding their economies back at the periphery of European modernization. And so, a resumption of regional economic and other cooperation has been long in the making. But some hopeful signs of a turn for the better, especially in central Europe, appear to be crystallizing and strengthening, considering the present horizon of regional cooperation.

There are, however, a number of outstanding issues that also weigh negatively on good neighborly relations between some EU members and some economies in transition. The divisive issue of the claims of *Sudeten* Germans or their descendants for property restitution or compensation from the Czech Republic offers a case in point, given the vocal position of that German group among the electorate in a key EU Member State. The protracted dispute over the status and rights of ethnic Italians who left Slovenia after World War II, including notably property settlements, which held up the signing of Slovenia's Europe Agreement until June 1996, is another concrete example of what may encumber accession and, in the interim, broader relations with the EU.

In the case of most transition economies, ensuring that there is concordance between the *finalité politique* of the EU and the applicant's aspirations is not as simple as it may seem at first sight. Declaring oneself to be 'in Europe' is not good enough. The EU is a quasi-supranational organization with ambitions that reach far beyond the intergovernmental level. This necessarily entails that yielding in particular essential elements of national sovereignty, not only in economic affairs, may cause severe existential problems. One cannot simply gloss over the fact that most of the transition economies have only recently regained their national sovereignty; in some cases, their independence for the first time in historical memory. Even more, they have done so only after a hard-won contestation and political struggle.

Yet, it should be clear as well that one cannot be a member of the Union without deferring essential elements of economic, and increasingly political, sovereignty to the *sui generis* communautarian echelons. This in and of itself may cause serious existential problems. Nonetheless, without enabling the transition economy to reduce the 'burden' of sharing eventually in the Union's benefits and to compress the costs to a level that the Union may be willing to support, accession of the transition economies to the Union's official integration framework would be postponed indefinitely if adjudicated largely on normal accession grounds. This suggests another reason why an alternative, more deliberative and pragmatic, approach to full accession recommends itself.

It is important to be aware of these rather subjective conditions too for they will eventually play a role in the summing up that policy makers will be forced to make once the present IGC has been successfully concluded. Suitably interpreted they can be invoked to speed up or to slow down the pace of the EU's expansion toward the eastern part of Europe. It is not helpful when policy makers in one transition economy or another (and the Prime Minister of the Czech Republic, Mr. Václav Klaus [1993/4], has gathered an enviable reputation for arrogance and intransigence in that respect), as was done by many pundits for that matter, claim that their economy is ready to join the EU, but that the latter is not yet 'ready' to receive them, and thus stalls and delays acting upon a request for accession with dispatch; Péter Balázs (1996) has referred to this as a "crawling" approach. On the whole, this may create good sound bites. But it misses the point: Even in the economy most advanced with its transformation, much remains to be done in terms of streamlining domestic policies and institutions before it can credible claim to reasonably fulfill the preconditions for accession.

Because so much of the integration endeavors of the EU depends on competition within the framework of market-based allocation of resources, the applicant must have a properly functioning market economy in order to be able to discharge the obligations of the *acquis*, and indeed to benefit fully from its advantages. Furthermore, to participate in the EU, it must have a civil service that can incorporate the *acquis* into the national legislative framework and public institutions, apply it reasonably smoothly, supervise implementation of the rules and regulations in a market context, and work positively within the *modi operandi* of the EU. One such requirement, for example, is that the country must be capable of servicing the agenda of the European Council and take a lead on other issues in the Council of Ministers if the presidency, which rotates every six months, were to befall it.

It is ironic in this context that most advocates of rapid transformation in the eastern part of Europe have explicitly sought to weaken the state and that the policies implemented since 1989 have left the civil service in many transition economies in considerable disarray. Surprisingly little has been done in recent years to strengthen the capacity of the state so that it can discharge the functions that are commonplace, including in the Union's Member States, in acting upon many EU endeavors as part and parcel of applying the *acquis*. I have little qualms about the argument that the civil service inherited from communist administration was not very well suited to discharge the functions incumbent upon a civil service in a rule-bound society with a market-based economy. Rather than utilizing this as an excuse to root out the old administration, I would have preferred looking upon it as a justification, certainly an inducement, for revamping and strengthening the civil service for the present and future tasks incumbent upon it.

This is not, of course, the place to elaborate on the role of the state in economic management, although in Chapter 6 I shall argue that the EU could usefully help to strengthen the state's governance capabilities in the transition economies as part and parcel of a pre-accession strategy or in streamlining its own assistance programs. Suffice it to note here that a reasonable adherence to the *acquis* presupposes a substantial and effective role of public agencies in socioeconomic life. That role cannot be limited to simply translating the articles of the *acquis*'s rules and regulations into the local juridical and administrative codes.

Implementing and abiding by the rules and regulations of the EU club is by no means easy or straightforward, or costless for that matter, as argued earlier (in Section 4). Concerns on that score have been repeatedly stressed, including on the core items of competition, most recently in connection with the impetus that the Conference is supposed to provide to easing access of transition economies to the EU. (For the expression of concern on these issues from prominent persons close to the Union, see the interview with Joseph Weyland, formerly Luxembourg's permanent representative to the Council and one of the members of the Reflection Group, in Interview 1996a, p. 9).

Even on the core issue of competition, doubts exist as to whether and when even the transition economies that are most advanced in their structural transformation will be able to withstand free competition from the EU. As argued in Section 1, the EU has intrinsically at best marginal interest in fostering membership of economies that would retrogress toward agriculture, the production of raw materials, or the exploitation of low labor and resource costs. Without the capabilities to participate in vibrant competition for the nuts and bolts of intra-industry trade, particularly in manufacturing which is highly specialized, it is hard to see how the EU could be challenged to bring the country in question under its integration umbrella. Declarations have their use. But deeds will have to be shown before credibility can be gained in the EU. Indeed, it would be useful to realize right up front that the path toward political pluralism and market-based decision making in their multiple EU dimensions is strewn with many palpable obstacles that can be overcome only over a protracted period of time, provided the socio-political consensus on the transition can be maintained.

Doubts have also been voiced by key decision makers in the EU, within the Commission, in Member States, and most recently by leading voices in the European Parliament, as to whether any economy in transition can truly claim to be a working democracy with a functioning market-based economic system. But some (such as the Czech Republic, Hungary, Poland, and Slovenia) are undoubtedly closer to fulfilling the cited political and economic preconditions for EU membership. They are therefore more credible candidates for business-like accession negotiations once the current IGC comes to an end. But even for the most ardent advocates of quick accession among leading eastern European policy makers, it is not always clear whether they are firmly committed to the overall ambitions of European integration. Some of the more likely applicants for early membership appear to be contesting the basic goals of the EU, insofar as they seem to equate them simply with a pure free-trade arrangement (Klaus 1993/4). That would certainly not be in the spirit of the "overall ambitions of European integration." In a rather extraordinary statement by Jacques Santer at a seminar held in Prague on 4 April 1996, he reportedly "warned Czech politicians who have criticized aspects of the EU's functioning" and stated that "joining the EU must be based on enthusiasm for membership," even though the "process of harmonizing laws with EU norms will be long and sometimes difficult" (reported in *OMRI Daily Digest*, 5 April 1996).

The requirements for viable candidacy of peaceful coexistence, of the rule of law, of political pluralism as a gateway to the establishment of fully-fledged democracy, and of moving decisively toward market-based allocation of resources are of course objectives, which entail obligations, in their own right as part of the process of forging ahead with the implementation of the transformation agenda. But in the context of potential EU membership, they take on a special dimension of significance because they lower the costs, qualitative and otherwise, that new members might otherwise inflict upon the existing Union. Such costs cannot all be reduced to unambiguous monetary values, however. Inability or reluctance to enact the EU's competition policy, for example, will inexorably lead to acrimony in EU relations, even though the losses sustained by claimants cannot be quantified with any precision.

Clearly, there are not only costs for the potential entrant. There are counterpart conditions to be met by the EU. The potential costs of assimilating new entrants within the EU are by no means trivial. The various agricultural, cohesion, regional, social, and structural funds managed by the EU for political reasons, whatever their intrinsic rationale and economic justification, cannot be abolished overnight and their appropriations can at best be increased only marginally. As a result, these facilities can be offered to the economies in transition only to the extent that the latter's claims remain 'manageable.' Second-class citizenship for economies in transition would not be acceptable to them nor, most probably, to a majority of the present EU membership. The process of convergence, not only in terms of per capita incomes but also in terms of economic structure between the applicant and the EU average or range of economies, will therefore have to proceed quite some way before the costs to EU members will become acceptable.

It is important to be clear that any eventual fusion of eastern and western Europe cannot simply be regarded as an economic matter. Instead, it is a highly political act revolving around some economic interests that can now be realized, after a long, divisive relationship especially in the postwar period. Previous EU enlargements, it should be recalled, have never been based solely (and in some cases not even mainly) on economic tradeoffs; political, security, and strategic considerations have also played their role, and not always in a transparent manner. There is no reason to believe that matters will be different for any of the economies in transition now or in the near term.

It could hardly be otherwise, given the fundamental political-economy features of the European Union. The latter is indeed a special club with statutes (the *acquis* and quasi-constitutional treaties), some of which are ill-defined, and are therefore interpreted on the go, as it were. It possesses also an evolving governance structure that is kept formally aligned with the organization's constitution. In point of fact, however, its formal authority provides a considerable degree of leeway regarding the decision when members should or could decide to consider an application for accession, and in what precise form, to negotiate in good faith; to admit an applicant; or to innovate and put in place an interim regime that will facilitate eventual full accession within a fairly well-defined transition period.

When all is said and done, however, those responsible for judging whether or not the economies in transition can realistically join the EU, when, and at what cost, must be aware of costs other than those associated with minimal compliance with the more qualitative conditions for membership. Even when full compliance has been achieved, both present EU members and applicants for accession will have to weigh the benefits and costs of union membership in terms of actual economic and financial repercussions, as cogently argued in Baldwin 1994. Although this calculation need not provide the final word on whether or not to seek accession, the benefits and costs considered separately for each Member State, as well as their aggregate, cannot be ignored. Although this is nowhere made explicit, the assimilation of the costs of an enlarged EU membership has always been at least implicit in the decision-making process on widening; it cannot be otherwise for the economies in transition.

The core problem besetting the relationship between the EU and the countries of the eastern part of Europe, then, is not whether or not to bring the economies in transition into the multilateral regimes of western Europe. Rather, it is how close these applicants will have to be to the 'average' or the 'worst' EU member with respect to fulfilling the conditions specified earlier in order to be accorded the same privileges *and* to be able and willing to discharge the same obligations as those now accruing to 'below-average' members. In other words, once the more fundamental aspects of a credible commitment to democracy, political pluralism, and market-based allocation of resources have been ascertained, the major focus will be on the economic or financial costs and benefits of accession.

4 – Accession Negotiations: Economics and Politics

Once reasonable fulfillment of the qualitative criteria is within reach, the accession negotiations can start. Judging by the previous four enlargements, from which some "classical" path of negotiating membership can be inferred, as done in an illuminating exercise by Christopher Preston (1995), these are dominated by several concerns. One is certainly that the applicant must accept in full the *acquis communautaire* and increasingly also the *acquis politique*. There can be no permanent exemption from this communautarian obligation. Second, most of the accession negotiations have been devoted to the practicalities of implementing these rules and regulations, normally leading to temporary derogations from the full application of the *acquis*. Third, problems resulting from widening the social and economic diversity of membership are as a rule addressed by creating new policy instruments without encouraging a fundamental, comprehensive revision of the existing programs. Fourth, accession is phased over time with the promise of a more fundamental review after enlargement. Fifth, in all previous enlargements concerns about maintaining equilibrium, both in time and across the membership, have shaped key components of the accession arrangements. This feature has recently been underlined once again by Carlos Westendorp y Cabeza (1995, p. 15), the Chairman of the Reflection Group (see Chapter 2). It is no exaggeration to assert that this

concern about balance has been at the roots of two overriding characteristics of the EU: gradual adjustment to widening on the part of
existing members; and a fair distribution of the expected benefits and
costs of increased membership. Finally, the EU negotiates with individual applicants but likes to review the applications of closely related
countries at the same time. There is no reason to believe that the shape
of the negotiations with the economies in transition, or with Cyprus and
Malta, will be any different.

At the heart of the accession negotiations, from the EU's point of
view, three major adjustment questions are likely to arise:

• First of all, what precise cost is western Europe willing to bear
by opening its markets further for goods, services, capital, and labor to
one or more economies in transition according to agreed rules and
regulations?

• Second, how quickly can this cost realistically be imposed and
absorbed, given the strength of the evolving integration movement and
the political will in Member States for further integration as well as
further enlargement?

• Finally, how will that cost be distributed within the EU, given its
existing or likely governance mechanisms?

The cost of enlargement is by no means confined to the impact on
income redistribution, although this is bound to be a critical factor in
considering how best to respond to new applications for membership.
But the answers to the three questions depend in part, in addition to
economic costs, on the EU's governance with respect to realizing its
longer-term aims. One can be fairly certain that there are rather firm
limits beyond which the material and other costs of adjusting structures
and absorbing income redistribution, the speed at which these costs
ought to be assimilated, and/or the feasible distribution of these costs
simply will not – and indeed cannot – be tolerated by a sufficiently large
number of the present EU members, if only because of political-economy reasons.

From recent policy pronouncements it is not at all clear whether the
EU is ready to undertake the adjustments required to absorb the economies in transition, even in small combinations (that is, subgroups of the
ten countries with a Europe Agreement) as members. Actual decisions
will depend crucially on whether Member States, both those that are

presently net contributors (especially France, Germany, Italy, the Netherlands, and the United Kingdom) and net beneficiaries (especially Greece, Ireland, Portugal, and Spain), are willing to support the required adjustments; among the beneficiaries, in particular those whose net gains will be eroded by any further enlargement to countries with a per capita income below the EU average will have to be taken into account very carefully. For example, structural supports depend, among other factors, on the gap between a Member State's per capita income and the Union's average. If new countries with a per capita level well below the average enter, the former beneficiary's gap will narrow, thus reducing the country's access to support from the Union. For a detailed account, see Dignan 1995.

A number of researchers as well as the European Commission have made estimates of the likely cost, in terms of supplementary budgetary expenditures, of various transition economies (usually the four central European ones or the ten countries with a Europe Agreement) becoming EU members. The estimates vary considerably for in each calculation assumptions have to be made as to the position of the potential entrant relative to the rest of the Union at the time of accession in terms of income, level of development, and economic structure. In other words, forecasts must be made of relative growth rates up to the date of accession; of the position of the applicant relative to the average income of the Union to obtain access to structural funds, for example; of the state of the potential entrant's agriculture; and so on. Furthermore, assumptions must also be made as to how the transfer programs will develop by the time the transition economies accede. Since a budgetary review is due in 1999 (see Chapter 2) and the further extension is hardly likely to be in place by then, it cannot be taken for granted that the shape and extent of the prevailing transfer programs will be extended in time or to the acceding transition economies. Estimations can therefore be at best highly hypothetical.

Since none of the parameters for preparing a firm cost estimate can be determined at present, a rough-and-ready method is usually resorted to by which the per capita support presently extended to the four Union members at the low end of the development scale (Greece, Ireland, Portugal, and Spain) is 'grossed up' with the population numbers of individual transition economies for various reference periods. It is not surprising that very different magnitudes of the "budgetary cost" are generated. The more credible numerical computations range from some 20 to 100 percent of the EU's budget projected for the Fifteen at some assumed future accession date, or some 20 to 100 billion ecu (about $36-130 billion) per year. These are very large, indeed staggering, annual sums, and considerably exceed the inflows of foreign investment into the economies in transition to date. The estimated share of structural transfers alone could exceed 12 percent of the GDP of the beneficiary countries in central Europe (see Gros and Steinherr 1995, pp. 503ff.; Rollo 1996 summarizes various measurements and suggests much higher transfer-to-GDP shares). It is not at all clear whether these countries actually possess the absorptive capacity to use such sizable funds productively. Jim Rollo (1996, slide 20) suggests that the share be restricted, perhaps to 5 percent of GDP, which is slightly below the shares currently applying to, say, Greece and Ireland. Clearly, absorptive capacity should be of concern to avoid making unproductive transfers, thus risking the creation of an undesirably rentier and dependency culture.

The point of the above hypothetical exercises is not really whether the net impact of the economies in transition on the EU's budget is going to be 20, 50, 70, or 100 percent of Union expenditures for the present membership. Actual costs will not be known in any case, not even approximately, until the instruments of accession have been fully negotiated and ratified. More important is the assessment of whether the existing Union members will be prepared in principle to raise their budget contributions by anything like the orders of magnitude suggested by these estimates; in particular, whether present contributors will shoulder the additional expenditures, whether present beneficiaries will agree to reductions in relative and perhaps absolute terms in their net gains, and whether reforms of the transfer systems, especially for agriculture and structural supports, are politically feasible (Begg, Gudgin, and Morris 1995, pp. 13ff.). At present, there appears to be little leeway with any of these otherwise flexible instruments, particularly in the case of early accession. But there could be more room for maneuver once the EU's next review of budgetary policies is completed.

Many observers have argued that the impact of the accession of the transition economies is likely to be small, given their comparatively low level of development, productivity, and population size, and that therefore the EU should adopt a magnanimous stance. The share of the transition economies in total Union trade is likely to remain marginal (perhaps 1-2 percent of Union absorption) and claims on Union resources in terms of overall GDP, using the estimates quoted above, will lie only between 0.25 and 1.3 percent. Even if these numbers were reliable, the argument based on them is not decisive. It is in any case the *relative impact* on the present EU as well as on new entrants that should be kept in mind. For the latter, such huge transfers relative to their GDP may be unwise: Their absorptive capacity is unlikely to be sufficient and adding to reserves is not a very productive exercise, except perhaps for those transition economies that continue to face stiff foreign-exchange constraints; but these are unlikely to figure among the early entrants anyway.

For the EU, it should be recalled that the budget, as determined at the Edinburgh Council, will amount to 1.27 percent of the Union's GDP through the end of the decade; but that agreement itself has not yet (end June 1996) been ratified by the United Kingdom (European Commission 1996o, p. 8). Accommodating the economies in transition may require raising this to perhaps 1.6 to 2.5 percent of GDP, an increase that does not seem to be feasible given the prevailing stance on fiscal policy in the core Member States of the Union. Note, however, that even if such a budgetary contribution were feasible, it would be wrong (as claimed in *Magyar Hírlap*, 21 March 1996, p. 7) to anticipate quick accession. Indeed, the budgetary transfers have very little to do with the ability of the potential entrant to live up to a reasonable degree to the *acquis*, and that, I submit when all is said and done, constitutes the crux of negotiating accession.

5 – Date of Entry

Here one is fully in the speculative arena. All that is officially known about timing is that no applicant will be considered for negotiations until after a satisfactory conclusion of the current IGC (the meaning of "satisfactory" being left deliberately vague, but presumably it implies some positive reform of the institutions and decision-making mechanisms of the EU, on the strength of the arguments made by well-placed decision makers in the Conference's deliberations, such as reported in Interview 1996a, pp. 8-9). It is also known from the decisions of the Cannes Council of June 1995 that accession negotiations with Cyprus and Malta will begin six months after the conclusion of the IGC. On an optimistic view, negotiations could also start at about the same time for at least the transition economies that are more advanced with their transformation agenda (probably the Czech Republic, Hungary, Poland, and Slovenia), though there are strong voices calling for holding simultaneous negotiations with all ten countries (NZZ 1996b, Southey 1996), presumably also implying simultaneous entry. Mr. Fraser Cameron (1996b), a well-placed adviser to Commissioner Van den Broek, has recently suggested that negotiations with the transition economies will be started up *after* the preliminary rounds with Cyprus and Malta will have been initiated and that after the opening round with the ten several meaningful subgroups will be constituted.

Following all of the above hints, the negotiations will most likely commence in early 1998. They can in reality be initiated only when the European Commission, after it submits its opinion – the so-called *avis* – on the application, receives a negotiating mandate from the European Council. This takes a minimum of six months, but often longer, as pointed out by the spokesperson for Commissioner Hans van den Broek, Nico Wegter (Interview 1996b, p. 23).

Note that on 26 April 1996, the European Commission handed over a questionnaire to each of the applicants, including "informally" Slovenia because it is "broadly expected to submit a formal accession request ... this June" (European Commission 1996n, p. 1). These contain some 200 questions on average (there is a core catalogue that is common for all and then specific annexes for each applicant) on a great variety of aspects around the *acquis*. The applicants have three months to submit their responses, but more time may be required to supply adequate answers. Indeed, the responses will be substantive inputs into the composite *avis* that the Commission will prepare for the Council.

If the date of the start of the process is uncertain, the duration of the negotiations is even more so. Some guidance can be obtained from considering four factors that have a bearing on the issue: (1) the time it took to arrange previous expansions of the Union; (2) the complexity of transferring the then prevailing *acquis communautaire et politique*, at least its core elements, to the aspiring entrant; (3) the large number of rather diverse countries seeking accession at approximately the same time; and (4) the political and security considerations and the extent to which the EU will be willing, or able, to consider tradeoffs between them and the financial and related costs of enlargement.

For the record, it is useful to recall that earlier accession negotiations generally took a long time. In the case of the United Kingdom (and by extension Denmark, Ireland, and Norway, which in the end decided not to join), negotiations were intermittent and spread over 12 years between first application and accession. For Greece the process lasted six and for Portugal and Spain nine years; it then took a minimum of ten, eight, and six years, respectively, to move from accession to full integration (Laurant 1994, p. 128), with formal exceptions for the CAP lasting in the latter two cases even longer – up to ten years. Recall that other facilitations were granted, such as for freeing capital flows by mid 1990 as required for other Member States. Naturally, within the relevant political-economy framework these experiences are not necessarily indicative of what is likely to happen for transition economies individually or as a group. Nevertheless, from all the admittedly limited information at hand, protracted negotiations and a long transition period seem to be in store.

One may object to the above categorization because it does not explicitly reflect the experience with the fourth enlargement of the EU. But the four EFTA countries (Austria, Finland, Norway, and Sweden) then negotiating had already adopted a lot of EU legislation as a result of their long association with the EU, which constituted their principal trading partner; the protracted negotiations about the EEA, which essentially permitted them full access to the four freedoms of the EU, but no role in EU decision making; and the history of these countries as a constituent part of western Europe. As a result, they were also thoroughly familiar with and integrated into the EU's economic and, often, sociopolitical networks. I feel therefore that their experience is not particularly relevant to the economies in transition phase.

Given the state of the transition economies, a rather lengthy transition after accession will be necessary. Several leaders of these economies have been pressing for a 'short' period, as they have for a brief period of negotiations to permit accession by the magical year 2000; but EU members, as well as outsiders (Ludlow 1996a, p. 73), judge it wiser to consider a longer period both for negotiations and for the transition. Perhaps a decade may be the sort of compromise that could emerge for the transition.

Nico Wegter, the spokesperson for Commissioner Van den Broek, has recently estimated that "at least two years" of negotiations will be needed before the ratification process can begin (Interview 1996b, p. 23). Fraser Cameron (1996b), a high-level adviser to the same Commissioner, recently suggested four to six years for negotiations. Just before going to press, the European Commission reportedly identified the year 2002 "as the earliest probably date of accession" for the more credible economies in transition (*Financial Times*, 17 June 1996, p. 18). Peter Ludlow (1996a, p. 74), who as Director of the Centre for European Policy Studies is close to the Commission, indicates at least three years for negotiations and several more for ratification. Given the EU's past record, the prevailing policy dilemmas around deepening and widening in the Union, and the long array of complex and rather obdurate problems to be addressed in the case of most economies in transition, anything less than five years appears to be highly optimistic indeed.

The special economic, political, security, environmental, labor, social, and other problems that will arise in bringing the transition economies to full membership argue for quick accession following a fairly brief negotiating period. Policy makers in central Europe, and also in Germany, have been arguing for the year 2000 as the magical date of entry. Given that there will be hardly more than two years between the start-up of accession negotiations (possibly early 1998) and the turn of the millennium, and given that the issues to be agreed upon are highly complex, and that the ratification process by the European Parliament and in each of the present EU Member States will take time, the year 2000 as the target for accession appears to be extraordinarily optimistic indeed. In my view, the year 2002 might be "probable" but not very likely for the same reasons.

The questions to be negotiated are not necessarily fundamental issues, which are part of the *acquis* and thus beyond the scope of compromise. Rather, leeway exists over how quickly those fundamental issues will have to be applied and respected by the new entrant and extended in full by existing members. Negotiations will therefore focus on the length of the period of transition; political representation; financial contributions; concessions in terms of social, regional, or structural supports ahead of time; and facilitation for the new member's existing trading arrangements, which was particularly important for some accedents. Thus in the case of the first enlargement for the United Kingdom, consideration was also given to the country's trading arrangements with its former colonies. This example suggests that if the central European countries were to enter the EU separately a temporary accommodation would be required to take their preferential arrangements in the CEFTA and with other countries into account. All of these matters are held to be very important determinants of the course of accession negotiations. For one thing, they alleviate the pressure of trade diversion for the new member. They also permit the present EU members to maintain their existing preferences and protective regime; or at least to space out adjustments over a fairly lengthy period of time.

At this stage, then, a probable date of accession for the transition economies is largely a matter of speculation. The Director of the Unit for Eastern Europe of the European Commission in 1995 suggested informally: "The most optimistic scenario for the associated countries of Central and Eastern Europe is full membership (that is, including transition periods) within 20 years, which would imply a very rapid passage compared with previous acceding countries" (Pearce 1995, p. 134). While it is entirely true that Ms. Joan Pearce, as claimed, was speaking in her own name, manifestly not on behalf of the Commission, it would nonetheless be unrealistic to assume that these views do not echo at all some of the sentiments prevailing in Brussels. Counting back on that evidence from 2015 and assuming that the transition period would be no longer than a decade, the earliest accession date for the most advanced economy in transition would be 2005. Even that target would require rather smooth accession negotiations and ratification procedures, and indeed "rapid passage," as Joan Pearce pointed out, but it would be within the time frame that Fraser Cameron (1996b) recently intimated, also in his own name: four to six years for negotiations followed by one to two years for ratification. The European Parliament has indicated that the year 2010 would be the more likely, if still optimistic, target for entry, even for the most advanced of the economies in transition (NZZ 1996b). A recent Hungarian assessment (*Magyar Hírlap*, 21 March 1996, p. 7) agrees with this earliest date of accession – "the end of the next decade."

In this connection, it bears to recall that the economies in transition find themselves in quite different economic, environmental, health, political, security, and social circumstances. If only for those reasons, it would seem unlikely that negotiations will be conducted simultaneously with all applicants; note however that the European Parliament has prodded the Commission and the Council to consider precisely such a strategy, thereby almost enforcing further delays in the reasonable horizon for accession for the more credible applicants. Whereas I can see the rationale for political maneuvering on this score, from a technical point of view there can be little justification for negotiating simultaneously with all transition economies and aiming at bringing them into the EU at the same time.

For one thing, the negotiating capacities of the Commission may be severely stretched if applied simultaneously to twelve bilateral rounds of accession negotiations that will somehow need to be coordinated in fairly minute detail (Ludlow 1996a, pp. 41-2). More important, however, the issues to be dealt with are sufficiently diverse that several negotiating tiers, hence different phases of negotiation and entry, are more likely to emerge, perhaps once the negotiations get under way (see also Cameron 1996b). This had already earlier been the case with Cyprus and Malta in the round with the other four EFTA applicants (Ludlow 1996a, p. 68).

No concrete proposals have yet been made on how best to stratify the economies in transition, but the first tier will almost certainly consist of the central European countries, including Slovenia, although it is not yet clear whether Slovakia will figure in that group. A second tier is likely to include those Baltic and Balkan States with a Europe Agreement, perhaps including Slovakia. A third tier might consist of Albania and the successor States of Yugoslavia other than Slovenia. A final group could encompass the western successor States of the Soviet Union judged to be 'European' (notably Belarus, Moldova, and Ukraine). It is unlikely that other economies in transition will either wish to apply for membership or that they would be accepted as European, with the possible exceptions, in principle, of Armenia and Georgia, if only in view of their western Christian heritage.

6 – Longer-term Facilitations

As emphasized on several occasions here and in my earlier writing, and of course by many other observers, the transformation of the former planned economies into 'normal' market economies with pluralistic democracy remains a daunting task. The achievements over the past six-seven years have been considerable and in many cases quite impressive. Yet popular disaffection with democracy continues to be quite strong; in fact, it appears to have recently risen in some countries (see European Commission 1996j for some quantitative measures), indicating that remaining gaps continue to be still quite striking. The normalization of these economies will occur only after a period of sustained growth to enable them to catch up with western European levels of development, a process that for many will take decades.

In the meantime, given the unusual features of these economies, a case can be made for instituting special arrangements for them which would extend beyond the official transition period after accession. What precisely that would entail cannot be spelled out in detail, for it would naturally depend on the actual negotiations and the accession format eventually agreed upon. But some elements can be identified, and it might be useful to consider them in the context of a longer-term EU assistance strategy, if only because the very nature of the long-term adjustment process in the transition economies may justify the formulation of a pre-accession assistance program (see Chapter 6).

Arguing for a longer-term facility specifically designed for the transition economies within the context of the period leading up to full membership, and even with full membership, is not as odd as it might appear at first blush. Indeed, in each new wave of accessions, the EU in its pragmatic approach to widening has previously innovated a special facility for the acceding countries and, in some cases, to accommodate their interests overseas. This was politics, of course. But it was also a recognition of the fact that without such a facility the accessions would not succeed in ushering the new Member States onto a constructive platform for them to be able to wage competition in intra-industry trade within the single market. Certainly, the entire debate around structural and cohesion funds in the second and third rounds of enlargement was based on that foundation.

With the very special characteristics of the economies in transition as backdrop, not only the ten most credible candidates but also the others that are likely prospectively to request entry, a special facility that recognizes both the economic and political interests of remaking Europe for the present EU as well as for the candidates for accession would seem entirely appropriate. It would provide an anchor for ensuring further progress with solidification of the market framework and indeed pluralistic democracy.

Conclusions

I have tried to show how complex accession negotiations for the economies in transition are likely to be, pulling together all the historical, institutional, logical, and other evidence that bears on the issue. Some readers may find that I have sketched an unduly pessimistic picture of the situation. I do not think so, though. I truly believe that none of the elements of the discourse I have touched upon, and perhaps others that I have inadvertently given short shrift, can be ignored in any serious – that is, realistic – debate around the remaking of Europe. That is not to deny that the European Commission has accomplished a great deal since the early 1990s and that much useful work of considerable quality with a great deal of commitment is being undertaken to turn the promise of enlargement to the eastern part of Europe into a reality without rocking the delicate EU boat so much that the fragile ship would be scuttled altogether. Even so, the road ahead remains very daunting in more than one respect.

Indeed the task is not just how best to bring the eastern part of Europe into 'Europe,' as if this were a finalized, solid, and irreversible, well-rehearsed play for a staid repertory theater in the western part of the continent. Without delving deeply into the admittedly murky issues revolving around good regional governance, such as is now the task of the sitting IGC, one is bound to err in assessing how best either to assimilate the economies of the eastern part of Europe into the Union or to foster a constructive cooperative relationship between the two groups. Neither ideology nor pure politics can help conclusively in focusing the discussion. Rather, it is the pragmatic reconciliation of inherently contradictory interests that has driven the (western) European integration process and that continues to provide the impetus to walking the trajectory leading toward EMU as an integral part of implementing the Maastricht Treaty.

Shopworn clichés of imparting credibility and security to the transition economies by 'absorbing' these countries immediately into the Union's framework without much preparatory work are not very helpful. Likewise, accusing western European policy makers of deliberately excluding these eastern partners from the Union for their own egoistic self-interests, or even worse arguments to the effect that the Union is now protecting the fragile eastern societies against their own self-destructive instincts, are neither persuasive nor very constructive. True, both approaches considerably compress the complexity of the real world in a reductive fashion, thus leading to rather easy – and, for some, appealingly straightforward – solutions. That sounds too good to be true. Precisely for that reason such suggestions are at this juncture not very helpful in deliberating about what *can* realistically be done in designing a pragmatic assistance program, in implementing such a set of actions, and in seeing to it that the measures embraced will be continually monitored, assessed, and fine-tuned. Such initiatives, which in fact amount to a particular form of 'social engineering,' should be attuned with a view toward maximizing the benefits that can be extracted for the transformation of the eastern part of Europe while ensuring steady progress with the completion of the EU's integration ambitions.

I turn now to considerations of such an alternative approach for at least some of the countries in the eastern part of Europe appear to be very keen on having a credible strategy in place leading eventually up to accession in a reliable fashion (Havel 1996, p. 40; WERI 1995, p. 187).

6

A Pre-accession Strategy and Beyond

In the preceding chapter, I have pointed to the range and nature of the obstacles, real and imputed, the EU will face in extending in particular some transfer programs to the economies in transition upon accession, the level and distribution of the adjustment costs to be defrayed by the present EU membership, as well as the problems that the transition economies are likely to incur in attempting to assimilate quickly the minimal *acquis*. In addition, I have emphasized the asymmetries in benefits and costs over time for the EU, for the EU Member States, as well as for the economies in transition. For the latter, ignoring the potentially sizable budget transfers if they will in the end materialize, most of these costs with all of their repercussions will have to be borne essentially before the benefits will become more tangible to broad layers of the population. All of these considerations prompted me to cast serious doubt on any suggestion that the accession negotiations will be smooth and progress quickly to full entry with access to the four freedoms (of movement of goods, services, people, and capital) any time soon. It will be well into the next century that by my estimation, subjective as it may well be, the first wave of transition economies will graduate into the EU; it may then take perhaps another decade before they will be full members.

It is also fairly clear that none of the economies in transition can wait till, say, the year 2010 before being enabled to reap most of the benefits of the single European market and becoming better prepared for assuming the obligations of the *acquis*, of a more stable security arrangement, and of bolstering the credibility of these transformation policies. Alternative options for fostering a closer relationship between the EU and the economies in transition, in the first place, but not only, those with a Europe Agreement, therefore deserve to be explored at the earliest opportunity. I want to make it crystal clear up front that I am manifestly *not* interested here in elaborating the case for alternatives to EU membership. Rather, my motivation is to advocate solutions that may forge soonest a closer symbiotic relationship between the EU and the transition economies – all of those prepared to work constructively toward such a new interim architecture, largely within the prevailing institutional setup. The goal is essentially full membership of the ten with a Europe Agreement and a constructive relationship with other economies in transition, both those that in time may join and others.

I first justify the overall approach pursued here. Then I plead for maintaining realistic aspirations by both sides. This is followed by a tentative strategy for the transition economies that presently have a Europe Agreement, consisting of eight clusters by way of illustration of what might realistically be envisioned once some political good will is mustered. Thereafter I project those suggestions against the desirability of developing more forceful regional governance in the EU. Before concluding, I underline the importance of doing something more coherent and constructive also for other transition economies, whether or not they will ever be able or willing to join the EU.

1 – The Rationale for a Pre-accession Strategy

The pre-accession strategy that the EU has been putting in place over the past year or so, at least since the Essen Council, and to the extent that it does not focus on preparing the EU's institutions and programs themselves for another enlargement, is largely geared toward acquainting the transition economies with the implications of EU membership, notably the obligations of the *acquis*, and familiarizing them with how the EU functions (see Chapter 4). None of the measures taken to date is likely to have a major impact on the more fundamental problems of moving toward membership identified earlier unless a more active and engaged stance on the part of the European Commission will be promoted. Thus, although the White Paper prepared for the economies in transition in 1995 has been most welcome, complying with all the legislation around the single market, which is deemed to be a prerequisite to accession (European Commission 1995f, p. 21; NZZ 1996b; Southey 1996), will take many years, in some cases very many years indeed. As with so many other considerations in contemplating accession, the

White Book can be utilized to accelerate the process or to slow it down, depending on how lenient the interpretation of "minimal compliance" with the *acquis* will in the end turn out to be. The latest salvos on that score, fired by the European Parliament, are not particularly encouraging.

The transition economies, however, cannot be left in limbo for very much longer, if only because of the economic, environmental, health, political, security, cultural, and other interests of the EU. Some of these priorities are of particular concern to individual Member States (Austria, France, and Germany in particular). Apprehensions about political stability and insecurity engendered by events in some of the more eastern economies in transition have recently led to several tentative initiatives on how best to map the future of the more likely entrants within a 'western,' possibly a 'European,' context. These could usefully be embedded in a more coherent and strategic – as well as ambitious – framework designed to address problems systematically over an extended period of time.

Without resorting to economic determinism, I would argue that economic interests as well support the claimed justification for innovating a more active, strategic approach to assisting the economies in transition. In what follows, however, I focus chiefly on the economic aspects as, in my view, they will be critical in facilitating accession of the economies in transition in particular. Beyond those areas, other matters can be considered and some have already usefully been tabled (for examples, see Altmann, Andreff, and Fink 1995; Altmann and Ochmann 1995; Baldwin 1994; Ludlow and Ersbøll 1996, pp. 59-61; Weidenfeld 1995). Without the economies in transition benefiting from a solid economic recovery that can be sustained into some catch-up dynamic over a substantial period of time, it is hard to see how the interests of the EU can be blended to a considerable degree with the aspirations of the economies in transition. While these considerations apply in particular to the potential ten entrants, I would argue for taking a broader scope and extending the approach, at least conceptually, to those eastern countries that may eventually become members of the EU, other than the ten with a Europe Agreement, as well as those that cannot reasonably be expected to join the EU as full members in any foreseeable future.

For the first group, that is, the economies with a Europe Agreement, the framework should preferably amount to a strategic sequencing of measures to be taken in both the potential entrant and the EU, the end result of which would be swift entry into the Union. Fixing an entry date up front may be useful for public relations, and it would undoubtedly impart some buoyancy in journalistic and political circles, as I have underlined in particular in Chapter 3 in connection with the prevailing EMU dilemmas. I reiterate, however, that setting such calendar deadlines is not very meaningful from the point of view of the broad political economy of EU accession and membership without having in place a credible strategy for meeting them.

The European Commission apparently disagrees with this assessment, as well as with the claims launched by several transition economies that the Commission specify soonest concrete entry conditions and dates, as it believes that "rather than drawing up specific criteria, it is far preferable to monitor progress toward the broad criteria set out at Copenhagen through sustained dialogue" (Pearce 1995, p. 136). It is of course necessary – indeed how could it be otherwise? – to monitor, assess, and fine-tune a constructive strategy in the light of actual events, including those that were not foreseen. Given the importance of what is at stake – the remaking of Europe, no less – it should be self-evident that the course ahead needs to be sensibly steered with a degree of flexibility, pragmatism, and purposefulness that has thus far been sorely lacking. But to have no strategy other than a structured dialogue around ill-defined criteria, such as those enunciated at the Copenhagen Council in mid 1993, is not particularly reassuring, including for the economies in transition. What other impression could be conveyed than that the EU itself does not have its priorities among its own activities clearly spelled out up front? Key actors in the economies in transition and of the European Parliament have recently made such observations, stressing the importance of having a realistic EU strategy for ushering the economies in transition into the Union in spite of political preferences that appear to dominate in one Member State or another, in Germany in particular.

Indeed, the EU could usefully elaborate such a strategy for itself, if only to clarify its own priorities and obligations at this stage. The Madrid Council recognized this need, in fact. It called for intensifying the pre-accession strategy under formulation "in order to create the conditions for the gradual, harmonious integration of those States, particularly through the development of the market economy, the adjustment of their administrative structures and the creation of a stable economic and monetary environment" (European Commission 1995e, chapter 3, p. 1). Likewise, the European Parliament has underlined in detail, in examining the 1995 White Paper (European Commission 1995f), that the Commission ought to address this issue soonest (NZZ 1996b, Southey 1996). Such strategic planning could also provide the potential entrant with a clearer vision of what needs to be accomplished in the near term, how to obtain appropriate assistance from abroad (including from the European Commission or individual EU Member States) to support the agenda of actions when desirable, and how best to mobilize the limited domestic resources to adhere to such a sequence of steps.

2 – Realistic Aspirations

There are three aspects of any coherent pre-accession strategy that deserve to be highlighted: economic benefits, gaining greater security in various dimensions, and strengthening and maintaining economic and political credibility for implementing the drawn-out transition agenda. As underlined in particular in Chapter 4, these have been the root aspirations of the transition economies from the moment they declared themselves keen on entering the EU at the earliest opportunity. Among the economic benefits to be expected, transfer gains can be separated from other economic advantages. Even if there is good reason to believe that the transfer bonus will not materialize soon, the other economic advantages from liberalized trade and factor movements (labor perhaps remaining subject to special constraints in view of the EU's unemployment problem and the vexatious migration pressures some of the Member States have been exposed to in recent years) can be quite substantial for the economies in transition and, on balance, significant for the EU Member States as well, regardless of the institutional and conceptual assistance frameworks envisaged. Those deserve to be accommodated soonest, especially to harden the crucial foundations for sustainable catch-up growth in the transition economies.

But these gains are not simply there for the taking. Successful transformation in the eastern part of Europe hinges critically on the ability of these economies to penetrate world markets on a competitive basis. That depends importantly, but only in part, on the domestic economic restructuring under way in these economies, including the policies, instruments, and institutional supports that are determinant of the transformation's successes and failures. It is also a function of the buoyancy of world markets and their openness to fair competition on a predictable basis. Much remains to be done in the latter respect. Some efforts have been made, notably in western Europe, to eliminate altogether discriminatory trade restrictions applicable in particular to the transition economies when they were still treated as state-trading countries and indeed to grant them in turn discriminatory preferences (see Chapter 4). However, more could and should be done. I consider it very important that the principals involved seize the opportunity provided by the historic turnaround in the eastern part of Europe to restore and reinforce basic elements of a multilateral trading world, notably by implementing quickly and as generously as possible the achievements of the Uruguay Round and by building further thereupon, including for sensitive manufacturing sectors and agriculture. Furthermore, trade can be hindered or promoted by various measures, many of which are not immediately identifiable – the intransparent, more qualitative nontariff barriers (NTBs) in particular.

In addition to seeking trade and other economic gains, the transition economies also desire a greater degree of stability and security, and indeed credibility, for their ongoing transformation programs. These aspirations definitely should not be disregarded. In this context, it should be stressed that considerable benefits, including increased security and policy credibility, as well as economic gains can be secured and safeguarded without rushing into hasty accession negotiations. Accordingly, a coherent pre-accession strategy reaching well beyond the EU's assistance efforts mustered since 1989 deserves to be worked out already prior to the start of accession negotiations.

Any such approach simply cannot be confined to 'structured dialogue' at the highest political level, however useful that may be in and of itself; to deliberations in special Association Councils, even though these are quite important in some respects; or to inventorying the

conditions each claimant must fulfill prior to exploring credible accession negotiations, however helpful and constructive such efforts may
intrinsically be. True, their payoff in the longer run should be beyond
contestation. The more strategic approach advocated here could have
a major impact on strengthening expectations both in and toward the
transition economies. This should be supported by well-targeted assistance on a much larger scale than has been forthcoming since 1989.
Major new funding might be welcome for some economies in transition, of course. But it would not be necessary for the most credible
applicants for accession. I contend, then, that major gains can be made
for very little, if any, extra budgetary expenses by the EU. Certainly for
the more plausible candidates for EU membership, the support needs to
be broadly based and encompass other areas, some of which are detailed below (see Section 3) by way of illustration.

Arguably the most important benefit of such an approach would be
confidence building. Expectations of policies and their likely outcomes
are very important in stances that economic actors, investors in particular, take. Enterprises in the transition economy and potential investors
from the EU should be more confident about the success of the transition process and of the country's eventual entry into the Union if such
a process were credibly elaborated in a coherent pre-accession strategy,
one that is furthermore steered in a confidence-inspiring mode. And if
households in the transition economies become more confident that
their levels of living are going to improve, however slowly during the
first phase, the social and political pressures on governments to abandon or dilute their transformation programs will be much reduced, thus
freeing up valuable time and other resources in strapped civil services
to get on with the tasks at hand rather than find ways and means of
acting in a more cautious, at times even surreptitious, manner. A well-
organized and strong commitment by the EU to such a strategy could
therefore play an important role in supporting and strengthening the
credibility of transformation policies advocated by government in the
transition economy.

Many of the requirements for maximizing the economic benefits can
therefore be met before tackling the more obdurate obstacles of moving
toward full entry if a coherent pre-accession strategy is put in place.
This is not the right place to advocate specifics in great detail, which in

any case will depend largely on political will and skillful negotiations by EU members and economies in transition alike, and indeed on country-specific circumstances. But it would not be unreasonable to expect such a program to be based on at least the following six principles:

(1) the EU must play a much more active role – as a robust, reliable partner – in the societal, especially the economic, transformation of the ten potential entrants;

(2) extend to them considerable technical assistance, in order to cope with the details and implications of membership, to support the convergence to EU institutions during the transition periods, and to strengthen the capacity and the role of public institutions in accomplishing such blending;

(3) reshape the external assistance programs, including especially easing further market access, and for infrastructure investment and industrial restructuring, with a view to underpinning robust and sustainable growth in eastern Europe;

(4) ensure that the gap in development levels between the two parts of Europe does not widen; this should be done regardless of the outcome of the current Conference, but it would be especially urgent if successful 'deepening' were to take hold soon;

(5) encourage intensification and widening of economic cooperation among the transition countries and the exploitation of all means available to strengthen the foundations of sustainable growth; and

(6) influence the psychological climate for 'Europe,' *inter alia* by collecting and disseminating appropriate information. The EU remains by and large a closed book to broad layers of the population in the eastern societies, and, conversely, the eastern economies remain a comparatively 'distant neighbor' in time and space for the vast majority of present EU citizens.

3 – A Tentative Strategy

A somewhat visionary, yet realistic, strategy for assisting the more advanced economies in transition with EU accession could include a large number of components reaching into many of the multiple dimensions of a constructive relationship. The following eight appear to me to constitute the most important steps in preparing such economies for accession and in ensuring that the entry barriers for them will not be raised as a result of the outcome of the current Conference, almost regardless of its outcome. Many other elements could of course be added (Altmann, Andreff, and Fink 1995; Altmann and Ochmann 1995; Baldwin 1994; Ludlow and Ersbøll 1996; Weidenfeld 1995), and indeed should be entertained in concrete negotiations on any such strategy. But I am sufficiently modest not to preempt – let alone, pretend to be the omniscient adviser, counselor, observer, or curmudgeon of – what should be substantive negotiations between the European Commission acting on behalf of the Union and one or more economies in transition among the ten favored ones.

1 – Trade and Commercial Relations

First, facilitating market access for exports from the eastern countries to the EU, providing trading outlets for products that these countries can offer on a competitive basis, however temporary that advantage might be for now, constitutes a critical support to transformation policies. It is arguably the most effective assistance that the EU, and the western countries more generally, can render the economies in transition. Not only that, its true economic cost, weighing present and future, as well as the interests of consumers and producers, will be the least of all forms of assistance.

Because the export base of the transition economies is at present rather shallow, and relatively concentrated on products that have been treated as somehow 'sensitive' in recent trade management, and even in the Europe Agreement, these countries are at a distinct disadvantage. Little change is likely to occur soon in the core export capacity of these countries based largely on comparatively cheap labor and, in some, raw materials as well as niches resulting from regulatory discrepancies. Gaining market access for the former products in particular, however small the import penetration remains at this stage, may displace EU production in areas that can exert strong and vocal electoral pressure, as demonstrated since the early 1990s; absolute magnitudes of import penetration are psychologically and politically less relevant than the pace of change in relative magnitudes, particularly at a time of unemployment levels that are deemed to be far too high and considerable sectoral interest-group pressures in the EU.

Nonetheless, strong and dependable trade outlets for products from the economies in transition must be found one way or the other if these countries are to sustain their ongoing economic recovery and experience an endogenous growth dynamic, thus permitting catch-up to levels of development in the Union. The EU's commercial policy with regard to the economies in transition could, for example, more closely take into account the peculiarities of the transition, including the unusual cost structure of enterprises in limbo between state and private ownership, and the difficulties of putting into place adequate corporate-governance mechanisms during much of the transition. It is not very helpful, for example, as is now the case in the context of the Europe Agreement, to implement strenuous contingent-protection clauses, leading to antidumping actions and safeguard clauses, or the imposition of strict countervailing duties, simply to protect EU producers in activities that themselves are in need of substantial restructuring and oftentimes downsizing. True, these have recently been sparingly invoked. But the sheer threat may already be enough of a deterrent.

The economies in transition deserve to benefit from the most generous and flexible interpretation of the EU's common policies notably regarding so-called sensitive products. Although EU quotas on all manufactures will be removed by late 1997, contingent-protection clauses are still part of the Europe Agreement. Whether one is willing or not to admit this, they loom large over the stance taken by some investors, particularly in economies where uncertainty is still as pervasive as in the economies in transition (WERI 1995, pp. 181ff.). I find it not particularly compelling when the European Commission (1995h, p. 11) argues that, because the transition economies are not nearly exhausting their quotas for sensitive products, "there is now little evidence that these countries are constrained suppliers." This may well be so in the short run. But it cannot hold in a longer-term perspective in which determinants of investment are factored in. Moreover, the cost of ascertaining the availability of unfilled quotas is said to be quite high, given the poor administrative infrastructure of economies in transition (WERI 1995, pp. 183ff.). If indeed the contingent-protection clauses were not constraining suppliers from the economies in transition, these stipulations would be redundant. It might therefore be good housekeeping to expunge them soonest from the Europe Agreement.

Reconsideration of these and related trade policies themselves could usefully be included among the policy considerations at the present Conference. Improved market access in this case would have to be combined with more determined efforts to clean up the books of state-owned firms in the transition economies, be it through divestment, restructuring the production process, or putting in place a standard corporate-governance framework, including transparent accounting practices. Assistance could focus on these issues in order to accelerate the arrival of the day when competition can be rooted overwhelmingly in genuine productivity differentials.

The protectionism afforded by many intransparent, invisible NTBs, which the "mutual recognition" principle of the single European market has actually intensified for third countries (Artemiev 1992, Brykman 1992, Grey 1992), could also be tackled. As argued earlier, notably in Chapter 4, the transition economies benefit in some cases from loopholes in regulatory regimes that are not available under the terms of the *acquis* to EU Member States. Mutual recognition under these conditions would undermine the minimum regulation deemed necessary to safeguard the contours of the EU's single-market approach. It would therefore be rather difficult to relax the hurdles these implied NTBs pose to one economy in transition or another. But there must be a number of areas for which certification procedures, for example, can be speeded up by the EU authorities and interpreted generously and expeditiously in the contingent 'mutual recognition' mode.

2 – Mobilizing Financial Flows

Second, official financial transfers, other than for emergency and humanitarian purposes, and various means of reinforcing the economic, political, and social environments in the economies in transition to bolster private capital inflows for financing productive investments, could be more carefully targeted at raising the capacity of these countries to sustain economic growth and indeed to continue to forge ahead expeditiously with economic restructuring. The successful economies in transition have demonstrated the importance of a resumption of net capital formation and the critical role played therein by domestic savings. Economic restructuring, as the experiences of a wide diversity of developed and developing countries have demonstrated, can be more easily undertaken at a time of economic expansion than when an economic recession or depression forms the environment.

Given the parlous state of the public-capital infrastructure, including that for supporting an expansion of trade to western markets, and fiscal constraints, sustaining growth will require major 'crowding-in' investments to enhance the environment for private capital formation and for attracting direct investment from abroad. Without such inflows, underlying productivity growth is unlikely to improve substantially, certainly not to the degree needed to stimulate self-sustainable growth and facilitate entry into the virtuous growth dynamic centered on vibrant intra-industry trade, given that most assistance has been in the form of loans to be serviced at market rates.

In order to avoid a further build-up of external debt, the EU could take the lead in formulating bankable investment projects as an integral part of a pre-accession strategy that can subsequently be financed through one of the regional or global official financial organizations and even by bilateral donors. Such projects could pave the way for the entry of substantial private capital inflows for productive purposes that do not exacerbate foreign debt. Thus far, such flows have trailed far behind expectations in the vast majority of transition economies. Such an approach would be perfectly compatible with the financial objectives tentatively set forth in the Europe Agreement, as briefly discussed in the context of the EU's present assistance format in Chapter 4.

I should like to emphasize most emphatically that the above component of the strategy, as indeed the strategy as a whole, is not intended to be prescriptive for the transition economies or to bring all assistance programs under one umbrella. At the same time, however, the mere existence of such a strategy could in and of itself provide a stimulus to more effective and spontaneous coordination. I shall elaborate on the merits and limits of this approach once I have advanced all elements that I deem to be of particular importance in forging ahead with a much more constructive relationship between the European Union and the economies in transition, both those with a credible claim on membership and others, on the way to more fruitful cooperation.

3 – Assisting with Industrial Restructuring

Third, both the likely applicants for membership and the EU itself are facing problems of enforced restructuring as a result of economic and technical change in the world economy. The EU has experience in dealing with these problems by means of a gradual approach to adjustment in industries such as iron and steel, coal, textiles and clothing, and agriculture. None has been a neat exercise conducted at minimal cost, in terms of the time required, social dislocations incurred, the financial concessions made, or the political compromises that needed to be hammered out to keep the endeavor sociopolitically viable. But useful lessons can be drawn from these efforts if only because EU decision makers can be expected to be aware of the major political, social, and technical obstacles and costs to be reckoned with. There is little point in holding the transition economies to a vastly more-rigorous adjustment process than western Europe has been prepared to accept for itself throughout the postwar period. Proceeding differently would yield an outcome that might involve aborting restructuring, hence promoting peripheralization of the economies in transition, precisely the kind of development that the "return to Europe" was meant to forestall. This would not, of course, be in the long-term interest of the economies in transition. Neither would it be constructive in remaking Europe as seen through the EU's perceptions of what really needs to be accomplished over the next several decades.

It would be useful to search for ways in which the potential applicants might already at an early stage be included in such prospective structural-adjustment programs in the EU, perhaps even sharing in some of the funds (grants as well as other financial provisions) earmarked in support of restructuring programs rather than being potentially or actually subjected to quotas or threatened with antidumping measures, notably in the case of the troublesome iron and steel sectors. Would it not be more constructive to explore ways in which the relevant enterprises from key economies in transition might already now be included in such adjustment programs in return for obtaining greater access to EU markets for some sensitive products on reasonably competitive terms? This applies in particular to the firms whose management may currently be more concerned about liquidity than augmenting net asset values, pending ownership and corporate-governance changes to proceed much further than they have to date. True, this is in a sense industrial policy, something that many contemporary economists are prepared to reject out of hand. I do not as a matter of principle, particularly when the process of "creative destruction" cannot possibly be expected to proceed smoothly on the strength of market incentives when the latter are still inadequate, if present at all (Brabant 1993).

Similar arguments can be made for other activities, including the construction of integrated energy systems; attempts to bring cross-border and other types of pollution under control; the establishment of integrated transport networks by land, air, and sea; the creation or strengthening of communications and computer linkages; and a host of other endeavors that can be readily imagined. Since the Essen Council of December 1994, only a few, rather limited measures have been enacted in the spirit of the above rationale for countries that then had a Europe Agreement in place (that is, ratified). For others, nothing as yet seems to be envisioned along such lines.

I am basing the foregoing advocacy essentially on the consideration that restructuring of the economies in transition (and indeed the repercussions of them joining the EU) should be seen primarily in the real sphere, that is, the production process, rather than nearly exclusively in macroeconomic-policy stances and institutions, however important the latter intrinsically are. It is there that the need for remedial action continues to be considerable. Any international assistance to alleviate matters and expedite the restructuring should be welcomed, particularly when private resource inflows on a predictable basis cannot yet be relied upon. Whereas this advice applies to all assistance providers, I have especially the European Commission, and indeed the EU at large, in mind. It is particularly important that it imparts best-practice positive effects to the agreed-upon transformation agenda, while containing negative repercussions for other countries. The vast bulk of appropriated assistance should act as a catalyst, both to bolster credibility of the transformation processes in transition economies and to cement firmly the groundwork for mobilizing private resources. But that may take quite some time and already proof of a solid economic recovery under way, as the recent recovery experiences of central Europe tend to suggest.

When considering accession to the EU, the complexity of the transformations in the ten candidates for accession justifies the adoption of a much more modulated, intrusive, and hands-on approach with a much longer time horizon in considering EU assistance, a matter to which I return in Section 4. That itself should recognize the specifics of the transformation agenda in the candidate countries, including in fine-tuning the strategy.

4 – Assisting with Institutional Transformation

Fourth, many 'market institutions' – defined broadly to include the infrastructure of institutions, laws, the attitudes of economic agents, and all the other elements that determine the particular shape of any 'market economy' – are still either missing in the eastern economies or function at best rather poorly. Strenuous efforts are still needed to bring about the structural transformations to improve the efficiency of resource allocation; macroeconomic stabilization, notably on the fiscal front; and to adapt existing institutions, such as they exist, to EU norms, notably the *acquis*. Often what is missing is a comparatively small component here or there that is nonetheless essential in ensuring the smooth functioning of the whole system.

Even in foreign economic relations, where the transformation of especially the more advanced economies in transition has been progressing most rapidly and arguably much farther than in many other endeavors, essential elements are still missing while others operate all too often dysfunctionally. Many more measures will be required to further liberalize trade and factor mobility. To cite only one example: The absence of certain foreign-trade institutions (such as functioning export-insurance and -guarantee agencies, credit facilities, efficient financial and foreign-exchange clearing units, and the like) places these economies at a competitive disadvantage in world markets, regardless of the institutions available in partner areas, but more so when they function poorly as in many eastern and southern partner countries. It is refreshing to read, in contrast to the claims made by many policy makers, that there are crucial institutions missing in bolstering, for example, CEFTA trade (see interview with Mr. Ladislav Dvořák, commercial counselor at the Embassy of the Czech Republic in Warsaw, as reported in *Trybuna*, 5 March 1996, pp. 9-10; Żukrowska 1996 only confirms this).

Furthermore, *ex ante* foreign-exchange constraints, particularly among the transition economies themselves, continue to inhibit the expansion of reciprocal, profit-based economic relations. The EU could take a more active role in bolstering this economic cooperation, in its own interests if the extension of membership is to succeed, perhaps through some kind of payment facility; the argument was made a long time ago, among others, in Brabant 1990, pp. 170-7; 1991, pp. 122ff.; UNECE 1990, pp. 147-50. Even at this late hour, the usefulness of these and related measures is now openly acknowledged by eastern European practitioners (see the cited interview in *Trybuna*, 5 March 1996, pp. 9-10). This should help to provide a more solid anchor for genuine current-transaction convertibility particularly in the countries that do not yet subscribe to, and abide by, Article VIII of the Fund's Articles of Agreement or that find it difficult for lack of adequate institutional infrastructure to ensure the smooth implementation of this important variant of currency convertibility.

It would be useful to synchronize the EU's involvement with this rounding off of market-based resource allocation in the economies in transition. The active participation of the EU in such improvements could also help to ensure that the hurdles to be jumped by the transition economies – the gap between the EU's sophistication and wealth and that of the potential members between now and accession negotiations – are not raised by several notches as a result of increased monetary integration and the deepening of integration that may otherwise come about as one of the outcomes of the IGC in progress. The danger that such more formidable hindrances may materialize with monetary integration and the outcome of the Conference is not at all remote.

5 – *Strengthening Policy Credibility*

Fifth, gaining credibility for sustained transformation efforts is a critical ingredient of policy making in the transition economies. It is desirable that rapid restructuring be continued for years to come. This in turn needs sustained support from continuing trade and foreign-exchange liberalization and from fuller integration into the global economic and other multilateral frameworks. A rapprochement with at least the spirit of the 'ecu,' and soon the 'euro,' regime would be most welcome once these economies achieve a reasonable degree of macroeconomic stability with inflation in single digits, even though it may still exceed the desirable target level of, say, 2 to 3 percent of regular members of the euro monetary union. Being closely associated with key mechanisms and policies of the EU would inevitably impart a constructive psychological boost. But pro-active financial measures in favor of currency stability in the transition economies can only be envisioned if the current obstacles to realizing monetary union are overcome. ERM II (see Chapter 3) could conceivably be adapted to accommodate some of the transition economies that are more advanced with their transformation and stabilization agendas.

However, bringing the more advanced transition economies into the ecu, and soon the euro, regime, does not solely depend on these countries attaining reasonable macroeconomic stabilization and the EU's resolving its own problems on the way to the effective functioning of the euro regime. Given the fragility of the financial sector, including in particular the banking sector, throughout the transition economies, much further progress must be made on a priority basis to lay the solid foundations for commercial-banking intermediation. Many issues are at stake beyond putting in place adequate prudential regulations and rules on banking supervision. The EU could play a constructive role in ensuring such progress with financial-sector reform. One element that has recently been advocated (Anderson, Berlöf, and Mizsei 1996, p. 71) is that the EU become much more involved in assessing and fine-tuning bank-supervision activities, not just exercising surveillance and issuing prudential regulations, in transition economies. Whereas the advocacy is for the EU to finance yet another round of consulting contracts with international auditing firms, I would plead a different case on the ground that having a firm commercial-banking sector in place is in part a public good. Public agencies, such as the Commission and the EU's specialized committees, notably ECOFIN, must therefore get actively involved together with private auditing firms if the latter have a comparative advantage in delivering core components of the required financial-sector assessment and fine-tuning exercise. I am not persuaded that this is always the case, though.

Assistance directed at meeting the convergence criteria for monetary integration would also be useful as the admission of new members is unlikely to be seriously contemplated without a firm commitment on their part to joining the monetary union within a reasonable period of time, as argued in Chapter 3. Of course, there is in fact for now no formal requirement that the applicants must be already in a position to meet the convergence criteria to be credibly considered for entry into the EU; but they certainly must have the institutions and policies in place – in other words, the capabilities – to eventually bring about compliance with the convergence criteria (Pearce 1995, pp. 136-7), either those presently binding the EU Member States or those that may be sought in the context of the euro regime, including notably for ERM II (see Chapter 3).

Such a strategy on convergence, preferably embedded in an encompassing program that extends beyond purely monetary and fiscal matters, could increase confidence that the process of closer economic, political, and security integration with the EU will not be deliberately stalled and that reviving regional cooperation on economic grounds, not just in commercial relations, would not be inhibited for overt partisan political motives (see point eight below). Of course, such a strategy would also make it more attractive, as well as urgent, for the EU to assume a major role in financing directly and indirectly, chiefly by issuing formal and other loan guarantees, a good part of the reconstruction costs of the economies in transition until they can attract larger inflows of FDI and generate sufficient savings at home for productive investments. Some justification of this position I have elaborated on in point two above.

6 – *Fostering Mutual Knowledge and Understanding*

Sixth, I have asserted earlier that broad layers of the population in both parts of Europe have limited knowledge and understanding of the continent's 'other half.' In the transition economies much of the posturing of core policy makers, for example, on their countries being 'European' more often than not involves a rather simplified set of assumptions about the origins of pluralistic democracies and market economies and how they actually work. It is still not generally understood that a market economy is not "a machine that goes all by itself, with its own laws and requirements," but a "voluntary mechanism for negotiation, where people enjoy the freedom to interact; the outcome may be success or failure, but the system works provided the rules governing the interaction are good ones" (Pavan 1993, p. 59). Educating the electorates in the transition economies about the western European institutions and practices, which they are in the process of adopting, should rank high on the list of priorities for assistance. Incidentally, the Union might also foster such acculturation among the broader public in its own Member States (see Moussis 1995, pp. 15-16).

Many initiatives in this direction could be envisaged; none need be very expensive. The assistance programs in place (such as PHARE and TACIS) already embody components of what is required, but they have tended to be poorly targeted and often their individual components work at cross purposes. Since the Essen Council of December 1994, these programs, PHARE in particular, are to be increasingly directed at preparing the potential entrants for accession within the context of the EU's pre-accession strategy (see Chapter 4). The Court of Auditors has interpreted this to mean "that a substantial part of the PHARE-program should be orientated toward a larger-scale and more adequate preparation of the administrations of the candidate States concerned for the understanding, the adoption and the implementation of the main Community policies and the related regulations" (European Commission 1995b, p. 216), thus underlining the desirability of acting upon the position argued here.

One essential step is to disseminate serious – objective and comprehensive – information about the EU in the relevant local languages of the economies in transition. Consultations with politicians, from all political parties, and with other groups (including nongovernmental) in economies in transition, going well beyond the fora already in place, could support a constructive deliberative dialogue. A pointed exchange of views between western institutions and the emerging civil societies in the eastern part of Europe would also be helpful in this respect (Reinicke 1992, p. 105). Bringing decision makers of these countries closer to the political EU institutions, especially the European Parliament and the Commission, where in fact most of the Council decisions are all but decided upon before the Council simply endorses them (Ludlow 1996a, pp. 71ff.), would contribute to disseminating information from west to east as well as ensuring some reciprocity. The Union could heed the interests of the economies in transition much more than has been the case in recent years. Foreign-policy matters and security aspects of their situation immediately spring to mind in this connection (for a perceptive analysis, see Timmermann 1993). The purported initiative in the European Commission to act upon the latter after the Florence Council, if true, I welcome, of course.

Promotion of the cultural patrimony of being 'European' would also be helpful. There is no need for cultural imperialism, however. But arranging for young people from eastern Europe to spend some time as students or interns in the European institutions at large could help to fashion a European consciousness that other EU members have developed over a long period of time, and even then only partially. This must necessarily be a two-way street. Although the feeling of being European first and, say, French or German second is not particularly widespread among the citizenry of the EU, there can be no doubt that the gap has narrowed to an astonishing degree as compared to what it was three or four decades ago. This change in psychology, in personal values, and in the behavior and thinking of the citizenry at large has to some extent been influenced by ever-closer economic integration and cooperation, by financial transfers, by an increasing range of 'European' political and cultural events, and, not least, by the wider educational opportunities now available in the EU.

But ignorance about the history and culture of the countries in eastern Europe is still widespread in western Europe, and the EU could help to defuse potential hostility toward the 'eastern cultures' by making better known their fundamentally European roots; likewise as far as ensuring a more realistic appreciation in the economies in transition of what the EU can and cannot do. Many other concrete actions could be suggested, preferably within a multilateral approach through the Europe Agreements.

This applies in particular to the elaboration of the purposes of the institutional machinery for monitoring and fine-tuning the Europe Agreement as a framework instrument for orchestrating this transfer of values. These contacts between the EU and partners with a Europe Agreement are now slated for agriculture, foreign affairs, finance, and transportation. That such consultative meetings will inevitably be beset by some acrimony, stemming largely from uninformed, at times spurious moral or historical, claims on entitlement to full membership at the earliest point in time, cannot be avoided. It will set the tone for later debates about integration proper. Likewise, claims on being exempted from the EU's "petty economic apartheid" (Bressand 1992, p. 15), for example, as embodied in textile, steel, agriculture, shipping, trucking, and other quotas, or threats of contingent protectionism, cannot be altogether avoided and should be digested with a sense of humor and *savoir-faire*. Much greater transparency and openness in clarifying the realistic room for proper negotiations in the EU as well as in the economies in transition would go a long way toward dissipating lingering but, on the whole, ill-founded suspicions.

7 – Strengthening Governance Capacities

It should be clear to all concerned that functioning within the single market, and indeed within the EU's machinery, requires appropriate capabilities at the legal, administrative, institutional, and other levels of governance. Thus, the *acquis communautaire*, whose rules and regulations forming the core part of the *acquis* are slowly developing into a veritable *Lex Europea*, calls for modifying the existing legal framework in the candidate states to conform to by now well over 10,000 EU laws and regulations. Some of these can, as a rule, be introduced during the transition phase negotiated as part of the accession deliberations, when they have not already been achieved in preparation for negotiations. All credible eastern candidates have already been doing so for some time. Even so, the European Parliament has recently underlined that the room for derogation in the case of the present candidates is very narrow (Southey 1996). But it should be emphasized that in earlier enlargements the adoption of the *acquis communautaire* did not require a massive revision of existing laws, administrative rules and regulations, and institutions on the part of the entrant. Even so, assimilating the *acquis* and ensuring that these rules and regulations become effective in the new entrant have never been simple matters. The task ahead in the economies in transition is bound to be much more formidable, given their postwar experience, in spite of the considerable progress made since 1989 (Ludlow 1996a, pp. 41-2). It is definitely appropriate to appreciate the substantial advances made in these countries over a comparatively short period of time. Yet, without the greater part of the rules and appropriate institutions in place and working effectively, it would be difficult for the economies in transition to make a credible commitment to abide by the given 'club rules' of the EU.

In this connection it is important to underline the role of the state and its civil service in supporting these types of activities. Unfortunately, the liberal bent that has held sway throughout most of the transition economies since 1989, in part at the behest of western assistance providers, has paid too little attention to the restructuring of the civil service and to redefining and transforming the governance capacities of the state to carry out its proper functions in a market economy. This weakness of public administration can only hamper the smooth integration of transition economies into the EU framework. A swift correction, if possible with the assistance of the EU, is urgently required.

This is not the appropriate place to elaborate on the role of the state in economic affairs (see Brabant 1993, pp. 142-70). I do wish to point out, however, that the need to reform the capacities of the state to govern also economic affairs, where it has, or should hold, a comparative advantage, and indeed to mobilize whatever capabilities for good economic governance are still within reach or in place to navigate the more difficult passages of the transition agenda, continues to be very considerable in all economies in transition. Rethinking the new role of the new state in all of its dimensions, including in coming to grips with the complexities of dovetailing these economies much more closely with those of the EU, is not something that can be postponed until the rudiments of incipient capitalist markets will have been assimilated and the needs for reining in the wilder sides of such an environment will have been forcefully expressed once again.

Rather, it is urgent to forestall the eventuality that these economies might retrogress into primitive capitalism – a state of affairs that these societies thought they had left behind at least with socialist industrialization. Ideological stances are unlikely to be very helpful in this regard. Determined pragmatism on the part of all actors involved in transformation policies would seem to be urgently needed. Under some conditions, only an authoritarian intervention in economic affairs, such as the so-called shock therapy, may successfully inch forward, and perhaps guide, the process toward the coveted new development path. But there can be no guarantee that this outcome will emerge from the shock.

It is also worth emphasizing in connection with the role of the state, and in contemplating how best the EU could help out in this respect, that the smooth integration of the economies in transition into the EU, or within the broader global economic framework for that matter, depends crucially on the availability of accurate and ample information on economic and other matters in these countries (UNECE 1990, pp. 16-17). The private sector as a rule does not provide such services; or if it does, it tends to focus on *ad hoc* studies motivated by private investment considerations. The provision of comprehensive and reliable statistics, for example, is in fact a public good that is essential for the efficient working of a modern market economy. But such provision also depends on a well-trained, -organized, and -equipped public administration. Improvements are well under way in many transition economies, often with expert help and advice from the EU's Eurostat, among other technical facilities of bilateral and multilateral assistance providers. But important gaps remain to be filled and shortcomings to be overcome. In this context it is unfortunate that a number of regional and international institutions have recently been cutting back on the resources devoted to the economic and statistical analysis of developments in the transition economies on the specious ground that the transition is over or 'others' are doing the legwork, thereby ensuring in a number of cases that it will not get done conscientiously.

Budget parsimony is the order of the day for public institutions. Its indiscriminate application, in lawn-mowing fashion, is particularly misplaced especially in this instance. In view of the still palpable uncertainty in many endeavors of the economies in transition, such a retrenchment may actually hamper the transfer to the private sector of some of the financing functions hitherto provided through official channels. The EU could usefully consider how to rectify this contraction in sources of information and analyses, particularly the more impartial ones devoted chiefly to examining available policy options, either through in-house developments or by supporting a revival of the capabilities in the organs that have traditionally earned their spurs in reporting on the economies of the eastern part of Europe. This may sound like pleading *pro domo*, but I manifestly do not encourage that impression. Monopolizing the information stream would definitely not be desirable, certainly not when the aim is to promote an open society.

In the same vein, a logical argument can be made in favor of enhancing the political dialogue in the context of the framework provided by the Europe Agreement, hopefully after harmonizing the provisions into a multilateral deliberative forum. Imparting a clearer view to the economies in transition on the role of 'market institutions' in the EU, their historical evolvement, their present functioning, as well as the advantages and drawbacks encountered at the present stage, would offer decision makers in the economies in transition, as well as the broader public, a more realistic perspective on what needs to be done, including in terms of creating the governance institutions that neither belong to the state nor are scrutinized in the marketplace.

8 – Encouraging a Revival of Regional Cooperation

Finally, a useful component of a pre-accession strategy would be to assist the transition economies with their reciprocal dialogue and mutual cooperation, including with those countries of the region that will not be candidates for EU accession at all or any time soon. This is admittedly a highly controversial issue. It is, however, definitely worth exploring not only in trade relations. Many serious commentators, as well as pundits of all ilk, have argued that strong intragroup ties, not only in the economic but also in the political and sociocultural spheres, will eventually emerge from being closer together within the EU. Worrying about the issue before adhesion, it is claimed, diverts attention from the current priority of securing EU membership, which is held to be the most desirable, even optimal according to some well-placed commentators, foreign-policy course to pursue at this stage of the complex transformation of these economies in transition.

This argument, however, is not especially compelling or persuasive for that matter. It would certainly not be very useful to enhance intragroup cooperation, let alone for the EU to promote it, if the goal were solely to deflect actual or potential trade away from the west. On the other hand, it is hard to imagine the economies in transition joining the

EU while their mutual ties remain in disarray or fragile. In fact, a case can be made for fostering close cooperation among the potential entrants while they await admission, simply to avoid infusing undesirable centrifugal forces into their tactical stances among themselves as well as with respect to the Union once the accession negotiations are successfully concluded (Martin 1994). Furthermore, accession will require time (see Chapter 5), and in the meantime these economies continue to be in need of sustaining their economic growth at the most rapid pace feasible. In view of the severity of the recession in these countries since the early 1990s, there must remain room for mutually supporting policies to shore up final demand.

Recent developments in intragroup cooperation have been especially gratifying to me personally. From early on in the transition debates, I have been unwilling to join the bandwagon of observers arguing the fruitlessness of bolstering intragroup economic cooperation, even of forging new commercial ties among these countries. From the very inception of transformation, in some contrast, I have underlined that the potential for such relations is far from negligible; it is certainly not nil. Though many of the former economic and other ties among these eastern countries have since 1989 been deliberately severed, I have expressed strong disagreements with those who argue that it is now too late to hope to benefit from any form of regional economic cooperation beyond what is likely to emerge spontaneously by letting economic agents pursue their own interests.

I feel that one can still marshal cogent arguments to buttress the proposition that markets with a population of between some 65 million (central Europe) and 130 million (traditional eastern Europe plus Albania, the Baltic States, and the Yugoslav successor States) with some positive purchasing power and a substantial import elasticity of demand simply cannot be ignored. For one thing, trade links among these countries justified on economic grounds have been ruptured and then a revival hindered by a variety of political and institutional obstacles. Also, these countries have traditionally not tried to reinforce reciprocal trade complementarities among their economies by more fully exploiting their present and evolving competitive economic strengths. Furthermore, these countries have focused too much, and chiefly in too narrow a fashion, on regaining rapid growth of trade with and quick entry into the EU – both rather unlikely events for some time to come. The point is manifestly not that such a market among the transition economies could possibly be autarkic or that it should be fashioned through intrusive discriminatory instruments. In fact, governments need to continue to take positive steps to ensure that obstacles presently created by still imperfectly functioning markets be reversed whenever justified on economic grounds (*Trybuna*, 5 March 1996, pp. 9-10; Żukrowska 1996). One could even argue beyond that: To restore a level playing field in trade among the economies in transition, as compared to their westward relations, positive discriminatory measures may be justified under some circumstances (Reinicke 1992, pp. 53-64).

The argument would be quite parallel to and symmetric with any justification of granting these countries a variety of discriminatory arrangements in the western part of Europe, such as the EU has done since 1989 and is indeed inherent in belonging to this integration format and organization. The point is simply that even if eventually that trade should amount to no more than, say, a quarter of the total trade of the economies in transition, but achieved at a high level of economic activity with steady economic expansion, it would amount to billions of dollars. What is more, given the external openness toward which the transition economies aspire, intragroup trade would count for a nonnegligible part of aggregate demand in these countries. For as long as the transition economies are not functioning against binding supply constraints, there should be room to accommodate such extra demand at a modest extra cost. Since potential supply is well ahead of actual output levels, given the low opportunity cost of mobilizing even outmoded production capacities in the short run, there should be room for profitable trade for all concerned, including the EU Member States.

With the collapse of the CMEA; the realignment of the various transition economies; and the fibrillating economic, political, and security realities in the eastern part of Europe, an altogether new system of alliances for countries wedged into the corridor running from the Baltic to the Adriatic and the Black Sea has been crystallizing. These efforts have been various and include most notably the Baltic Sea States Council, a sort of outgrowth of Nordic cooperation, which has found it difficult to fuse the new Baltic States with the established Nordic Council, and the Baltic Council, which has been in need of credibility;

the Visegrád forum with the CEFTA; the Central European Initiative, which was preceded by the Alps-Adria cooperation (with Austria, Hungary, Italy, and the former Yugoslavia, and for a while in 1989 also Bavaria) and the *Pentagonale-Hexagonale* (the *Hexagonale* with Poland; the *Pentagonale* with Czechoslovakia and the four Alps-Adria participants); and the Black Sea Economic Cooperation Region. Most of these regional formats have remained very weak and fragile. One should best look at these undertakings as potentially affording interim forms of cooperation that may or may not survive evolving events. Most probably will not as stronger ties are built up over time with core cooperation partners. Unlike others (see Baldwin 1994) I do not see much purpose in promoting new institutional-organizational forms of either intragroup or east-west cooperation beyond streamlining the Association Councils and making them the operative institutional platform for developing, monitoring, assessing, and fine-tuning the pre-accession strategies under discussion here.

It can be shown that transaction costs in trade among the transition economies are still unusually high. The infrastructure for mediating and supporting commercial links continues to be poorly developed (*Trybuna*, 5 March 1996, pp. 9-10), and often western intermediaries are mobilized, such as for effecting payments, at significant fees for what could largely be taken care of by a regional clearing institution. Fears of political and strategic entanglements that could conceivably divert attention from moving into the world economy are quite pronounced. Nonetheless, greater credibility and targeted institutional supports could be provided at a sensible cost. This should be a critical motive to investigate in earnest the most desirable ways and means of assisting these economies in reentering the global economy through international economic cooperation.

I am prepared to argue that both conditions apply to an unusual degree in the case at hand. True, the transformation processes in the eastern part of Europe have been palpably hampered by the willful destruction of intragroup economic relations that had been built up during the forty-odd years of cooperation in the CMEA framework, which *in se* were economically warranted, at least in the short to medium run. That is now history, and we should not be prisoners of a redolent past that never was. But the pertinence of such, from an economic perspective, intrinsically warranted advantages even at this stage should be recognized for what it is.

The paramount motivation for action at this juncture should be the search for how best to exploit the current and prospective room for rebuilding commercial ties on economically warranted principles. But legacies of the technological snobbery (for examples, see Paweł Bożyk, who is director of the Institute for International Economic Relations of Poland, no less, in *Rynki Zagraniczne*, 27 January 1996, p. III; Richter and Tóth 1996) so prevalent in communist posturing continue to cloud the decision-making horizon and current thinking about economic, political, and social transformations to a much larger degree than need be. It may well be true that firms in one transition economy or another continue to have only a weak interest in importing from their eastern neighbors. But that should be seen as a transitory aberration. Once the profitability of bolstering intragroup trade becomes clear, this penchant for favoring one market over another with spare capacities, or resources available to expand such capacities, will disappear once arbitrage in functioning markets shows profitable opportunities forgone.

Trade among these countries intermediated by western middlemen offers but one illustration of such arbitrage; that may well be efficient pending the creation of a rudimentary institutional infrastructure, as noted earlier, but it cannot be justified in the longer run as the total cost of building institutions is likely to be smaller than the cost of intermediation through western middlemen. But it remains highly imperfect because of temporarily high transaction costs for lack of experience and uncertainty in these markets. These costs could be substantially lowered by improving the 'institutions' for direct trade, as argued earlier (Brabant 1995a).

Bringing about such credibility requires at a minimum: (1) a reasonable guarantee to the effect that virtually all discrimination between domestic and foreign agents and among various groups of foreign agents will be abolished over a comparatively short period of time; (2) a good chance of that goal being achieved at a cost worth incurring, given the objectives pursued and the gains in savings with transaction costs that can be realized; and (3) that both insiders and outsiders to the transformation policies remain committed to steering the economies in transition resolutely in the direction of market-based resource allocation in a pluralistic political environment without jeopardizing the still-delicate sociopolitical consensus.

Any of these arguments, and certainly when all are taken together, could justify EU support for policies to improve the specialization of the transition economies, individually *and* collectively, and thus mitigate some of the existing obstacles to their eventually joining the EU. This applies especially to weak intermediation, particularly through financial markets, and the crisis in the banking system in many transition economies. Assistance for strengthening the banking and financial systems could be very important for enabling the transition economies to participate effectively in the single market. (This argument is set out as well in Altmann, Andreff, and Fink 1995, pp. 241-4. It has been made on a number of occasions since 1989 in various issues of *Economic Survey of Europe* and *Economic Bulletin for Europe*.)

4 – A Hands-on Approach?

Underneath the argument I have made here lies the contention that the EU constitutes a natural center for exerting 'subtle' pressures on the transition economies perhaps in exchange for a commitment to broader assistance from and collaboration with the EU. This could most fruitfully be formulated to shore up and impart a new impetus to intragroup cooperation, while smoothing whatever rough edges there are for now, linked directly to the integration of the economies in transition into the global community in general and into 'Europe' in particular. Providing support for intragroup cooperation through financial transfers, macroeconomic surveillance, and diverse forms of technical assistance would in and of itself inject a crucial measure of credibility into intragroup cooperation at this juncture, prior to merging more fully into the Union.

Adherents of the notion that it is desirable to foster only the purest market relations may object to such 'intervention,' particularly since it emanates from the outside. I disagree with this stance in principle. On reasonably realistic grounds and historical experience, the measures I have been advocating can be considered an integral component of good regional governance and indeed of just plain good policy making in the economies in transition themselves. Positive intervention where warranted by the adversities and distortions of the transitions, not to forget by the various instances of EU discrimination in favor of the eastern economies, would be particularly appropriate in the context of easing the economies in transition into the Union. Of course, such should not even be contemplated simply for the benefit of reviving intragroup cooperation. Rather, it could be an integral element in the strategy for strengthening democracy and market-based decision making in the eastern part of Europe *and* preparing selected economies in transition for moving eventually more fully into the global economy in general and the EU in particular to obtain especially economic security, but also some political and military security.

It should be clear, however, that such an assistance package, including its domestic requirements, cannot be foisted upon any transition economy. But an unwillingness to cooperate on the latter's part would diminish its claim for assistance beyond the level that the EU may wish to safeguard for reasons of 'national security.' This approach too forms part of good regional governance and of what is required to facilitate, not to delay, the entry of economies in transition into the EU.

The agenda points advocated in the preceding section are deliberately meant to be suggestive and incomplete, and thus to prompt further discussion. All I hope to accomplish in the process is to emphasize the importance of devoting more than casual attention, by the EU leadership in particular, to what can and should be accomplished in terms of forging a more realistic rapprochement between the economies in transition and the EU than what the latter would seem to have seen fit to undergird since 1989. It emphasizes in particular what could be done comparatively quickly and with minimal incremental budgetary expenditures on the part of the EU for those transition economies that have applied, or will soon apply, for EU membership with a view to minimizing the possible damage that the current IGC and further progress with integration among the Fifteen may inflict by raising the barriers to accession.

Much more could be done, of course. I suggest, however that the eight areas outlined in the preceding section are those in which progress is feasible with some political good will and at tolerable cost; parametric details of those broad areas can be further elaborated, depending on the situation in the individual transition economy. They may provide a solid start to cementing, and then anchoring more robustly, a closer and a much more durable relationship, one based on realistic compromises rather than arid acrimony. If only for that reason, the tasks should rank very high on the agenda of the present IGC.

The proposal is not, of course, prescriptive. Nor is it aimed at centralizing all western assistance under the EU's umbrella, as indicated in connection with mobilizing resources for financing crowding-in investments. There is just no need for that. Quite the contrary: An articulated strategy that is comprehensive, well coordinated, and credible is required. By leading up to the accession of the transition economies with a Europe Agreement, but not necessarily at the same date, such a program will, in and of itself, act as a coordinating mechanism. Other partners in global cooperation are likely to pay attention to the program's components of direct interest to them and their repercussions. Since they support the basic objectives of the transition process anyway, they should see the advantage of orienting their own efforts to its basic structure, if only because the latter forms the *raison d'être* for the pre-accession strategy to begin with. As a result, rather than aggravating bureaucratic turf battles, wasting assistance, or creating overlap in different approaches, such a coherent program would provide the basis for a more spontaneous format of coordination among the various actors assisting the transition process. It would also constitute a useful guideline for assisting the transition economies and the preparing the EU for another enlargement.

5 – Assisting Other Economies in Transition

Aside from the ten countries with a Europe Agreement, which can thus be expected to be credible claimants for full EU membership sometime in the foreseeable future, there are at least two other groups of economies in transition of strategic significance to the EU. This holds not only for the EU as a regional organization. If anything, it is even more germane to individual Member States, notably those on the EU's present eastern borders (Austria, Finland, Germany, and Sweden in particular).

One group consists of Albania and the successor States of Yugo-slavia other than Slovenia. Presumably after suitable socioeconomic restructuring and the normalization of relations in the Balkans, these countries too will eventually seek entry into the EU, and be allowed to do so, once the next round(s) of enlargement will have been concluded. In addition there are other economies in transition, notably in the CIS, that are unlikely (especially those that can hardly be classified as Euro-pean) or unwilling for their own reasons (for example, Russia might well take such a stance) to consider membership. Especially the western-most of these countries – notably Belarus, Moldova, Russia, and Ukraine – are strategically located *vis-à-vis* the EU. Some of these countries are large and potentially significant trading partners for the EU. Without exception, all have been benefiting from some types of assistance, notably via TACIS, from the EU.

The obstacles to recovery and sustainable growth that these two groups of economies in transition face are quite different from those prevailing in the candidates for EU entry and they affect the agenda of the ongoing Conference only marginally. Even so, the latter's outcome is potentially of great importance for shaping the future relationship of the EU with these economies. Mr. Hennadii Udovenko, Ukraine's Minister of Foreign Affairs, on 6 May 1996 pleaded openly for such assistance from the EU to help his country become economically strong, and thus reach a platform from which it could then seek full accession to the Union (*OMRI Daily Digest*, 7 May 1996).

To the degree that the Conference, as many observers anticipate (or hope?), will set major markers on the path to remaking Europe, the outcome of the deliberations will in one way or another affect the process whereby the relationship between the EU and these other economies in transition can be streamlined into a constructive partner-ship for years to come. At least in commercial, environmental, human rights, transportation, security, and related matters, the EU has funda-mental interests with respect to these countries at stake that cannot be ignored. In fact, in certain positions taken by leading political parties, such as the CDU/CSU in Germany, extension toward the eastern part of Europe and avoiding the emergence of a vacuum in the area by maintaining a constructive relationship with other economies in transi-tion, notably the other successor States of the Soviet Union, figure among the core tasks of shaping the Union's future (see, for example, Biedenkopf 1995, Lamers and Schäuble 1995).

In the Balkans, the successor States of Yugoslavia (except Slovenia) have an immediate need for reconstruction and basic development as well as for making headway with the rudiments of a coherent transformation agenda (notably stabilization, privatization, fiscal reform, governance issues, financial markets, and restructuring). Their potential for being brought under the EU's umbrella as full partners is therefore more latent than is the case for the Baltic or other Balkan economies with a Europe Agreement. There is little doubt, however, that at some point in the future these countries too will, on present policy stances, hope to become credible candidates for entry.

In that perspective, it might be useful for the EU to think strategically about how best it can earmark available funds, even if only from within existing assistance budgets, and target them at expediting economic recovery in the area; establishing a democratic political culture with at least minimal respect for human rights; accelerating the sociopolitical and economic transformation processes, including the role of the state and the public sector in economic affairs, in such a way that the countries will be able to deal constructively with the prospect of eventually integrating with the EU; and regaining sustainable economic growth with substantial structural change over the next several years. In terms of economic development, these countries are now even less capable than the present candidates for EU membership of engaging in open competition in a single market, such as the EU's, and of integrating themselves into the virtuous growth cycle around vibrant intra-industry trade. That anchor is still largely absent. A priority therefore is to construct programs that will reduce the risks of peripheralization, which would be undesirable in itself and counterproductive in regard to EU integration (see Chapter 5).

Such a compact would, of course, be different in nature from the one that could usefully be entertained with respect to the economies in transition farther east, just as it would be quite different from the pre-accession strategy I have advocated for the ten countries with a Europe Agreement in place. If there were to be any likelihood of some of the western successor States of the Soviet Union being eventually considered for accession, and some like Moldova and Ukraine have already underlined their desire to be so chosen, those countries could be dealt with separately from the other successor States that will not be so treated because they are not European or will not wish to solicit membership for their own political reasons. Comprehensive trade and cooperation agreements are probably the most useful way of dealing with the core issues at stake in a first revamping of their relations with the EU. They would also seem to offer the most suitable way of assisting the most western members of the CIS over the next several years. But, eventually, more substantial assistance may be required to check the decline in support for economic transformation. The latter could not but have repercussions on other reforms, notably in the political and strategic arenas.

Indeed, comprehensive, well-targeted assistance might well be warranted to ensure that the lukewarm transformations that have kept these countries on a path of socioeconomic decline for all too long now will not further deteriorate and hollow out whatever penchant for pluralistic democracy and market-based resource allocation might still be rescued and strengthened, if only to overcome the prevailing state of vacillating indecisiveness. Once such a recovery path will be within reach, the scenario of moving toward the kinds of support programs just outlined for the Balkan countries, suitably interpreted, of course, could again be seriously contemplated.

In one way or another, then, all of these arrangements will involve working out to mutual satisfaction some degree of preferential access to the EU's market and to its financial resources, possibly at the explicit expense of other beneficiaries of preferential arrangements with the EU . Their impacts on EU members and present beneficiaries of the various preferential arrangements will need to be reconciled with the EU's economic, environmental, health, political, security, and other interests in formalizing relations with both these groups of transition economies. For those economies in transition that remain outside the EU framework altogether or will conceivably enter into this organization only in a very remote future, the consequences for the present arrangements of the EU will naturally be less severe and daunting than those that may arise in fusing the other economies in transition into the EU framework as full members. Just the same, the EU can hardly afford to ignore them, if only because of its own interests.

Conclusions

As I have argued on several occasions during this political-economy excursion, there is no simple choice between 'widening' and 'deepening' integration in the EU. Both objectives must be pursued simultaneously, even though widening remains contingent on a critical minimal commitment to deepening, in such a way that any delay in integration among the present and near-term members will not infringe too much on the delivery of the economic, political, security, and other benefits that Union membership eventually holds out for a range of transition economies. That poses a number of critical governance issues, hence the salience of the current IGC and the need to thoroughly prepare for the remaking of the Union's decision-making mechanisms. That is part of the deepening that should take place over the next several years if at least a minimal consensus can be hammered out at the present IGC.

But there are also deep-seated governance issues relating to the orderly preparation of these countries for assuming in the near term the costs of membership in the EU in order to be able to benefit maximally from what the EU has to offer; budgetary transfers can at best be only one, and rather short-term, consideration. Similar governance issues are at stake in managing assistance delivery to all economies in transition. Some are not unlike those that the Union members have had to face over the years to manage prior episodes of enlargement and to anchor more firmly regional integration beyond achievements of a rudimentary customs union.

The range of acute issues that crop up with any enlargement toward the eastern part of Europe is unique in a number of respects (Ludlow 1996a, pp. 34ff.). Even the fundamentals of democracy and market-based resource allocation still leave a lot to be desired. They also present thorny, and at times baffling, problems of how one can compromise on fundamental precepts, either those pertaining to the core, the very essence of the transformations in the eastern part of Europe (such as sound macroeconomic policy, competition, and the role of the state in a viable market economy) or those at the heart of European unification, or perhaps both.

I have argued here that both the EU and the economies in transition, as well as a broad range of other actors involved with assisting the region in the broad sense of technical and economic interaction, could benefit from putting in place a coherent pre-accession strategy at the earliest possible moment as well as a more comprehensive assistance program for economies that cannot expect to join any time soon or do not want to do so at all.

Conclusions

At the end of this journey, the reader may legitimately ask where precisely I stand on the accession of the economies in transition to the EU individually or in one or multiple groups. I want to stress candidly at this stage that I have been, and remain, an ardent advocate of reasonably staggered membership in the EU at the earliest possible time for most economies in transition. How best to govern this process of remaking 'Europe,' while the Union itself is being recast in several dimensions and the economies in transition progress with the implementation of their transformation agenda, has been my central purpose here. In short, there are at present too many obstacles to forging ahead with consolidation of the integration achievements obtained to date and moving into new areas of common policies in the EU, as well as with encumbering the transformation agendas in the eastern part of Europe with the EU's *acquis*, putting it briefly, to permit early membership justified largely on economic grounds. However, I realize that political sentiment and *raison d'état* may well dictate a different course. Of course, the hurdles to be overcome would intrinsically not be substantially different, and the obstacles will have to be confronted one way or the other in any case.

I am fully aware that high politics may act swiftly upon any political calamity in the eastern part of Europe. That might well precipitate setting aside some of the more technical and organizational concerns in the deliberations about accession that I have been concerned with here. Their implications for how the economies in transition will function within the EU, and indeed encumber the prevailing imperative nature of deepening the EU's integration processes, will not be so easily dispelled, however. It is against the above backdrop as well as the fact that the EU is presently actively redesigning some of its own 'architecture' that I have concentrated the discussions in this volume.

Because an IGC is as a rule a seminal event, and as such rarely convened, the one that was initiated in late March 1996 provides a signal that important decisions on the future shape of the EU, and by extension of Europe as a whole, are afoot. This is certainly so as far as the institutional setup, decision-making powers, and broader governance issues of the EU's endeavors are concerned. Progress on these issues, at least their underlying principles, needs to be made over the next several months as, according to EU insiders, holding another IGC to deal with such issues is unlikely to be agreed upon for years to come (Interview 1996a, p. 9). Expectations are arguably even more ambitious, they certainly reach even further, because of the daunting array of obstacles that the process of integration has been facing notably since the conclusion of the Maastricht Treaty in 1991. What happens at the ongoing Conference, however, is not just the concern of the present EU members; it will also exert a major impact notably on shaping the format through which the ten transition economies with a Europe Agreement will eventually be able to proceed toward accession.

Although the concrete agenda for the IGC is as yet unknown, I have argued here that it is bound to be informed by three sources of concern: (1) the review of the Maastricht Treaty, which was its original purpose, in particular on institutional and decision-making issues; (2) unforeseen events since 1990, notably the transformations in eastern Europe and the former Soviet Union, the turbulence in financial markets that undermined earlier arrangements for moving toward the completion of EMU, and the slowdown in economic activity at a time of already very high levels of unemployment with tight restrictions on government budgets; and (3) the need to make arrangements to come to grips with the difficulties encountered during the ratification of the Maastricht Treaty.

Attempts to confine the Conference's agenda solely to institutional and governance reforms of the EU, as the Commission and some Member States have been attempting, will probably be unsuccessful because deepening cannot realistically be pursued at the express expense of widening, even though the latter remains contingent on the former; and the reverse is simply not possible if the EU's basic objectives are not to be abandoned. In that light, rather than second-guessing the ongoing debates, this book has sought to paint the backdrop of the policy deliberations at the ongoing Conference, including the needs for institutional and governance reforms, monetary integration, budgetary matters, the policies underlying the transfer programs, and assisting all economies in transition.

Whatever transpires at the Conference, the strategic decisions taken there, if only by default, by the time it ends sometime in 1997 will be of major importance not only for western Europe and its immediate neighbors, but also for the global community as a whole. This will certainly be the case if the Conference is successful in moving the EU's integration agenda forward. But failure to reach consensus on the most critical challenges facing the Union would also have major consequences with respect to the structure of European cooperation. Similarly affected would be the EU's economic and other relations with nonmember countries, especially those benefiting from preferential arrangements; in other words, for the remaking of Europe and for repositioning the continent as a constructive partner in the global concert of nations. After all, the EU is *de facto* an important actor in coordinating global affairs, including in economic matters.

Arguably, the outcome of the Conference will nowhere be of more significance than for the transition economies of eastern Europe and the CIS, both individually and as a group, and regardless of whether they will be able or want to join the Union in the foreseeable future. Any enlargement of the Union without a *modus vivendi* on its deepening in the near term can lead only to a weakening of the commitment to integration beyond some variant of free trading. From a longer-term perspective, seen within the context of the ambitions on European integration in the successive treaties of the EU, however, this would be detrimental. It would be especially so for the economies now aspiring to membership in the EU. A retrogression in the EU's commitment to deepening integration would reduce the attractiveness of the EU to those transition economies whose ambitions for membership are based on wider considerations than the benefits of free trade.

There is no need for any doomsday scenario, though. Trading and broader economic relations among the present EU membership are highly interdependent, particularly for intra-industry trade. This degree of interlacing cannot, nor need it, be unraveled because of lack of progress with deepening integration. But such stagnation could exacerbate uncertainty in markets as to the future framework for economic relations on the continent. That would affect the expectations of economic agents in a number of respects, most notably in their investment decisions. Precisely because the transition economies are not yet so firmly tied into this intricately laced network of intra-industry trade in the EU, the repercussions of failure to move ahead with deepening integration in the Union might be more serious. Indeed the attempts of these countries to exploit international trade as an engine sustaining recovery and moving economic expansion forward at a steady pace for some time, thus delivering them with their coveted catch-up dynamic toward western levels of income per head, wealth, technology, and so on, may be in partial jeopardy.

Bringing the transition economies into the EU framework as full members will take time. It will also involve substantial costs in the short run both for the EU and the new entrants. Estimates of this burden cannot simply be confined to budgetary contributions or receipts. A wide range of costs and benefits ought to be considered, given especially that their distribution for existing EU members and for the candidate members, both contemporaneously and over time, is asymmetric, which will complicate the negotiations. All economies in transition have a long way to go before they can reasonably claim to have reached the position of, say, Portugal or Spain in the mid 1980s, in relation to the *acquis* and their ability to abide by it.

But a closer, more streamlined and strategic relationship between the EU and the economies in transition, especially with those presently seeking EU membership, needs to be elaborated soon in order to meet at least to some extent the expectations of the candidates for entry as regards economic benefits, largely those emanating from market access but also subsidies to some extent; and greater security, as well as to underpin the credibility of their transformation policies. Several channels are available to ensure that expectations on the part of the transition economies, notably on policy credibility and security, can be met to a significant degree without engineering membership in an overhasty manner. Many of the economic benefits can be harvested and some of the costs forestalled in particular by working in a more strategic manner toward easing the process of gaining membership.

I have here elaborated in particular on the development of a strategic pre-accession program in which a detailed sequence of steps to be followed in terms of adjusting policies and institutions, in both the economies in transition and in the EU, should be laid out. The answer to the frequently posed question of *when* accession can be contemplated should then preferably follow logically from complying with the components of the strategy, which may have to be intermittently fine-tuned to ensure its continued relevance. It should be clear to all concerned that fulfilling those conditions would be tantamount to qualifying for membership – no more nor less.

Such an approach would offer an opportunity to reverse the fairly widespread dissatisfaction with the way in which international assistance has been dispensed to the economies in transition in general and with the programs the EU has seen fit to launch since 1990 in particular. If western Europe is serious about its own and the continent's 'architecture,' it simply cannot afford to disregard the eastern half of the continent, regardless of the eventual suitability for membership of these countries. At the very least, the growing perception in several eastern European countries that they are being deliberately kept 'on the doorstep' of the EU needs to be reversed. Likewise, if the economies in transition are firmly bent on joining the 'Europe' that the EU embodies, they will have to formulate credible programs for constructing the institutional and policy foundations necessary for discharging the objectives and benefiting from the privileges of full membership. If the need for such a transition period can be recognized by both partners, a realistic compromise may then be in the offing, if perhaps not quite within immediate reach. A detailed, well thought-out strategy could thus provide the transition economies with a credible insurance that mutually beneficial membership will soon be in the offing.

The international community at large can only hope that western Europe at this critical juncture in its own affairs as well as with respect to its historical role in refashioning the continent, and as a result a major component of the global framework, will rise to the task in depth and in breadth, and with magnanimity. It would, however, be unwise to harbor the illusion that the present Conference will formulate solutions for decades to come, except possibly in its institutional, decision-making, and governance dimensions. For those the Conference simply *must* succeed. As regards the other policy issues confronting the EU, however, the decisions made in the course of the Conference will exert a determining influence, hopefully a positive one, on the evolving long-term nature of European integration and its relation to the rest of the world. It is incumbent upon the Member States to embrace measures that will make the current Conference neither a *pro forma* event nor stretch it out indefinitely far into the future; nor that it be conducted with a great deal of secrecy and behind-the-scenes deal makings.

Unfortunately, the first months of the deliberations of the Conference have been far from transparent, at least to observers like myself who have no privileged access to the intramural debates. If only from that private perspective, the calls for openness and transparency in EU matters, such as they emerged after the Maastricht Treaty was agreed upon, still seem to be largely unheeded. The EU's governance bodies might well take note of this observation for it probably applies to most outside observers of the EU scene.

Apprehension on the part of the leadership of the economies in transition that virtually any proposal falling short of membership in the EU at the earliest moment is tantamount to "keeping their countries out" should be dispelled with dispatch; it is a bogus complaint that deserves to be rejected on solid grounds. True, resistance to the idea of promoting cooperation in the eastern area has waned somewhat as the realities of the economic, global, and social transformations, as well as of the hurdles to be overcome in joining the EU, have taken ascendency over ideology, politics, or any misguided moral or facile historical claim. Rather than frowning at any offer from the EU that would credibly promise to move the economies in transition onto a clearly hewn path with a fairly comprehensive pre-accession strategy, at the end of which membership would ensue, it could, in fact, provide a plausible insurance that mutually beneficial membership will soon jell.

The proposals advocated here by way of illustrating what *could* be done to accelerate a meaningful accession of the ten privileged economies in transition in particular and to strengthen the EU's cooperation with other such economies are intended to be helpful in selecting the framework of discourse for the relevant policy discussions and concrete negotiations about the formulation, implementation, assessment, and fine-tuning of such a strategy. I am fully aware of the fact, and I do wish to underline it here once more, that much more thought deserves to be given regarding how best to set about formulating and implementing, let alone negotiating expeditiously, any pre-accession and cooperation strategies along the lines discussed in Chapter 6; providing a stronger safety net for transition economies, in terms of economic, political, and security matters, involves many diplomatic and political issues that cannot be settled in advance, certainly not by an outsider like myself.

Moreover, I manifestly underline that any such strategy cannot be foisted upon any of the applicants for accession. Such a pre-accession process *must* be voluntarily entered into. To clarify the policy options at stake, however, the Commission should first of all set the broad framework of such a strategy, as might have been the intention when the Council mandated the development of the EU's pre-accession strategy, and the Commission is now perhaps considering delivering upon under the inappropriate label of "partial membership," and then invite the applicants, if interested, to embark on concrete negotiations to identify the specifics of a program tailored to the circumstances of each candidate.

The present Conference's outcome, whatever it will be, will undoubtedly clarify matters in this regard and, it is hoped, in so many other EU endeavors.

Bibliography

Note: I have made extensive use of Internet postings especially by the European Commission and some of its Member States. These notices are not always clearly dated and page references must, by force of circumstance, depend on one's computer equipment and oftentimes the time frame during which one has access to these various home pages. I have tried to date everything as accurately as possible. This was easier for new appearances. It was not always possible to do likewise for inventory items, however.

Adam, Rudolf G. (1995), "Wo ein Wille ist, gibt es viele Wege," *Frankfurter Allgemeine Zeitung*, 5 December, 16.

Allsopp, Christopher, Gareth Davies, and David Vines (1995), "Regional macroeconomic policy, fiscal federalism, and European integration," *Oxford Review of Economic Policy*, No. 2, 126-44.

Altmann, Franz-Lothar, Wladimir Andreff, and Gerhard Fink (1995), "Die zukünftige Erweiterung der EU in Mittelosteuropa," *Südosteuropa*, No. 5, 235-58.

_____ and Cornelius Ochmann (1995), "Central and eastern Europe on its way into the European Union – a report on the state of readiness for integration," in *Central and eastern Europe on the way into the European Union – problems and prospects of integration*, edited by Werner Weidenfeld (Gütersloh: Bertelsmann Foundation Publishers), pp. 9-20.

Anderson, Ronald W., Erik Berglöf, and Kálmán Mizsei (1996), *Banking sector development in central and eastern Europe – forum report of the economic pollicy initiative no.1* (London: CEPR and New York: Institute for Eastwest Studies).

Anon (1996), "Das europäische Haus braucht mehr als nur einen Fassadenputz," *Neue Zürcher Zeitung*, 3-4 February, 31.

Artemiev, Igor (1992), "The Single Market, intellectual property, technology transfer and global competition," *Journal of Development Planning*, No. 22, 137-57.

Atkinson, Rick (1996), "A story of love, betrayal and revenge," *Inter-*

national Herald Tribune, 15 March, 2.

Balázs, Péter (1996), "The 'globalisation' of the eastern enlargement of the European Union: symptoms and consequences" (paper prepared for the "Third Ghent Colloquium on The Relations Between the European Union and Central and Eastern Europe: The Political, Economic and Legal Dimension," Ghent [Belgium], 7-8 March).

Baldwin, Richard (1989), "The growth effects of 1992," *Economic Policy*, No. 9, 248-81.

_____ (1992), "European monetary union and its ramifications for the international monetary system and non-member countries: the micro-economics of EMU," *Journal of Development Planning*, No. 22, 41-52.

_____ (1994), *Towards an integrated Europe* (London: CEPR).

Barber, Lionel (1996), "Taciturn diplomat in Russian thriller," *Financial Times*, 26 February 1996, 2.

Begg, Iain, Graham Gudgin, and Derek Morris (1995), "The assessment: regional policy in the European Union," *Oxford Review of Economic Policy*, No. 2, 1-18.

Bempt, Paul van den (1993), "L'adhésion des pays d'Europe centrale et orientale à l'Union Européenne: espoirs et problèmes," *Revue du Marché Commun et de l'Union Européenne*, No. 369, 579-86.

Benelux (1996), "Mémorandum de la Belgique, des Pays-Bas et du Luxembourg en vue de la CIG" (Brussels: European Commission, 8 March).

Berthold, Norbert (1995), "European currency union – do we need a centralized fiscal stabilization policy?" *Aussenwirtschaft*, No. 3, 399-422.

Besançon, Alain (1995), "Les frontières orientales de l'Europe – le cas russe," *Commentaire*, No. 71 (Autumn), 493-500.

Biedenkopf, Kurt (1995), "Rethinking the European Union I – a German perspective," *The World Today*, July, 130-3.

Bilger, François (1993), "Europäische Währungsordnung," *ORDO*, Vol. 44, 15-54.

Bini-Smaghi, Lorenzo and Paolo del Giovane (1996), "Convergence of inflation: a necessary prerequisite for EMU?" *Open Economies Review*, No. 2, 117-26.

Bofinger, Peter (1995), "The political economy of the eastern enlargement of the EU" (London: CEPR Discussion Paper No. 1234, August).

Boissieu, Christian de (1995), "Éditorial," *Revue des Affaires Européennes*, No. 4, 3-10.

Borko, Y. (1996), "Intra-European relations and Russia"(paper prepared for the "Third Ghent Colloquium on The Relations Between the European Union and Central and Eastern Europe: The Political, Economic and Legal Dimension," Ghent [Belgium], 7-8 March).

Bourlanges Jean-Louis and David Martin, rapporteurs (1995), *Report on the functioning of the Treaty on European Union with a view to the 1996 Intergovernmental Conference – implementation and development of the Union* (Brussels and Strasbourg: European Parliament, document A4-0102/95/PART I.A of 4 May).

Brabant, Jozef M. van (1990), *Remaking eastern Europe – on the political economy of transition* (Dordrecht, Boston, MA, and London: Kluwer Academic Publishers).

_____ (1991), *Integrating eastern Europe into the global economy – convertibility through a payments union* (Dordrecht, Boston, MA, and London: Kluwer Academic Publishers).

_____ (1992), *Privatizing eastern Europe – the role of markets and ownership in the transition* (Dordrecht, Boston, MA, and London: Kluwer Academic Publishers).

_____ (1993), *Industrial policy in eastern Europe – governing the transition* (Dordrecht, Boston, MA, and London: Kluwer Academic Publishers).

_____ (1995a), *The transformation of eastern Europe – joining the European integration movement* (Commack, NY: Nova Science Publishers).

_____ (1995b), "Integration and the 1996 Intergovernmental Conference," *OneEurope Magazine*, No. 8, 24-5.

_____ (1995c), "The transition economies and accession to the European Union," *OneEurope Magazine*, No. 9, forthcoming.

_____ (1996a), "A tale of bridging two Europes," in *Fifty years after Bretton Woods: the new challenge of east-west partnership for economic progress*, edited by Bernard Snoy and Miklós Szabó-Pelsőczi (Aldershot: Avebury), forthcoming.

_____ (1996b), "Remaking Europe – the accession of transition economies," *Economia Internazionale*, forthcoming.

_____ (1996c), "Bonding the EU and the transition economies," *Economia Internazionale*, forthcoming.

Bressand, Albert (1992), "A pan-European community in the making?"
in *European reunification in the age of global networks*, edited by
Albert Bressand and György Csáki (Budapest: Institute for World
Economics of the Hungarian Academy of Sciences), pp. 7-17.

Brown, L. Neville (1993), "A personal view from Britain: disunity in
the Union," *Common Market Law Review*, No. 6, 1089-94.

Brykman, Liliana (1992), "The Single Market, technical standards and
certification, insiders-outsiders and global competition," *Journal of
Development Planning*, No. 22, 161-73.

Buerkle, Tom (1996), "EU agrees to form new currency grid and
cements EMU," *International Herald Tribune*, 15 April, 13, 15.

Buiter, Willem H., Giancarlo Corsetti, and Nouriel Roubini (1993),
"Excessive deficits: sense and nonsense in the Treaty of Maastricht," *Economic Policy*, No. 16, 58-90.

Cameron, Fraser (1996a), "The European Union and the challenge of
enlargement"(paper prepared for the "Third Ghent Colloquium on
The Relations Between the European Union and Central and Eastern Europe: The Political, Economic and Legal Dimension," Ghent
[Belgium], 7-8 March).

_____ (1996b), "EU Commissioner Van den Broek's adviser: we have
to be very patient with Slovakia" (translated from *Narodna Obroda*
in JPRS, *Daily Report – East Europe*, 10 May, document
AU1305123696).

Camps, Miriam (1966), *European unification in the sixties – from the
veto to the crisis* (New York: McGraw-Hill).

Caporale, Guglielmo Maria, Christis Hassapis, and Nikitas Pittis
(1995), "Excess returns in the European Monetary System: Do
'weak' currencies still exist after the widening of the fluctuation
bands?" *Weltwirtschaftliches Archiv – Review of World Economics*, No. 2, 326-38.

Chaltiel, Florence (1995), "Enjeux et perspectives de la Conférence
Intergouvernementale de 1996," *Revue du Marché Commun et de*

l'Union Européenne, No. 393, 625-36.

Chavagnac, Hughes de (1993), "Le programme PHARE d'appui aux réformes économiques dans les PECO – l'exemple des pays baltes," *Revue du Marché Commun et de l'Union Européenne*, No. 369, 569-78.

Chirac, Jacques (1995), "Pour une Europe forte," *Revue des Affaires Européennes*, No. 1, 27-32.

Cobham, David (1989), "Strategies for monetary integration revisited," *Journal of Common Market Studies*, No. 3, 203-18.

Corbey, Dorette (1995), "Dialectical functionalism: stagnation as a booster of European integration," *International Organization*, No. 2, 253-84.

Corden, W. Max (1986), *Inflation, exchange rates and the world economy – lectures on international monetary economics* (Chicago, IL: University of Chicago Press and Oxford: Oxford University Press, 3rd ed.).

Davidson, Ian (1996a), "The absent agenda," *The Financial Times*, 21 February, 12.

_____ (1996b), "Orthodox doctrine reversed," *Financial Times*, 6 March, 10.

Dignan, Tony (1995), "Regional disparities and regional policy in the European Union," *Oxford Review of Economic Policy*, No. 2, 64-95.

Dutheil de la Rochère, Jacqueline (1995), "Au-delà de Maastricht – le financement de la future Europe," *Revue des Affaires Européennes*, No. 1, 101-4.

Eatwell, John (1992a), "European monetary union: problems remaining after Maastricht," in *Supplement to World Economic Survey 1990-1991* (New York: United Nations Publications, Sales No. E.92.II.C.2), pp. 32-55.

_____ (1992b), "European monetary union and its ramifications for the international monetary system and non-member countries: the macro-economics of EMU," *Journal of Development Planning*, No. 22, 53-70.

Edwards, Richard W., Jr. (1985), *International monetary collabor-*

ation (Dobbs Ferry, NY: Transnational Publishers).

Eichengreen, Barry (1993), "European monetary unification," *Journal of Economic Literature*, No. 3, 1321-57.

_____ and Charles Wyplosz (1993), "The unstable EMS," *Brookings Papers on Economic Activity*, No. 1, 51-143.

Erkel-Rousse, Hélène (1995), "Les problèmes posés par les disparités régionales dans la transition à l'Union Monétaire européenne et au delà," in *Économies en transition*, edited by Jean-Pierre Gern ([Paris]: Éditions Maisonneuve et Larose), pp. 163-211.

European Commission (1993), *Traité sur l'Union européenne – Traité instituant la Communauté européenne* (Brussels and Luxembourg: Office des publications officielles des Communautés européennes).

_____ (1995a), *Intergovernmental Conference 1996 – Commission report for the Reflection Group* (Brussels and Luxembourg: Office for Official Publications).

_____ (1995b), "Annual report concerning the financial year 1994 together with the institutions' replies," *Official Journal of the European Communities*, C303, 14 November.

_____ (1995c), "Intergovernmental Conferences: an overview" (Brussels: European Commission, 1 December).

_____ (1995d), "Summary of positions of the Member States of the European Union with a view to the 1996 Intergovernmental Conference" (Brussels and Luxembourg: European Commission, 8 December).

_____ (1995e), "Conclusions of the European Council, Madrid, 15-16 December 1995" (Brussels: European Commission [undated document, but probably from late December]).

_____ (1995f), *Preparation of the associated countries of central and eastern Europe for integration into the internal market of the Union* (Brussels: European Commission, 3 and 10 May 1995 [COM(95)163]).

_____ (1995g), "The pre-accession strategy" (Brussels: European Commission [undated communication, but probably towards December]).

_____ (1995h), *Towards greater economic integration – the European Union's financial assistance and trade policy for central and eastern Europe and the New Independent States* (Brussels: European

Commission, October).

_____ (1996a), "Reinforcing political union and preparing for enlargement" (Brussels: European Commission, 28 February).

_____ (1996b), "Commission presents opinion on the IGC: 'political will is the overriding requirement'" (Brussels: European Commission, press *communiqué* of 28 February).

_____ (1996c), "Speech of M. Jacques Santer: opinion of the Commission on the IGC – European Parliament, 28 February 1996" (Brussels: European Commission, press *communiqué* Speech/96/53 of 28 February).

_____ (1996d), "Turin European Council, 29 March 1996, presidency conclusions" (Brussels: European Commission [undated communication, probably 30 March]).

_____ (1996e), "Calendar: (EU) main European activities – 96: April-May" (Brussels: European Commission, communication of 15 April).

_____ (1996f), "The working of the single market in 1995" (Brussels: European Commission [undated communication, probably of March]).

_____ (1996g), "Relations between the European Union and central and eastern European countries (CEEC)" (Brussels: European Commission [undated communication, but probably February]).

_____ (1996h), "Représentants personnels des Ministres des Affaires Étrangères pour la Conférence intergouvernmentale 1996" (Brussels: European Commission, 26 March).

_____ (1996i), "Together in Europe – European Union Newsletter for Central Europe Number 86 (April 1st, 1996)" (Brussels: European Commission, communication of 1 April).

_____ (1996j), "Central and Eastern Eurobarometer No. 6, March" (Brussels: European Commission).

_____ (1996k), "The European Union's single market" (Brussels: European Commission, undated communication [probably late April]).

_____ (1996l), "Calendar: (EU) main European activities – 96: May-June (Brussels: European Commission, communication of 15 May).

_____ (1996m), "Together in Europe – European Union Newsletter for Central Europe Number 87 (April 15, 1996)" (Brussels: European Commission, communication of 15 April).

_____ (1996n), "Together in Europe – European Union Newsletter for Central Europe Number 88 (May 1st, 1996)" (Brussels: European Commission, communication of 1 May).

_____ (1996o), "Together in Europe – European Union Newsletter for Central Europe Number 89 (May 15, 1996)" (Brussels: European Commission, communication of 15 May).

_____ (1996p), "Together in Europe – European Union Newsletter for Central Europe Number 90 (June 1st, 1996)" (Brussels: European Commission, communication of 1 June).

_____ (1996q), "Together in Europe – European Union Newsletter for Central Europe Number 91 (June 15, 1996)" (Brussels: European Commission, communication of 15 June).

Faini, Riccardo and Richard Portes, eds. (1995), *European Union trade with eastern Europe – adjustment and opportunities* (London: CEPR).

Fisher, Andrew and Peter Norman (1996a), "Finding way through Emu ins and outs," *Financial Times*, 11 April, 2.

_____ and _____ (1996b), "Bundesbank outlines plans for EU currency stability," *Financial Times*, 11 April, 10.

France (1996a), "Entretien du ministre délégué aux affaires européennes, M. Michel Barnier, avec 'R.F.I.'," *Bulletin d'Information du 19 mars 1996 (56/96)*, 1-2.

_____ (1996b), "Débat à l'Assemblée Nationale sur la CIG – discours du ministre délégué aux affaires européennes, M. Michel Barnier," *Bulletin d'Information du 13 mars 1996 (52/96)*, 6-13.

_____ (1996c), "Débat à l'Assemblée Nationale sur la CIG – discours du premier ministre, M. Alain Juppé," *Bulletin d'Information du 14 Mars 1996 (53/96)*, 9-13.

Fritsch-Bournazel, Renata (1992), *Eruope and German unification* (New York and Oxford: Berg).

FT (1996), "The ins, the outs and Emu," *Financial Times*, 11 April, 9.

Garrett, Geoffrey and George Tsebelis (1996), "An institutional critique of intergovernmentalism," *International Organization*, No. 2,

269-99.

Gautron, Jean-Claude (1995), "L'élargissement de l'Union européenne aux pays de l'Europe centrale et orientale," *Revue des Affaires Européennes*, No. 1, 105-10.

Germany (1995), "Germany's position with respect to the 1996 IGC" (Luxembourg: European Parliament, 8 December).

_____ (1996), "Vortrag des Staatsministers im Auswärtigem Amt Dr. Werner Hoyer bei einer Vortragsveranstaltung des Bundesministeriums für Wirtschaft und der EU-Kommission am 10. Januar 1996 in Berlin" (Bonn: Auswärtiges Amt [undated release, but probably from January]).

Ghymers, Christian (1995), "La coordination des politiques économiques dans la communautée européenne – une évaluation en vue de la conférence intergouvernementale," *Revue du Marché Commun et de l'Union Européenne*, No. 385, 76-82.

Giscard d'Estaing, Valéry (1995), "Manifeste pour une nouvelle Europe fédérative," *Revue des Affaires Européennes*, No. 1, 19-25.

Glick, Reuven and Michael Hutchison (1993), "Fiscal policy in monetary unions: implications for Europe," *Open Economies Review*, No. 1, 39-65.

Grauwe, Paul de (1993), "The political economy of monetary union in Europe," *The World Economy*, No. 6, 653-61.

_____ (1996a), "Une union monétaire à deux vitesses risque de faire capoter tout le processus d'intégration européenne," *Journal de Genève et Gazette de Lausanne*, 4 March, 11.

_____ (1996b), "The economics of convergence: towards monetary union in Europe," *Weltwirtschaftliches Archiv – Review of World Economics*, No. 1, 1-27.

Grey, Rodney de C. (1992), "The Single Market and financial services," *Journal of Development Planning*, No. 22, 117-32.

Gros, Daniel (1989), "Paradigms for the monetary union of Europe," *Journal of Common Market Studies*, No. 3, 219-30.

_____ (1993), "Seigniorage and EMU – the fiscal implications of price stability and financial market integration," *European Journal of Political Economy*, No. 4, 581-601.

_____ and Niels Thygesen (1992), *European monetary integration* (London: Longman).

_____ and Alfred Steinherr (1995), *Winds of change – economic tran-sition in central and eastern Europe* (Harlow: Longman).

Gudin, Charles-Étienne (1995), "Éditorial," *Revue des Affaires Eur-opéennes*, No. 1, 3-4.

Guigou, Élisabeth (1995), "Les enjeux de la Conférence de 1996," *Revue des Affaires Européennes*, No. 1, 35-42.

Havel, Václav (1996), "The hope for Europe," *New York Review of Books*, No. 8 [*sic*! probably 11], 38-41.

Heinemann, Friedrich (1995), "Bailout- und Bonitätseffekte in der Wirtschafts- und Währungsunion," *Zeitschrift für Wirtschafts- und Sozialwissenschaften*, No. 4, 605-22.

Henig, Stanley (1983), "The European Community's bicephalous poli-tical authority: Council of Ministers-Commission relations," in *Institutions and policies of the European Community*, edited by Juliet Lodge (New York: St. Martin's Press), pp. 9-20.

Hoekman, Bernard and Simeon Djankov (1995), "Catching up with eastern Europe? The European Union's Mediterranean free trade initiative" (London: CEPR Discussion Paper No. 1300, Novem-ber).

Howe, Geoffrey (1996), "No longer part of the convoy," *Financial Times*, 11 March 1996, 14.

Hughes, Kirsty (1996), "The 1996 intergovernmental conference and EU enlargement," *International Affairs*, No. 1, 1-8.

IMF (1996a), "EMU on the runway, preparing for takeoff," *IMF Sur-vey*, 15 April, 137-40.

_____ (1996b), "Tunisia concludes association agreement with EU," *IMF Survey*, 4 March, 77-9.

Inotai, András (1994), *The system of criteria for Hungary's accession to the European Union* (Budapest: Institute for World Economics of the Hungarian Academy of Sciences).

Interview (1996a), "La CIG 96 – réponses à quelques questions," *Re-vue du Marché Commun et de l'Union Européenne*, No. 394, 8-14.

_____ (1996b), "The selfish Union," *Central European*, No. 2, 22-3.

Islam, Shada (1995), "EU and ACP agree on revised Lomé pact," *AfricaRecovery*, No. 4, 13.

Kaminski, Matthew (1996), "Consultancy blooms in Ukraine's sunnier climate," *Financial Times*, 18 April, 2.

Klaus, Václav (1993/4), "The Czech Republic and European integration," *Perspectives – Review of Central European Affairs*, No. 2, 7-11.

Kramer, Heinz (1993), "The European Community's response to the 'new eastern Europe'," *Journal of Common Market Studies*, No. 2, 213-44.

Krichel, Thomas, Paul Levine, and Joseph Pearlman (1996), "Fiscal and monetary policy in a monetary union: credible inflation targets or monetized debt?" *Weltwirtschaftliches Archiv – Review of World Economics*, No. 1, 28-54.

Krimm, Roland (1996), "Un SME bis axé sur l'euro verra le jour en 1999," *Journal de Genève et Gazette de Lausanne*, 15 April, 15.

Labhard, Vincent (1996a), "The controversy over the Maastricht convergence criteria – a synthesis" (Geneva: Institut Universitaire de Hautes Études Internationales, 25 January, mimeographed).

_____ (1996b), "A primer on costs and benefits of European monetary union" (Geneva: Institut Universitaire de Hautes Études Internationales, 25 January, mimeographed).

Lachmann, Werner (1993), "The creation of the European Central Bank – expectations and problems seen from the German vantage point," *Il Politico*, No. 3, 375-93.

Lamers, Karl and Wolfgang Schäuble (1995), "Réflexions sur une politique européenne," *Revue des Affaires Européennes*, No. 1, 9-17.

Lamfalussy, Alexandre (1995), "La mise en place de l'union monétaire: progrès et défis," *Revue des Affaires Européennes*, No. 4, 11-14.

Laurant, Pierre-Henri (1994), "Widening Europe: the dilemmas of the Community success," *The Annals of the American Academy of Political and Social Science*, No. 1, 124-40.

Lengyel, Ákos (1995), "Trade between the European Union and the Visegrád countries" (Budapest: mimeographed, no date [but probably late 1995]).

Lieven, Anatol (1993), *The Baltic revolution – Estonia, Latvia, Lithuania and the path to independence* (New Haven, CT and London:

Yale University Press).

Ludlow, Peter (1982), *The making of the European Monetary System – a case study of the politics of the European Community* (London and Boston: Butterworth Scientific).

_____ (1996a), "Preparing for membership," in *Preparing for membership: the eastward and southern enlargement of the EU*, edited by Peter Ludlow *et al.* (Brussels: Centre for European Policy Studies).

_____ *et al.*, eds. (1996b), *Preparing for membership: the eastward and southern enlargement of the EU* (Brussels: Centre for European Policy Studies), pp. 1-82.

_____ *et al.*, eds. (1996c), *Preparing for 1996 and a larger European Union: principles and priorities* (Brussels: Centre for European Policy Studies).

_____ and Niels Ersbøll (1996), "Towards 1996: the agenda of the Intergovernmental Conference," in *Preparing for 1996 and a larger European Union: principles and priorities* (Brussels: Centre for European Policy Studies), pp. 1-61.

Maas, Cees (1995), "L'introduction de la monnaie unique – analyse des aspects pratiques," *Revue des Affaires Européennes*, No. 4, 37-47.

Major, John (1994), "The future of the European Union, speech by John MAJOR in Leyde, 7 septembre [*sic!*]1994" (Brussels: European Commission [undated communication, but probably September]).

Marglin, Stephen A. and Juliet B. Schor, eds. (1990), *The golden age of capitalism: reinterpreting the postwar experience* (Oxford: Clarendon Press).

Martin, David, rapporteur (1995), *Report on the functioning of the Treaty on European Union with a view to the 1996 Intergovernmental Conference – implementation and development of the Union* (Brussels and Strasbourg: European Parliament, document A4-0102/95/PART I.B2 of 12 May).

Martin, Philippe (1994), "A sequential approach to regional integration: the European Union and central and eastern Europe" (London: CEPR Discussion Paper No. 1070, November).

Mayhew, Alan (1992), "Fact sheet on the association (European) agreements between the Czech and Slovak Federal Republic, Hungary, Poland and the European Community," in *The association process: making it work – central Europe and the European Community*, edited by Richard Portes (London: CEPR), pp. 13-16.

McDonald, Frank and George Zis (1989), "The European Monetary System: towards 1992 and beyond," *Journal of Common Market Studies*, No. 3, 183-202.

Moravcsik, Andrew (1993), "Preferences and power in the European Community," *Journal of Common Market Studies*, No. 4, 473-524.

Moussis, Nicolas (1996), "Au-delà de la CIG de 1996: les grands enjeux de l'Union Européenne," *Revue du Marché Commun et de l'Union Européenne*, No. 394 (January), 15-20.

NZZ (1996a), "Euro-Zentralbank als Powerhouse der EU? – Britischer Widerstand gegen neues Wechselkurssystem," *Neue Zürcher Zeitung*, 15 April, 7.

_____ (1996b), "Strassburg gegen raschen EU-Beitritt Osteuropas – Palamentsdebatte über das Weissbuch," *Neue Zürcher Zeitung*, 18 April, 2.

OECD (1996), *Assistance programmes for central and eastern Europe and the former Soviet Union* (Paris: Organisation for Economic Co-operation and Development).

Økonomiministeriet (1996), *EU's udvidelse mod øst – økonomiske perspektiver* (Copenhagen: Økonomiministeriet).

Olson, Mancur (1984), *The rise and decline of nations – economic growth, stagflation, and social rigidities* (New Haven, CT and London: Yale University Press).

Padoa-Schioppa, Tommaso *et al.* (1987), *Efficiency, stability, and equity – a strategy for the evolution of the economic system of the European Community* (Oxford: Oxford University Press).

Passell, Peter (1996), "Central Europe is unsettled by a currency union for West Europe," *The New York Times*, 16 May, D2.

Pavan, Antonio (1993), "Europe and the transition in the eastern countries: democracy and development," *Aula – Society and Economy*, No. 2, 54-61.

Pearce, Joan (1995), "Comments," in *From association to accession –*

the impact of the association agreements on central Europe's trade and integration with the European Union, edited by Kálmán Mizsei and Andrzej Rudka (Warsaw, Prague, Budapest, Košice, and New York: Institute for Eastwest Studies), pp. 133-8.

Peel, Quentin, Robert Preston, and Caroline Southey (1996), "Bewilderment turns to despair," *Financial Times*, 23 May, 15.

Persson, Torsten and Guido Tabellini (1996), "Monetary cohabitation in Europe" (Cambridge, MA: NBER Working Paper No. 5532, April).

Pisani-Ferry, Jean (1995), "L'Europe à géométrie variable: une analyse économique," *Politique Étrangère*, No. 2, 447-65.

Pöhl, Karl-Otto (1995), "International monetary policy: a personal view," in Yegor Gaidar and Karl-Otto Pöhl, *Russian Reform/ International Money* (Cambridge, MA: The MIT Press), pp. 55-140.

Pomfret, Richard (1991), "What is the secret of the EMS's longevity?" *Journal of Common Market Studies*, No. 6, 623-33.

Portes, Richard, ed. (1992), *The association process: making it work – central Europe and the European Community* (London: CEPR).

Preston, Christopher (1995), "Obstacles to EU enlargement: the classical Community method and the prospects for a wider Europe," *Journal of Common Market Studies*, No. 3, 451-63.

Reflection Group (1995), *Reflection Group's Report* (Brussels: European Commission, 5 December 1995, SN 520/95 [Reflex 21]).

Reinicke, Wolfgang H. (1992), *Building a new Europe – the challenge of system transformation and systemic reform* (Washington, DC: The Brookings Institution).

Richter, Sándor (1996), " The Visegrád group countries' expectations *vis-à-vis* western Europe," *Russian & East European Finance and Trade*, No. 1, 6-41.

_____ and Lászlo Tóth (1996), "Prospects of economic cooperation among the Visegrád group countries," *Russian & East European Finance and Trade*, No. 1, 42-94.

Rodrik, Dani (1992a), "Foreign trade in eastern Europe's transition: early results" (London: CEPR Discussion Paper No. 676, June).

_____ (1992b), "Making sense of the Soviet trade shock in eastern

Europe: a framework and some estimates" (London: CEPR Discussion Paper No. 705, July).

Rollo, Jim (1996), "The economics of EU enlargement to the east" (slide materials prepared for the "Third Ghent Colloquium on The Relations Between the European Union and Central and Eastern Europe: The Political, Economic and Legal Dimension," Ghent [Belgium], 7-8 March).

Silguy, Yves-Thibault de (1996), "Discours de Yves Thibault [*sic!*] de Silguy à la table ronde sur la monnaie unique, 22 janvier 1996, Bruxelles" (Brussels: European Commission [undated communication, but probably January]).

Slim, Assen (1993), "L'aide de la CEE aux PECO: modalités et contraintes," *Le Courrier des Pays de l'Est*, No. 378, 3-24.

Southey, Caroline (1996), "MEPs caution on the pace of EU enlargement," *Financial Times*, 18 April, 2.

Švejnar, Jan, "Economic transformation in central and eastern Europe: the tasks still ahead," in *Economic transformation – the tasks still ahead*, edited by Thomas Walter (Washington, DC: Per Jacobsson Foundation, 1995), pp. 3-15.

Tangermann, Stefan (1993), "Some economic effects of EC agricultural trade preferences for Central Europe," *Journal of Economic Integration*, No. 2, 152-74.

Tell, Gillian (1996), "Call for non-EMU currencies to be allowed loose link," *Financial Times*, 15 April, 1.

_____ and Andrew Hill (1996), "Verona stages a victory for all," *Financial Times*, 15 April, 2.

Tew, Brian (1967), *International monetary cooperation – 1947-67* (London: Hutchinson University Library, 9th ed.).

Thomas, Ingo P. (1994), "Finanzausgleich und Kohäsion in der Europäischen Union," *Die Weltwirtschaft*, No. 4, 472-91.

Thygesen, Niels (1989), "The Delors Report and European economic and monetary union," *International Affairs*, No. 4, 637-52.

_____ (1993), "Towards monetary union in Europe – reforms of the EMS in the perspective of monetary union," *Journal of Common Market Studies*, No. 4, 447-72.

_____ and Daniel Gros (1990), "The institutional approach to monetary union in Europe," *Economic Journal*, No. 402, 925-35.

Tietmeyer, Hans (1996), "Stabiles Geld für Deutschland und Europa,"
Deutsche Bundesbank – Auszüge aus Presseartikeln, No. 29, 1-5.

Timmermann, Heinz (1993), "Europa – der zentrale Bezugspunkt für
die Länder des Ostens: Erwartungen, Möglichkeiten, Konzepti-
onen," *Osteuropa*, No. 8, 713-25.

Triffin, Robert (1991), "The IMS (International Monetary System... or
scandal?) and the EMS (European Monetary System... or
success?)," *Banca Nazionale del Lavoro Quarterly Review*, No. 4,
399-436.

UNECE (1990), *Economic Survey of Europe 1989-1990* (New York:
United Nations Publication, sales No. E.90.II.E.1).

_____ (1991a), *Economic Survey of Europe 1990-1991* (New York:
United Nations Publication, sales No. E.91.II.E.1).

_____ (1991b), *Economic Bulletin for Europe – vol. 43* (New York:
United Nations Publication, sales No. E.91.II.E.39).

_____ (1992), *Economic Survey of Europe 1991-1992* (New York:
United Nations Publication, sales No. E.92.II.E.1).

_____ (1993), *Economic Survey of Europe 1992-1993* (New York:
United Nations Publication, sales No. E.93.II.E.1).

_____ (1996a), *Economic Survey of Europe 1995-1996* (New York:
United Nations Publication, sales No. E.96.II.E.1).

_____ (1996b), "Purchasing power parities for eastern Europe" (Geneva: UNECE Press Release ECE/GEN/7 of 14 February).

United Kingdom (1996a), *A partnership of nations* (London: Foreign
and Commonwealth Office, 12 March).

_____ (1996b), "Statement by the Prime Minister, Mr John Major,
House of Commons, 1 April: Turin European Council, 29 March"
(Brussels: European Commission [undated communication, but
probably April]).

Vandenbussche, Hylke (1996), "Is European antidumping protection
against central Europe too high?" *Weltwirtschaftliches Archiv –
Review of World Economics*, No. 1, 116-38.

Vignes, Daniel (1994), "Le calcul de la majorité qualifiée, un casse-tête pour 1996," *Revue du Marché Commun et de l'Union Européenne*, No. 382, 561-3.

Vrbetić, Marta (1995), "European Union and its neighbors in the east and south," *Euroscope Reports*, December, 3-7.

Weidenfeld, Werner, ed. (1995), *Central and eastern Europe on the way into the European Union – problems and prospects of integration* (Gütersloh: Bertelsmann Foundation Publishers).

WERI (1995), *Poland – international economic report, 1994/95* (Warsaw: Warsaw School of Economics).

Westendorp, Carlos (1995), "Die wirtschaftlichen Unterschiede zwischen Nord und Süd in der Europäischen Union," *West-Ost-Journal*, No. 3-4, 15.

Winters, L. Alan (1992), "The Europe Agreements: with a little help from our friends," in *The association process: making it work – central Europe and the European Community*, edited by Richard Portes (London: CEPR), pp. 17-33.

Woyke, Wichard (1993), "Die Politische Union der Europäischen Gemeinschaft," in *Gesamteuropa – Analysen, Probleme und Entwicklungsperspektiven*, edited by Cord Jakobeit and Alparslan Yenal (Bonn: Bundeszentrale für politische Bildung), pp. 362-77.

Żukrowska, Katarzyna (1996), "Probleme der regionalen Zusammenarbeit der CEFTA-Staaten," *Osteuropa-Wirtschaft*, No. 1, 38-51.

Index

absorptive capacity, 202-3
accedents to the European Union (EU), 6, 207
accession criteria, 188-199
  ability to comply with the *acquis*, 20, 34, 35, 107, 192, 194-7, 213
  acceptance of overall ambitions of European integration, 34, 192-3, 197
  budgetary impact, 12, 19, 31-4, 38, 96, 97, 183, 185, 192, 199-203, 251
  democratic maturity and political stability, 34, 193, 197, 199
  domestic political pluralism, 34, 96, 192, 196, 197, 199
  European identity, 4, 12, 19, 34, 41, 50, 99, 192, 245
  functioning democracy, 34, 192
  good neighborly relations or peaceful coexistence, 34, 192, 193, 197
  qualitative or subjective ones, 31, 34, 179, 190, 192-4, 198, 199
  reasonably effective market-based allocation of resources, 34, 96, 175, 192, 194, 196, 197, 199, 226
  respect for human rights, 34, 79, 158, 161, 190, 192, 243, 244
  rule of law, 34, 192, 197
accession negotiations, viii, 10, 12, 21, 28, 35, 46, 49, 56, 95-6, 106, 141, 175, 179, 188, 191, 196, 199-209
  see also pre-accession strategy
accountability in the European Union (EU), 3, 30, 39, 61, 67, 72, 84, 87, 94
accounting in the European Union (EU), 118, 121, 123
accounting unit in the European Union (EU), 123

acquis, 6, 23, 33, 34, 35, 38, 90, 92, 93, 96, 97, 98, 100, 153, 164, 169, 170, 177, 184, 185, 192, 194, 195, 199, 203, 204, 206, 212, 213, 214, 222, 226, 232, 248, 251
acquis communautaire, 6, 19, 22, 80, 90, 97, 113, 174, 188, 190, 198, 232
acquis communautaire et politique, 6, 12, 19, 89, 190, 198, 205
adjustment burden, 146-7
  see also assistance to other economies in transition, Partnership and Cooperation Agreement, preferential arrangements of the European Union (EU), transformation policies
Africa, Caribbean, and Pacific (ACP), *see* Lomé Convention, preferential arrangements of the European Union (EU) with nonmembers
agenda of the Intergovernmental Conference (IGC), 2, 10, 24-31, 49-51, 53, 55, 56, 65, 67, 70-101, 107, 143, 156, 242, 243, 249-50
  see also mandate of Extraordinary European Council, Intergovernmental Conference (IGC), Turin mandate
Agreement on Social Policy, 62
  see also Maastricht Treaty, pillars and social agenda, Social Protocol, social union
agriculture in Europe Agreement, 161, 163, 164, 168, 224, 231, 232
  see also agriculture in the European Union (EU), common agricultural policy (CAP), Europe Agreement
agriculture in the European Union (EU), 32, 68, 88, 97, 120, 170, 171, 182, 201, 202, 217, 224

of the ins, 115-18
of the outs, 30, 89, 115-18, 133, 185, 228, 229
of the semi-outs, 30, 115-18, 133
see also common monetary policy, Economic and Monetary Union (EMU), European Monetary System (EMS), exchange-rate mechanism (ERM), fiscal federalism, fiscal policy in Economic and Monetary Union (EMU), monetary policy
monetary union, 4, 11, 18, 19, 24, 26-30, 38, 43, 54, 61, 65, 71, 72, 82-3, 89, 91, 100, 102-33, 184, 185, 228-9
monetary union, first attempt, 54, 109
monetary union, fourth attempt, 29, 131
monopoly of foreign trade and payments, 138
moral claims to European Union (EU) membership, 9, 43, 175, 192, 233, 253
Moussis, Nicolas, 110, 230
Mr. CFSP, 80
Multi-fibre Arrangement (MFA), 163-4
see also contingent protectionism, Europe Agreement, textiles and clothing
multilateralism, 137, 147, 148, 153, 167, 169, 199, 217, 228, 231, 234, 235

national security, 9, 22, 36, 134, 136, 141, 144, 158, 178, 179, 180, 211, 212, 216, 217, 229, 231, 237, 241, 246, 251, 254
national sovereignty, 23, 84, 85, 86, 95, 119, 189, 193, 194
negotiating mandate for accession of transition economies, 95, 96, 204
negotiating mandate of the Council for the Intergovernmental Conference (IGC), 10, 67, 70, 73, 77-81
Netherlands, 32, 48, 66, 92, 201
neutrality in post-Cold War period, 59

noncooperation policy, *see* British non-cooperation
nongovernmental organizations (NGOs), *see* civil society
nontariff barriers (NTBs), 217, 222
Nordic Council, 237
Norway, 64, 85, 162, 205

Oostlander, Arie, 171
Oostlander Report, 171
see also acquis, entry of transition economies, European Parliament
openness in the European Union (EU), 3, 30, 39, 75, 84, 232, 237, 253
optimum currency area, 11, 26, 103, 105, 110, 114, 128
Organisation for Economic Co-operation and Development (OECD), 152, 155, 187
Ostpolitik, 136
Orthodox heritage, 7

Paris Treaty, 48, 52, 89
partial membership in the European Union (EU), 171, 254
Partnership and Cooperation Agreement, 157-9
peaceful coexistence, 34, 192
Pearce, Joan, 207, 215, 229
Pentagonale, 238
Petersberg tasks, 80-1
PHARE, 153-4, 159, 166, 170, 185, 230
pick-and-choose Europe, 92
see also constitution of the European Union (EU), *à la carte* Europe, *finalité politique*, Intergovernmental Conference (IGC), inter-governmentalism, quasi-constitutional treaties of the European Union (EU), variable geometry
pillar, first, 56, 61, 93
pillar, fourth, 52
see also Agreement on Social Policy, common social policy, pillars and

International Studies in Economics and Econometrics

1. T. Harder: *Introduction to Mathematical Models in Market and Opinion Research.* With Practical Applications, Computing Procedures, and Estimates of Computing Requirements. Translated from German. 1969 ISBN 90-277-0096-6
2. A.R.G. Heesterman: *Forecasting Models for National Economic Planning.* 2nd rev. and ext. ed. 1972 ISBN 90-277-0224-1
3. A.R.G. Heesterman: *Allocation Models and Their Use in Economic Planning.* 1971 ISBN 90-277-0182-2
4. M. Durdağ: *Some Problems of Development Financing.* A Case Study of the Turkish First Five-Year Plan (1963-1967). 1973
 ISBN 90-277-0267-5
5. J.M. Blin: *Patterns and Configurations in Economic Science.* 1973
 ISBN 90-277-0203-7
6. A.H.Q.M. Merkies: *Selection of Models by Forecasting Intervals.* Translated from Dutch. 1973 ISBN 90-277-0342-6
7. H.C. Bos, M. Sanders and C. Secchi: *Private Foreign Investment in Developing Countries.* A Quantitative Study on the Evaluation of the Macro-Economic Effects. 1974
 ISBN Hb 90-277-0410-4; Pb 90-277-0439-2
8. R. Frisch: *Economic Planning Studies.* A Collection of Essays. Selected, introduced and edited by Frank Long, with a Preface by Jan Tinbergen. 1976 ISBN Hb 90-277-0245-4; Pb 90-277-1194-1
9. K.L. Gupta and M. A. Islam: *Foreign Capital, Savings and Growth.* An International Cross-Section Study. 1983 ISBN 90-277-1449-5
10. C.A. van Bochove: *Imports and Economic Growth.* 1982
 ISBN 90-247-3052-X
11. O. Bjerkholt and E. Offerdal (eds.): *Macroeconomic Prospects for a Small Oil Exporting Country.* 1985 ISBN 90-247-3183-6
12. D. Weiserbs (ed.): *Industrial Investment in Europe.* Economic Theory and Measurement. 1985 ISBN 90-247-3270-0
13. J.-M. Graf von der Schulenburg and G. Skogh (eds.): *Law and Economics & The Economics of Legal Regulation.* 1986
 ISBN 90-247-3377-4
14. S. Pejovich (ed.): *Socialism: Institutional, Philosophical and Economic Issues.* 1987 ISBN 90-247-3487-8
15. R. Heijmans and H. Neudecker (eds.): *The Practice of Econometrics.* Studies on Demand, Forecasting, Money and Income. In Honor of Jan Salomon Cramer. 1987 ISBN 90-247-3502-5
16. A. Steinherr and D. Weiserbs (eds.): *Employment and Growth.* Issues for the 1980s. In Honor of Albert Kervyn de Lettenhove. 1987
 ISBN 90-247-3514-9
17. M.J. Holler (ed.): *The Logic of Multiparty Systems.* 1987
 ISBN 90-247-3515-7

18. J.M. van Brabant: *Regional Price Formation in Eastern Europe.* Theory and Practice of Trade Pricing. 1987   ISBN 90-247-3540-8
    See also below under Volume 23
19. A.M. Wesselman: *The Population-Sample Decomposition Method.* A Distribution-Free Estimation Technique for Minimum Distance Parameters. 1987   ISBN 90-247-3603-X
20. P. Coffey (ed.): *Main Economic Policy Areas of the EEC − Toward 1992.* The Challenge to the Community's Economic Policies when the 'Real' Common Market is Created by the End of 1992. 3rd rev.ed., 1990   ISBN 0-7923-0810-7
21. A. Breton, G. Galeotti, P. Salmon and R. Wintrobe (eds.): *The Competitive State.* Villa Colombella Papers on Competitive Politics. 1991
    ISBN 0-7923-0835-2
22. S. Pejovich: *The Economics of Property Rights.* Towards a Theory of Comparative Systems. 1990   ISBN 0-7923-0878-6
23. J.M. van Brabant: *Remaking Eastern Europe.* On the Political Economy of Transition. 1990   ISBN 0-7923-0955-3
24. J.M. van Brabant: *Privatizing Eastern Europe.* The Role of Markets and Ownership in the Transition. 1992   ISBN 0-7923-1861-7
25. J.M. van Brabant: *Integrating Eastern Europe into the Global Economy.* Convertibility through a Payments Union. 1991
    ISBN 0-7923-1352-6
26. G.W. Kołodko, D. Gotz-Kozierkiewicz and E. Skrzeszewska-Paczek: *Hyperinflation and Stabilization in Postsocialist Economies.* 1992
    ISBN 0-7923-9179-9
27. P. Mihályi: *Socialist Investment Cycles.* Analysis in Retrospect. 1992
    ISBN 0-7923-1973-7
28. A. Breton, G. Galeotti, P. Salmon and R. Wintrobe (eds.): *Preferences and Democracy.* Villa Colombella Papers on Competitive Politics. 1993   ISBN 0-7923-9321-X
29. K.Z. Poznanski (ed.): *Stabilization and Privatization in Poland.* An Economic Evaluation of the Shock Therapy Program. 1993
    ISBN 0-7923-9341-4
30. P. Coffey (ed.): *Main Economic Policy Areas of the EC-After 1992.* 4th Revised Edition. 1993   ISBN 0-7923-2375-0
31. J.M. van Brabant: *Industrial Policy in Eastern Europe.* Governing the Transition. 1993   ISBN 0-7923-2538-9
32. H.J. Blommestein and B. Steunenberg (eds.): *Government and Markets.* Establishing a Democratic Constitutional Order and a Market Economy in Former Socialist Countries. 1994   ISBN 0-7923-3059-5
33. S. Pejovich: *Economic Analysis of Institutions and Systems.* 1995
    ISBN 0-7923-3214-8

34. R. Holzmann, J. Gács and G. Winckler (eds.): *Output Decline in Eastern Europe.* Unavoidable, External Influence or Homemade? 1995   ISBN 0-7923-3285-7
35. P. Coffey: *Europe – Toward 2001.* 1996
                                  ISBN 0-7923-3891-X; Pb 0-7923-3892-8
36. M. Mejstrik (ed): *The Privatization Process in East-Central Europe*, 1996   ISBN 0-7923-4096-5
37. J.M. van Brabant: *Integrating Europe*, 1996

                                          ISBN 0-7923-9806-8

KLUWER ACADEMIC PUBLISHERS – DORDRECHT / BOSTON / LONDON